The rIng
companion

The Ring Companion
1 84567 001 8

Published by
Titan Books
A division of
Titan Publishing Group Ltd
144 Southwark St
London
SE1 0UP

First edition October 2005
2 4 6 8 10 9 7 5 3 1

Picture Credits
Grateful acknowledgement is made to the following for the use of their visual material, used solely for the advertising, promotion, publicity and review of the specific motion pictures and television programmes they illustrate. All rights reserved. AFDF, ApolloMedia, Applause Pictures, Bandai Visual Co Ltd, Buena Vista International, Bungei, Columbia Pictures Corporation, Daei Studios, Dark Horse Manga, DreamWorks SKG, Edward Arnold Ltd, Fuji Television Network Inc, HarperCollins Ltd, Hugh Carey, Kadokawa Shoten Publishing Co Ltd, Kadokawa-Daiei Eiga KK, Kindai Eiga Kyokai, Masulpiri Films, Omega Project, Oz Company Ltd, Paramount Pictures, Popcorn Films, Shintoho Company Ltd, Shochiku Films Ltd, Toei Video Co Ltd, Toho Company Ltd, United Artists, Vertical Inc, Warner Bros. Any omissions will be corrected in future editions.

Visit our website:
www.titanbooks.com

Did you enjoy this book? We love to hear from our readers.
Please e-mail us at: **readerfeedback@titanemail.com** or write to Reader Feedback at the above address.

To subscribe to our regular newsletter for up-to-the-minute news, great offers
and competitions, email: **titan-news@titanemail.com**

A CIP catalogue record for this title is available from the British Library.

Printed and bound in Great Britain by MPG, Bodmin, Cornwall.

The rIng companion

Denis Meikle

Research Associate: Javier Lopez

TITAN BOOKS

To Sarah
For a time when she is no longer troubled by nightmares.

Acknowledgements

Those who helped with the acquisition of material related to the *Ring* films were David Barraclough, Brian D Horrorwitz, Richard Klemensen and Mark A Miller. I thank them all. A special thanks on this occasion goes to Javier Lopez, Head of Translations for ADV Films and web-master of 'ringworld' (www.theringworld.com), who not only helped on a practical level, but whose ready assistance from his home base of Houston, Texas, proved invaluable in clarifying some of the more esoteric aspects of Japanese language and culture. There are not many subjects for which an author requires the services of a translator, but this most certainly was one!

No book of this kind is feasible without the input of those who first ventured to set foot in the spook-house. I have referenced articles and interviews by journalists and academics from all parts of the globe, including Ian Berriman, Norman England, Richard Harlan Smith, Deborah Hochberg, Jay Holben, Henry J Hughes, Lisa Kuwamura, Clyde Mandalin, Tadayuki Naito, Donald Richie, Norman A Rubin, Tim Screech, Jasper Sharp, Den Shewman and others, most of whom have been credited in the text; to any I may have missed, I offer my apologies and my appreciation for their daring and diligence.

Titan Books would also like to thank Project Editor Stefan Jaworzyn for his invaluable work on the manuscript of this book.

Foreword

In any book on a subject as esoteric in principle as that of Japanese horror films, there inevitably arises the question of semantics. Many of the films dealt with in this text can be referred to in the West in a number of alternative ways, few — if any — of which were literal translations of the original titles to begin with. In addition, many Far Eastern nations traditionally refer to individuals by means of their surname first, forename last, a contravention of Western convention which can be exacerbated by a media that varies in its adherence to the precept, some choosing to conform to it and others switching the names around again in accordance with Western practice.

I have therefore opted to adopt the accepted English form for proper names over that of Japanese, which places the surname first. I have also chosen to refer to films by their most widely accepted British or American title, with their original Japanese titles following on in parentheses. Film purists might howl in protest, but *The Ring Companion* is intended for a Western lay readership, first and foremost, and not for that elite band of brothers who have seen Kon Ichikawa's *Genji monogatari* a dozen times each and spend their days nit-picking over errors in the subtitling. On this last point, all dialogue quotes from the films themselves are derived from the Anglicised versions to which the public at large has most common access; no attempt has been made to redefine the work of their original translators, or to acquire obscure native prints, unless otherwise stated in the text.

Mamillius: A sad tale's best for winter: I have one
Of sprites and goblins.
- **William Shakespeare**, *The Winter's Tale/Act 2, Scene 1* (1611)

The tale of terror... has found its best medium in the film.
- **Mario Praz**, *Three Gothic Novels*/Introductory Essay (1968)

Contents

Prologue: Seven Days

Ring.
Ando thought it over, recalling what he knew about the English word. He was most familiar with its use as a noun to mean 'circle'. But he also knew that it described the sound a bell or a telephone makes; it could be a verb meaning 'to cause a bell or a telephone to sound', and by extension, could mean calling someone on the phone or summoning someone by means of a bell.

- Koji Suzuki, *Rasen* (1995)

In the modern world, the term 'horror film' has become a catch-all for a multitude of cinematic sins. In the 1940s, such classification was confined to films with a Gothic or supernatural bent; in the 1950s it was extended to include the giant monster fantasies; in the 1960s, iconoclastic 'atrocity' movies were appended to the roster; by the 1970s, the horror film was anything with an X or an R rating which was not strictly sexual in nature. Nowadays, the horror film is everything from predictable 'slasher' flicks of the teens-in-peril variety to effects-laden space operas and serial-killer thrillers.

In the process of this homogenisation, much of the great and good in the associated field of supernatural fantasy has been denied more appropriate analysis through being lumped together with lesser offerings under the label of 'horror film'. Principal among these have been the Terror-movies which were adapted, or derived inspiration, from classic works of what English scholar David Punter christened 'The Literature of Terror', whether they be John Barrymore's strikingly original take on *Strange Case of Dr Jekyll and Mr Hyde* in 1920, Jack Clayton's visually inventive version of Henry James' *The Turn of the Screw* — *The Innocents* — in 1961 or Hideo Nakata's *Ring* in 1998.

The Terror film stands at one remove from the film of horror, whose main purpose is to depict *guignol*esque acts of physical violence and, in so doing, to provide visceral shock. The Terror film is more thoughtful in tone, as befits the thematic nature of the literary sub-genre to which it owes its allegiance, and its horrors are usually unseen

or, at best, only partially perceived. Its particular thrills are of a more cerebral kind, and it demands a degree of intellectual interaction on behalf of the viewer which invariably is absent in run-of-the-mill horror fare, where the sole requirement placed on an audience is for it to gasp and gag. In short, the film of Terror requires imagination.

Above: The Ring *(2002): Rachel Keller (Naomi Watts) watches the 'cursed' video.*

Films of Terror have existed since the dawn of cinema itself — indeed, many of the very earliest productions drew on Gothic literature for their plots — but the template for a *cinema* of Terror was first set in motion in the 1940s by producer Val Lewton, whose films, though few qualified as tales of Terror in themselves, nevertheless operated to a dramatic schema which would become *de rigeur* for exponents of the Terror film ever afterwards. From *Cat People* to *Bedlam*, Lewton's series of miniature masterpieces for RKO, filmed between 1942 and 1946, were mood-pieces suffused in shadow-play, allusive hints and a palpable sense of dread, whose climactic frights often took place off-screen: horror 'by suggestion', rather than by illustration. But his tasteful essays in the art of fear established the rules by which the film of Terror was enabled to distinguish itself from its cruder stable-mate in the field of genre filmmaking.

In a literary context, the term Terror is employed to mean *spiritual* fear, as opposed to instinctive concern for one's physical well-being in times of crisis, and spiritual fear has traditionally best been expressed by the 'ghost' story. But the ghost story is the one tale of Terror which rarely succeeds as well in film as on the printed page. That strange sixth sense of awareness of 'shadowy thirds' — as Robert Browning and T S Eliot had it — is less sustainable in cinema than it is in novel or short story form, where the impulse to *reveal* runs counter to the notion that what is *not* revealed in a ghost story is often what makes it frightening. Film, as a visual medium, has trouble coming to terms with the idea of the 'Unseen'; a film about the Unseen is, in effect, an oxymoron. Thus the straight 'horror' film, with its raucous circus of monsters and vampires and walking dead-men, has tended to dominate the field at the expense of more thought-provoking excursions into the supernatural.

Notwithstanding the medium's inability to do justice to the ghost story, the cinema of Terror has long been overdue a renaissance. All that was needed was the right set of circumstances. In the late 1990s they came about through a combination of millennial angst, thematic exhaustion in the horror genre as a whole and widespread fear of a new unknown, as represented by the insidious creep of high technology. The cultural icons of new wave Gothic were destined always to be spawned among the darker outcrops of science fiction dreams which inexorably gave way to nightmare reality, and there is no small irony in the fact that the resurgence of interest in ghost stories should have come about in a continent which unarguably is one of the most technologically advanced on earth. The catalyst for their revival as cinematic super-genre in Japan and the Far East in recent years was the very hi-tech science to which the form naturally is antithetical, and the movement was spearheaded by a single feature film which belatedly had been adapted from an unsuccessful novel published half a decade earlier.

In its skilful handling of the supernatural element of the novel, the film bridged the aforementioned gap between story and screen. By going against the precept established by Lewton that things seen are never as scary as things left *unseen*, it lifted the veil on its ghost in a famous final scene that no one who saw it is ever likely to forget. It was a veritable *tour de force* of terror, and it was achieved with no make-up and with minimal special effects. But for the first time since William Friedkin's *The Exorcist* in 1973, the expectations of an audience in relation to what purported to be a scary movie, a film of Terror, were matched — if not exceeded — by the imagination of its creators.

The film, like the novel which sired it, was entitled simply *Ring*. But with its arrival in the last decade of the twentieth century, the cinema of Terror finally came of age.

Okayama-born director Hideo Nakata's supernatural chiller *Ring,* from a novel by Koji Suzuki, was nothing less than a sensation when it premièred in Japan in 1998. The reason? *Ring* was considered to be the most frightening film for a generation, and was so successful that it sired two television serials, an immediate Korean remake (*The Ring Virus*), three home-grown sequels (*Rasen* [*Spiral*], *Ring 2* and *Ring 0: Birthday*) and a Hollywood remake in 2002 (*The Ring*), which has now been delivered of a sequel of its own under the full-circle direction of Nakata. In addition, Suzuki has contributed two more novels and a collection of short stories to the mythos, and novels and films have inspired *manga* comic adaptations, a Sega Dreamcast computer game, countless cross-media spin-offs, and a legion of devoted fans world-wide — the Internet version of whom refer to themselves as 'ringworms'. All this from an idea that not only caught the imagination of the public but also the mood of the moment.

The premise of *Ring* is an urban legend of a supposed 'cursed' video, which brings death to those who dare to watch it exactly seven days later. But not just any old death. Oh, no... Those who view the tape are fated to die of *fright*. The death-dealing videotape ultimately is revealed to be the posthumous creation of a young girl with telepathic powers — Sadako in the originals (except for the Korean remake), Samara in the American versions — who was slain by her stepfather and disposed of down a well. That is merely the overture, however: *Ring*'s equivalent to Count Dracula taking up residence in his Carpathian castle and waiting for unwary passers-by.

Nakata's approach to the story was equivocal and represented in part a return to the 'horror by suggestion' ethos of producer Lewton. But it was paired to the uniquely Japanese iconography of the vengeful female ghost, and the coalition of the two themes brought about a new and novel twist in the film of Terror which also acknowledged the influence of all that had passed since. Thematically, Suzuki's novel is part of the great tradition of ghost fiction which was popularised by turn-of-the-century writers like M R James and expatriate Irish-American Lafcadio Hearn (who took up residence in Japan in 1890), but Nakata invested his film with a resolutely modern tone, far removed from former classics of Japanese supernatural cinema, such as Masaki Kobayashi's *Kwaidan* (1964, from four tales by Hearn) or Kaneto Shindo's *Kuroneko* (1968).

That the Ring cycle of five films, two TV series, a made-for-TV movie and two American remakes of sort has since become something of a cult among aficionados of the genre — not only in the domestic theatre of the original productions but globally as well — almost goes without saying. Single-handedly, these supremely inventive forays into the clammy realm of the Gothic ghost story have revived interest in the subtle *frissons* of Asian horror cinema at a time when the impact of digitally inspired monsters has at last begun to pall through repetition and their own overblown sense of luminance. *Ring* and its various spin-offs were proof positive of the adage that less is more — that what is only vaguely glimpsed can be infinitely more fear-inducing than what is held up to the unblinking gaze of scrutiny. M R James, the acknowledged master of the English ghost story, encapsulated the rules by which Terror cinema plays most effectively in a reference to the vengeful ghost in his own 'A Warning to the Curious': 'I always saw him with the tail of my eye on the left or the right, and he was never there when I looked straight for him', adding, for good measure, 'all the same I daren't face him.'

In the case of *Ring*, face *her* would be more appropriate.

In what follows, that is what *you*, the reader, will be required to do also. ○

Day One: The Curse

You need to use your imagination in order to enjoy terror. For instance, at night in the bathroom you feel someone is right behind you but it's all in your mind. The thought 'there might be someone behind me' develops into a ghost and gives people fear. I managed to write a good horror story because I don't actually like horror. If I liked it and was always reading it, I would have written typical horror. Instead, the story was original and fun.

- **Koji Suzuki**, interview with Akemi Yokoyama (2004)

Author Koji Suzuki was a 'new man' in Japan before the idea became fashionable in the West in the early 1990s. Like much in Japanese society, he is also a contradiction in terms: a scientific rationalist who is fascinated by the supernatural, a 'macho' man in the Ernest Hemingway mould who remains resolutely in touch with his feminine side, and a writer of romantic adventures who paradoxically has become best-known on the international stage for his horror stories. Each of these attributes is reflected in *Ring*, the novel which Suzuki created on a wing and a prayer in 1990 from a single, simple idea, and which went on to become the biggest horror sensation in his nation's literary history, inspiring a host of imitators, seven feature films to date and a new cinematic sub-genre in the process.

Koji Suzuki was born on 13 May 1957, in Hamamatsu, an industrial city situated in the same prefecture as Mount Fuji, home to household names like Honda, Yamaha and Suzuki (no connection), and affectionately considered by its denizens to be 'in the middle' of Japan due to its equidistance from Tokyo in the east and Osaka in the west. Foreign tourists might more readily equate this largest city in the Shizuoka district with the annual kite festival which is held there every 3-5 May. After reading European literature at Keio University, Suzuki took up a teaching post at a *yobiko* — a 'cram school', where high school students enroll for supplemental lessons to facilitate the passing of exams — but eventually decided that he wanted to become a full-time writer instead. By then, he was married and the proud father of two baby daughters, but he persuaded his wife to return to her profession as a teacher of Japanese history while he took on the role of writer and 'house-husband', a concept which was virtually unheard of in Japan (or anywhere else) in the mid-1980s.

By 1988 Suzuki had written a first novel, *Paradise* (*Rakuen*), which was published two years later and won him the Fantasy Novel award for 1990. This auspicious start to his fledgling career spurred him to continue in the same vein and in 1989 he set about crafting what he ambitiously determined would be an 'epoch-making story; something extremely interesting'. "I didn't intend to write horror," he said (despite the fact that he used to entertain the pupils at his cram school by telling them scary stories). "I wanted to write a new type of novel, because I was a new type of father in Japan in the way that I took care of my daughters, and I think it's very important for a novelist to write about his own experiences."

Above: Koji Suzuki.

Influenced as much by European and American writers of fiction as he was by his native Japanese, Suzuki posed himself a conundrum out of which he began to concoct his own, intricate 'Chinese box' mystery: "The idea that started it was what if four men died in different places at the exact same time? Then I had to think of what these men had in common; something they had caught. A virus? Maybe a virus that kills exactly one week after someone is infected. So they had to be together in the same place at that time. Then the problem became one of deciding what the virus was. A toxin in the food? No, it would have to be something you could see. A ghost? No, not in this day and age…"

The result was *Ring*, which was invested with its now-familiar title as something of an afterthought. "I'd got about halfway through and I hadn't thought of a title yet," the author recalled. "I happened to be thumbing through an English-Japanese dictionary when I thought it was about time to decide on something. Then the word 'ring' passed my eye. I had the strong feeling that it would fit. 'Ring' is usually used as a noun, but there is also a verb usage of ring, meaning 'to call someone' or 'to call out', such as an alarm clock or phone ringing. I liked this." The novel was published in June

1991 by Kadokawa Shoten, a Fujimi-based media conglomerate that was founded in 1946 and whose fingers are now to be found in every pie from books and magazines (Kadokawa publishes Japan's best-selling TV guide, *Shukan*, whose weekly sale is in excess of 1.3 million copies) to computer games and movies, but sales got off to a slow start. Only when *Ring* was issued as a *Kadokawa Bunko* mass-market paperback two years later did it begin to build the momentum which went to make it the publishing phenomenon of the decade. The springboard for Suzuki's tale of terror was to be an 'urban myth', so it was fitting that in the early days of its publication, *Ring* would become something of an urban myth in its own right.

> At seventeen Tomoko didn't know what true terror was. But she did know that there were fears that grew in the imagination of their own accord. *That must be it. Yeah, that's all it is. When I turn around there won't be anything there. Nothing at all…*
>
> - **Koji Suzuki**, *Ring* (1991)

Part 1: Autumn.

Ring begins with the unaccountable deaths of two students, one in Yokohama and one in Tokyo, followed immediately by those of another two from the same areas, who are both found inside a locked car. It subsequently transpires that all four died of heart failure at the very same instant, their features 'contorted with terror'.

One of the four is Tomoko Oishi, by coincidence a niece of the wife of *Daily News* reporter Kazuyuki Asakawa. Sensing the potential of a story in the affair, Asakawa sets out to investigate. His hard-headed approach to a seemingly inexplicable set of events leads him to speculate that some sort of virus might have been responsible. Tracing the last known movements of the four, he finds that they all shared a weekend together in a rented cabin at a leisure resort named Villa Log Cabin; following in their footsteps, he rents the same cabin.

Part 2: Highlands.

Before settling in for the night, Asakawa happens upon a cryptic note from one of the four in the visitor's book. It reads in part: *Consider yourself warned: you'd better not see it unless you've got the guts. You'll be sorry you did.*

Asakawa puzzles over what 'it' might be but notices that there is a VCR below the television set in his cabin. He borrows the same tape which he ascertains that the four students had watched on the night in question and slots it into the machine. A series of strange images flicker onto the screen.

First, there is an exhortation: *WATCH UNTIL THE END. YOU WILL BE EATEN BY THE LOST…* As Asakawa tries to decipher the last word, the image changes to a

sea of red-hot lava and a shot of an erupting volcano, followed by the Japanese char-acter for 'mountain'. Next, he is shown two dice in a lead bowl, on which the num-bers one and five are uppermost. This is replaced by shots of an old woman talking to camera in an unfamiliar dialect, and the face of a newborn baby. Another change and the screen is filled with faces, kaleidoscopically multiplying from dozens to hundreds, and then to thousands — all of them berating the viewer with accusations like 'Liar!' and 'Fraud!' The next shot is of a television set, on which appears the character for 'Sada'... Suddenly, there is the face and upper torso of a man — sweating, intense. For a moment, he moves out of frame; when he returns, his shoulder is bleeding from a deep wound. Blood drips towards the camera, as though he is towering above the viewer. A blank screen gradually reveals a small, bright circle at its centre, like a ring of light. The face of the man appears briefly inside the circle, and then is gone. The ring dims, and the screen fades to black...

Above: Covers of the Ring *book trilogy.*

Finally, there is another caption: *Those who have viewed these images are fated to die at this exact hour one week from now. If you do not wish to die, you must follow these instructions exactly...*

No instructions. Only a commercial for mosquito repellent.

Asakawa is stunned. Something about the tape has affected him profoundly; he had felt, while watching it, almost as though he were a participant in the events which it depicted — that he had *been there* himself.

At that very moment, the phone rings also. Asakawa picks it up and listens. No one is there. A *confirmation* call...

Given the unquestioned deaths of the four viewers of the tape prior to himself, and at the exact hour predicted, Asakawa now considers that he has no choice but to take the warning seriously. Stuffing the tape in his bag, he heads back to Tokyo.

'Asakawa put the car in motion, but he couldn't help glancing in the rear-view mirror. No matter how he floored it, he couldn't seem to get up any speed. It was like being chased in a dream, running in slow motion. Over and over, he looked at the mirror. But the black shadow chasing him was nowhere to be seen.'

Part 3: Gusts.

Asakawa contacts an old high school friend named Ryuji Takayama, and they begin to look into possible sources for the unnerving videotape. Ryuji is made of sturdier stuff than Asakawa and is not subject to the same irrational fears; consequently, he has no qualms about viewing the video in an attempt to discover its origin. Asakawa copies it for him and the first thing they establish is that the 'mountain' on the tape is Mihara, an active volcano situated on Oshima Island. On closer inspection, some of the scenes seem not to have been captured by any kind of camera at all, but instead were reproduced on the tape by means of 'psychic' photography — mental images transferred by thought alone: regular blackouts within the scenes seem to Ryuji to mimic the action of the human eye when it *blinks*…

In his haste to unlock the secrets of the video, Asakawa had left the original version of the tape in the VCR at his home. During one of his increasing absences, his wife and daughter had stumbled upon it and also watched it. All of them are now cursed to die, seven days from the point when the end of the tape was reached. It is suddenly doubly imperative for Asakawa and Ryuji to come up with a solution to the mystery.

The pair decide to search out known psychics, and they meet with the son of Professor Miura, a psychic investigator who has compiled a countrywide list of people reported to have exhibited paranormal abilities. This avenue also points them in the direction of Oshima Island and a powerful telepath named Shizuko Yamamura, whose public debunking had led to her committing suicide in 1956 by throwing herself into the same Mount Mihara. However, Shizuko had left behind a daughter, whose name was Sadako: the 'sada' of the tape, Asakawa speculates. Convinced that they are on the right track at last, the two head for Oshima. "It's a grudge," Ryuji suggests (meaning a 'curse'). "Imagine how Sadako must have felt when her mom threw herself into Mount Mihara."

With only two days left on the countdown clock, Asakawa asks a rival journalist to conduct some research into the background of Sadako Yamamura while he and Ryuji continue to dig up what they can about Shizuko on the island. One of Miura's precepts about the nature of paranormal activity keeps playing on Asakawa's mind: '*Thoughts have energy…*' In the close-knit Oshima community, they soon turn up a distant cousin of the deceased woman, who tells them the whole tragic story…

It transpires that from 1950 to 1955, Shizuko had been involved in scientific trials to try to ascertain the extent of her supposed psychic abilities; her daughter Sadako had been born in 1947 and naturally had attended these events, though not as a participant. By 1955, the media was demanding a demonstration in order to decide the debate one way or the other. Shizuko was unprepared; the year before, she had given birth to a second child — a boy — who had died at four months. But the clamour for her to prove herself was insistent, and the task was a simple one: all she had to do was to read the numbers of two dice placed inside a lead bowl. Came the day, and Shizuko's power deserted her in front of a hostile audience and the full glare of a cynical press. The numbers were one and five, but she saw nothing at all. She had failed the test, and the following day's headlines hammered home the ignominy: 'A FAKE AFTER ALL... FIVE YEARS OF DEBATE ENDED. VICTORY FOR MODERN SCIENCE'.

As a result, Shizuko was comprehensively discredited and consequently humiliated, though local legend persisted that her psychic power was genuine and had come from the statue of an ancient mystic named En no Ozunu, which she had recovered from where it had been deposited in the sea during the American occupation of the country.

After listening to the story, Asakawa and Ryuji reach the same conclusion. *One and five*. The numbers on the two dice in the video. Shizuko might not have seen them, but her daughter Sadako *did*.

As the two are forced to wait out a storm before they can board a return ferry to the mainland, Asakawa receives a fax from his colleague which fills in more blanks about what happened to Sadako after her mother's death. According to those who knew her, she grew to be tall, slim and exquisitely beautiful. Eventually, she left her island home for Tokyo where, aged eighteen, she joined a theatre troupe. Despite her angelic appearance, the theatre director had felt that there was something 'creepy' about her: one day, he had found her standing in front of a television set whose screen showed only static. On closer inspection, he had noticed to his surprise that the set was unplugged from the wall socket at the time... Soon after this incident, Sadako left the troupe and nothing further was heard of her.

That trail having gone cold for the moment, Asakawa and Ryuji turn their attention to Sadako's notional father, who turns out to have contracted smallpox and died in a sanatorium. They trace the doctor who treated him during his last days and pay him a visit. But as soon as they set eyes on Dr Nagao, they realise that their quest must be nearing its end: he is the man *in the video*, whose face can be seen to bear down on the viewer!

Ryuji grabs hold of Nagao and forces a confession out of him. It does not make for pleasant listening. Sadako, they hear, had taken a post at the sanatorium to help with the treatment of her father, whose eventual death afforded him the dubious distinction of being the last person in Japan to die of smallpox. Sadako nevertheless continued in her post until one day she found herself walking in the grounds with Nagao. Giving in to a sudden, uncontrollable urge, he had forced himself upon her and brutally raped her. As she tried to gather herself together after the assault, Nagao noticed something peculiar about her: the girl had *testes* below her vagina. Being a medical man, he knew at once what that meant: Sadako was afflicted with testicular feminization syndrome. In effect, she was an hermaphrodite — half-woman, half-man. His passion now replaced by rage, Nagao had throttled her, dragged her to an old well nearby and thrown her bodily down its shaft. "The well was dark," he tells them. "and from where I stood at the top I couldn't see the bottom very clearly. From the smell of soil wafting up, it seemed that there was a shallow accumulation of water at the bottom. I let go. Sadako's body slid down the well into the earth, hitting the bottom with a splash." A shower of rocks had followed on, to bury all trace of the deed.

In addition to the horror of the rape and murder, both men now realise something else: Nagao had himself contracted smallpox through working with his patients, though he was subsequently cured. But he was infected with the virus when he raped Sadako. The girl had therefore been infected with smallpox prior to being killed. Assuming that she *had* been killed before being thrown down the well... For if not, she had lain there for who knows how long, incubating a deadly contagion.

Before he and Asakawa leave Nagao to his guilt, Ryuji asks him the whereabouts of the sanatorium at which the murder of Sadako had taken place. It no longer exists, they are told; it was torn down to make way for the building of a resort complex — the very Villa Log Cabin at Pacific Land where the four unsuspecting students had watched the video in one of its rented cabins!

Asakawa and Ryuji believe they now have all the pieces of the puzzle. Sadako, in her rage against an unjust world which had humiliated and ultimately destroyed both of her parents, had projected her dying thoughts onto the ether where they had laid in wait for a suitable vessel through which they might find form again. Something over which, in life, she had been able to exert control. Television. A television whose picture, at the very instant of psychic transmission, was being recorded onto videotape by students on a weekend break. With only a matter of hours to spare before the deadline runs out for Asakawa, they head back to Pacific Land and the cabin where he first had watched the video six days before.

Ryuji has reasoned that to lift the curse, Sadako's remains must be properly laid to rest. They have also figured out that the old well in which she breathed her last must lie beneath the floor of the rented cabin. Time is fast running out, but they manage to gain access to the cavity under the floorboards and lo and behold, there it is! Taking it in turns, they lower themselves into the well to scoop out buckets of water in the search for Sadako's corpse. Eventually, Asakawa lays his hands on a skull...

In his desperate attempt to find the remains, Asakawa has lost track of time. Ryuji now gleefully informs him that the deadline has passed, six minutes before. In the nick of time, the curse has been lifted; Asakawa and Ryuji are free.

The two men return the bones of Sadako to the Yamamura cousin on Oshima Island for burial and set off back to Tokyo.

Part 4: Ripples.

All is not as it seems, however. On the following day, at the appointed hour, Ryuji begins to sense that something is wrong. He feels suddenly unwell; his chest constricts; his heart races... He calls his girlfriend on the telephone. She answers, but all she hears is a piercing scream...

When he hears the news that Ryuji is dead, Asakawa is left in a quandary as to how *he* managed to survive while his friend died. He turns the problem over in his mind; the only logical solution is that inadvertently he must have done something along the way which Ryuji did not. Eventually, the truth dawns: Asakawa had watched the tape from the cabin at Pacific Land, but he had made a *copy* for Ryuji to see. Without realising it, he had transferred the curse. It was more than a 'grudge': it was a *virus* — just as he had thought at the start. Sadako's will had somehow conjoined in death with the smallpox with which she unwittingly had been infected. To survive the curse, the next 'carrier' had to pass a copy of the tape on to another unsuspecting victim. And they, to another again. And on and on, until the whole world was contaminated. What then? Could it be passed back to one who had seen it already?

Asakawa cannot think that far ahead. His concern now is to save his wife and child: it is their turn next. Unless... He has his wife make two more copies of the video. He explains that he wants to show it to her parents... As he sets off towards the home of his in-laws with the deadly tapes at his side, Asakawa's thoughts are in turmoil...

'Asakawa kept his foot steady on the accelerator and the car pointed towards Ashikaga. In his rear-view mirror he could see the skies over Tokyo, receding into the distance. Black clouds moved eerily across the skies. They slithered like serpents, hinting at the unleashing of some apocalyptic evil.'

"At first, I didn't have the story," Suzuki recalled for Norman Englund of *Fangoria* magazine. "I didn't even have the idea. I'd started out with four people who were going to share a strange experience, but I was just writing off the top of my head, not knowing where I was going. In my study, I had music playing and sunlight was streaming in from a window. An odd feeling came over me and, looking to the side of my desk, I saw a videotape. That's when it hit me. Why don't I have them watch a video together?"

Suzuki may not have been in possession of the whole of his story at this stage, but he did have cultural and historical references on which to draw in order to provide himself with a *back* story of sorts. When it came to developing the history of the 'cursed' tape, he decided to seek out cases of psychic phenomena in the paranormal history of Japan, in the same way that Bram Stoker had added verisimilitude to Count Dracula by blending his own character's résumé with an intricate weave of fact and fiction which he was able to cull from the archives of the British Museum about a real-life Wallachian warlord from the fifteenth century by name of Vlad Tepes. Suzuki reportedly chanced upon the psychic experiments of one Tomokichi Fukurai, an assistant professor of psychology at Tokyo University from 1908 to 1913, who decided to devote himself to the study of telepathy and clairvoyance. Among several supposed mediums upon whom Fukurai was able to call to further his investigations was a young woman from Kumamoto, on the island of Kyushu. Chizuko Mifune was twenty-three years old by the time she came to the attention of the professor, but already she was famous in her locality for her alleged powers of 'second sight' and ability to identify objects hidden from her view. Fukurai's experiments with Mifune and others of similar bent, like Kohichi Mita, Ikuko Nagao and a Briton by the name of William Hope, formed the basis of a book on the subject which he published in 1931, entitled *Clairvoyance and Thoughtography*.

> How, then, can the spirit operate on matter? I maintain that it can do so by the willing. When the spirit wills to produce a picture on plates, then that picture will appear on it... It follows that the camera is of no use for spirit-photography, any more than for thoughtography, because the spirit, being a pure reality, transcends the physical law of light and acts directly upon the plate, without going through the camera.
> - **Tomokichi Fukurai**, *Clairvoyance and Thoughtography* (1931)

Mifune was a woman of strong religious beliefs, but she was also ill-educated, had suffered from tinnitus since the age of twelve and was known to harbour grudges. The 'experiment' which had caught the eye of Suzuki took place in Tokyo in August 1908, when what Fukurai refers to as the medium's 'dishonesty' in front of a panel of learned observers resulted in accusations of fraud, and a cloud of suspicion being cast over the whole of Fukurai's thesis. The episode of the dice occurred on 18 November 1910, in Kumamoto City, with Fukurai as the sole witness. Mifune correctly predicted, six times out of nine, the numbers which were facing up on two dice that were shaken after being sealed inside a black cigarette case. Suzuki chose one and five for his numbers, as this was one of the combinations which did *not* feature in the original experiment.

Fukurai's enthusiasm for the pseudo-science of *nen*-telegraphy — the transference of thought to a solid medium, such as an unexposed photographic plate — was not shared by his faculty colleagues, however. His demonstrations were rarely conducted with the kind of rigour normally demanded of scientific experimentation and Mita, for instance, was better known as one of a group of theatrical magicians. Fukurai cited blemishes on one such plate as proof that Nagao could imprint a mental image onto it from afar, but when another image produced by Nagao was advanced as being a psychic photograph of 'Kwanjeon, God of Mercy', Fukurai's explorations of the paranormal were felt to be more to do with spiritualism than science and no longer consid-

Above: Sadako Takahashi.

ered supportable by the Imperial hierarchy; he was forced to resign his post and take up one at the Shingon-run university in Koyasan, the home of esoteric Buddhism. Chizuko Mifune, his notional protégé, had committed suicide by ingesting poison on 18 January 1911, and a tomb in her honour stands in Kumamoto's Rokujizo Park. On the morning of her death, she had read a newspaper article inspired by a failed experiment of Nagao's, which concluded that 'Thoughtography is doubtful' and spoke of her also in derisive terms. "It is no use trying," she told her brother Takeo, and she took her own life a few hours later.

(The story of Fukurai and Mifune and their respective falls from grace parallels that of William Crookes and Florence Cook, one an eminent Victorian psychic investigator and the other his pet medium. While in a state of trance, Cook allegedly was able to bring about the materialisation of a phantom in her own image, which she referred to as Katie King — an unprecedented achievement which Crookes validated. However, Cook had a sister of similar height and build, who was also a medium and capable of a little duplicity. Crookes used his experiments with Florence Cook as a springboard to found the Society for Psychical Research in 1882 and, in stark contrast to the fate which later befell Fukurai, went on to become President of the Royal Society and the recipient of a knighthood.)

"I put myself in Asakawa's shoes to analyse the video images I had described," Suzuki explained. "I realised that the images could be separated into two categories: images that are floating or hidden in the scenes, and images that can actually be seen with the naked eye. I had to make some distinction between the two. How could I do this? Some of the images pass through your retina, but you don't actually see them,

Mount Mihara.

and so you don't blink. The images that you can see with your naked eye cause you to blink and are held inside by the black curtain of that blink. And then later I inserted these blinks into the story. Well, these images that you can see as they pass into your eye, how were they copied onto the tape? Were they broadcast from somewhere? Were they the result of pirated signals? No. Then I began to think that it could be *nensha*. Alright, so I'll go with *nensha*... I began to read up on ESP. Before that, I hadn't been thinking of putting a psychic in the story. I wasn't really interested in it in the beginning, but I did some reading on the topic... About Professor Fukurai and so on. The story of *Ring* really began to unfold from there."

Scant information of substance is available on this aspect, other than Fukurai's own take on the subject in his monograph and anecdotal evidence concerning the mediums who were involved. Much of what has since been dispersed around the Internet in relation to Professor Fukurai and his dealings with Chizuko Mifune is akin to the urban legends that intentionally were contrived to give credence to *The Blair Witch Project* in 1999. More verifiable is Suzuki's sea-born psychic progenitor, En no Ozunu, who was based on a real mountain ascetic of that name (or, variously, En no Gyoja, En no Odunu and more) who is venerated as the founder of Shugendo, an esoteric Buddhist religion that combines Shinto folk-tales with Taoist beliefs and Chinese Yin-yang magic. Like many such religious fountainheads, En 'the Ascetic' became a focus for legend after having been banished to Izu province in 699 AD, ostensibly for practising sorcery; it was said that he could hover in the air, walk on water, perform all manner of miracles and exert his will over others by the power of thought alone.

Notwithstanding the validity or otherwise of claims made on behalf of his historical sources, Koji Suzuki pulled all these disparate influences together to lend his novel an air of scientific credibility and mystic resonance: En the Ascetic was incorporated into the narrative in relatively unaltered form, while Fukurai and Mifune became Ikuma and his lover Shizuko Yamamura, mother of Sadako. Having given Asakawa something to investigate, Suzuki added other cultural elements into the mix, such as the real eruption of Mount Mihara in 1950, which his reporter confirms by checking an entry in Mitsuro Yoshimoto's *Volcanoes of Japan*. (In popular mythology, Mihara was also the volcano into which movie monster Godzilla was lured at the climax of *Godzilla 1985* [*Gojira*, 1984].) For his conceptual 'virus' and actual cause of death from viewing the video, he utilised the fact that smallpox had been eradicated from the Asian continent in 1975; it was officially declared dead by the World Health Organisation in 1980. The symptoms of smallpox were quickening of the pulse, intense headache, convulsions, delirium and pustulous

sores that produced desiccated scabs which fell away to leave reddish-brown scars. *Above: Sadako Sasaki.* Death was often as a result of asphyxiation, due to inflammation of the larynx or windpipe. These symptoms, greatly accelerated, are identical to those to which Ryuji is climactically subject in the novel — not the more theatrical but largely unfeasible death by *fright*: 'The cheeks were yellowish, dried and cracked, and hair was falling out in clumps to reveal brown scabs,' Suzuki writes of Ryuji's plight, as the latter contemplates his fate in the mirror.

There was still the matter of a name for his reluctant villain, and with some sense of irony, Suzuki picked Sadako, after Sadako Sasaki, in memory of all the children who had ever been wronged by adult folly. Sadako Sasaki was born on 7 January 1943 — a child of Hiroshima. When she was two years old, the first atomic bomb to be deployed in anger fell on her city, at 8.15am on the morning of 6 August 1945. Sadako's home was only a mile away from the centre of the blast. In November 1954, while in the sixth grade of her Nobori-cho elementary school, she was diagnosed with leukaemia. Sadako was admitted to the Red Cross hospital in January the following year. That August, a gift of brightly coloured *origami* cranes was sent to the hospital by well-wishers. This, in turn, inspired some of the patients to make their own, including

Sadako. By the time she succumbed to the disease on 25 October 1955, at the age of twelve, little Sadako had made more than a thousand paper cranes. They were buried with her. The story spread and was elaborated into a more idealised version, which had Sadako make only 644 of the cranes before her death, the rest being completed by her classmates. A memorial to Sadako Sasaki was erected in Hiroshima's Peace Park, emblazoned with the legend: 'I will write Peace on your wings and you will fly all over the world.' A second memorial stands in the Peace Park in Seattle, Washington DC (which coincidentally became the setting for the American remake of *Ring*). Sada means 'chaste' in Japanese, while ko means 'child'.

But there was a dark side to this particular choice of name. Just before his dismissal from Tokyo University, Professor Fukurai had encountered another dubious medium by the name of Sadako Takahashi. Takahashi supposedly was a descendent of Noh dramatist Juro Motomasa, author of *The Madwoman at the Sumida River* (*Sumidagawa*), but she was subject to physical seizures and seemed on occasion to Fukurai to be possessed by a secondary personality of a 'long-nosed *goblin*'. "At first it stood behind the medium and gave her advice about illness or psychic work, usually through dreams, visions, or planchette-writing. Afterwards, however, it used to appear before the screen and talked directly with us..." he wrote. On 27 April 1911, Sadako Takahashi produced an image of 'feathers in a vortex' on an unexposed photographic plate — the feathers being those of the goblin's wings. Invited to participate in further experiments, she declined and in the summer of 1913 returned with her husband to her birthplace of Okayama; she was never heard from again.

"For scenes such as those in the video to exist, I felt that there had to be someone with the power to do this kind of thing," Suzuki elaborated. "Someone with the ability to impress such images onto tape. To this end, I created Sadako. In order for the tape to do what it had to, I needed Sadako to explain its existence."

(Videotape is an analogue medium and not a digital one, however, so the quality of copies would degrade to the degree that the image would become unwatchable and the viewer would be relieved of its injunction to dupe, unless Sadako's particular way with *nensha* was somehow able to overcome that technical impediment!)

With the various pieces of the puzzle assembled, all that remained for Suzuki to do was to work out the mechanics of the plot and come up with his ambiguous title. "From the beginning, I didn't exactly use the name *Ring* in the circular sense," he explained. "But since I gave it that title, a lot of circular things have come up in the story — the spiral, the DNA double helix, the loop, and so on. I guess it's a good thing that I chose that title."

For all its skilful employment of modern technology, *Ring* is a Gothic novel, in that it conforms to the precepts set down for the Gothic by Mario Praz in his

Introductory Essay to *Three Gothic Novels* (Penguin English Library, 1968): 'An intro- *Above:* Onibaba
ductory story in order to produce an old manuscript where the happenings are writ- *(1964): the*
ten down, a Gothic castle forming a gloomy background with its secret corridors and *woman (Nobuko*
labyrinthine network of subterranean passages, a mysterious crime frequently con- *Otowa) retrieves*
nected with illicit or incestuous love, and perpetrated by a person in holy orders, a vil- *the Noh mask*
lain (as a rule an Italian or a Spaniard) who has pledged himself to the devil, who final- *from the dead*
ly hurls him into the abyss; ghosts, witches and sorcerers, nature conspiring to effects *samurai.*
of terror and wonder, portraits endowed with a mysterious life, statues which suddenly are seen to bleed...' For Praz's manuscript, read videotape; for his castle, read
Oshima island, the rental cabin in the woods or any other locale central to the action;
the mysterious crime connected with illicit love is that of rape and murder; the villain
is Sadako, a girl with powers gifted by the devil; the remainder is accounted for by the
palette of paranormal effects with which Suzuki imbues his tale. One could add to the
above that the Gothic staple of a curse hangs over the proceedings, and that Asakawa's
quest is a redemptive one — albeit cloaked in the ironic garb of postmodernism.

The examination of the pseudo-science surrounding the concept of the Ring
'virus' is a blind, and a contemporary adoption of the sleight-of-hand technique that
was much used by H G Wells in novels like *The Invisible Man* (1897). In that story, Wells
took the old alchemical dream of a cloak of invisibility and dressed it in the garb of science fiction, but there is no overlooking the fact that the trick itself is achieved by
magic; by a serum, a 'powder', in the manner of Dr Jekyll's transformation into Mr Hyde
(in fact, Griffin's passage into invisibility occurs between chapters). Much convincing
prose is then given over to the everyday effects of invisibility, which affords the tale a
scientific air, but it is pure Gothic horror in truth. In *Ring*, the same supernatural 'magic'

enables Sadako to metamorphose her rage into images on a videotape, virus or no virus.

Suzuki cleverly mixes the old in with the new, drawing on an assortment of cultural allusions along the way: the casting of Sadako's body into a handy well echoes Nagisa Oshima's *In the Realm of Passion* (*Ai no borei*, 1978), in which an adulterous couple dispose of a murdered husband in a similar manner. Asakawa's own descent into the well at the climax recalls Nobuko Otowa's midnight clamber into the pit in the reed beds to retrieve the *Noh* mask from the dead samurai in Kaneto Shindo's *Onibaba* (1964). The Kabuki *Bancho Sayarashiki* also makes use of a well. In Japanese mythology, water is viewed as the realm of the dead and areas of association are often regarded as passages to the underworld.

If the novel has a failing, it is in the matter of its climax (or epilogue, in fact), when the pair discover that the charm has not been fulfilled and the curse of Sadako is visited upon Ryuji. After such an elaborate build-up and the palpable sense of dread which has accumulated as a result, the much-anticipated payoff to all that has gone before never actually materialises, and Sadako's 'grudge' comes off as something of a let-down. Interviewed for JapanReview.net, Suzuki declared, "I don't believe in devils, demons, or evil." His inability to bridge that philosophical divide for the sake of his novel is only too clear in its closing pages. Suzuki's reticence in conjuring a vision that could produce the heart-stopping effect on its victims which he describes so vividly in the early chapters is the single greatest deficiency in *Ring*; in the event, he merely has Ryuji stare into a mirror at the face of (his own) death:

'The face in the mirror was none other than his own, a hundred years in the future. Even Ryuji hadn't known it would be so terrifying to meet himself transformed into someone else.' This last reference relates to the earlier description of the sight which greets Ryuji in the mirror; the image is meant to emulate the effects of smallpox, but the previous reference to 'a hundred years in the future' is simply inexplicable.

(There is a sidebar in the novel to the effect that Ryuji had been a rapist, the reason for which becomes clear when he is able to prise a confession to the rape of Sadako out of Nagao through his intimate knowledge of the psychology of such a crime; however, Suzuki withdraws this charge at the end of the tale by having his girlfriend Mai declare him to be a virgin. This curious recanting of something which the reader has been led to believe throughout appears to serve no purpose beyond an attempt to elicit sympathy for the only one of the two protagonists to die from the curse of Sadako.)

From this summary, it can be seen that the novel of *Ring* contains *no* actual ghost. The *will* of Sadako survives in some form, to imprint itself on the ether and ultimately onto radio-waves, but this could be classed as a paranormal rather than

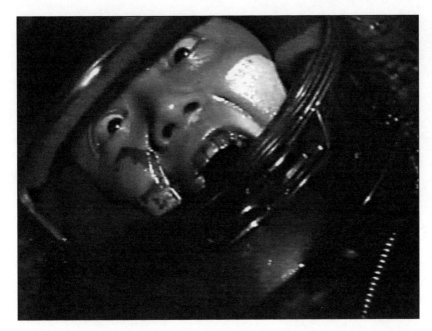

Ring: Kanzenban
*(1995): the biker
dies.*

a supernatural phenomenon — as Suzuki goes to some pains to classify Sadako in
life. Certainly, there is nothing in *Ring* to support the contention that Sadako herself
has somehow survived decease. Her will, or whatever — the 'residue' of her rage —
could conceivably have lain dormant since the moment of her death, awaiting acti-
vation by any set of circumstances similar to that which sets the plot in motion.
There is no 'conscious ghost' at work, as the species is delineated by Michael Cox
and R A Gilbert in their introduction to *The Oxford Book of Ghost Stories* (1986).
Thus, no climactic apparition is possible, despite the many allusions to it in which
Suzuki teasingly indulges.

To hedge his bets, Suzuki at least posits the *possibility* that Sadako is the agent
of a devil. The novel states that the ancient mystic, En no Ozunu, was possessed of
occult power, and that part of this power was transferred to Sadako's mother Shizuko
when she recovered his statue from the sea; in turn, it was bestowed on Sadako
through the gene pool. When the true nature of the curse is finally revealed and the
contagion is set to spread, Suzuki tentatively abandons science in favour of a more
irrational reading: 'In every age, the devil reappears in a different guise,' he has
Asakawa muse. 'You can stamp it out, and stamp it out, and he'll keep coming back,
over and over.'

"I'm not so interested in the concept of evil," Suzuki explains. "But for a novel,

it is necessary to have evil: you have to have good things and bad things for a novel to work. I strive to write the good parts of the human experience. If there is no dark, there is no contrast and it doesn't highlight what you're trying to show: dark and light." Like all professed agnostics, he is nevertheless fascinated with the fundamentalist doctrines of organised religion, the inability of science to uncover the secrets of life and death, and the rationale behind the idea of the soul.

"I do wonder what happens when people die," he revealed to Akemi Yokoyama of *60 Seconds.* "At present, science cannot explain everything that happens. Some things simply defy explanation. Nevertheless, I think most paranormal stuff is rubbish. But who cares — so long as it's fun."

Ring: Kanzenban

> Arima: Shigemori... died.
> Asakawa: Died?
> Arima: Yes. From heart failure...
> - *Ring: Kanzenban* (1995)

In 1995, Fuji Television purchased the rights to Suzuki's novel and turned it into a 95 minute, Friday night 'movie of the week', directed by Chisui Takagawa. Despite a small number of (relatively minor) changes which were implemented to improve pace and accommodate the need for ad breaks on behalf of programme sponsors Nescafé and Pola cosmetics every ten minutes, the film remained faithful to its source — almost reverentially so. Asakawa's daughter Yoko was eliminated and his wife made pregnant instead, and a sub-plot which saw Sadako engaging in an incestuous relationship with her father was introduced late in the proceedings, primarily to establish her ability to kill by thought alone when she 'wills' to death a would-be boyfriend who catches them in the act. In all other respects, *Ring: Kanzenban* ('The Complete Edition', as it was to become known) is an accurate rendering of the novel as written.

The prologue is pure Suzuki. A young girl sits at home, alone. She begins to sense something untoward; suddenly, the lights flicker and dim... She starts to panic and goes downstairs. From the expression on her face, she has become aware of another person in the room; she looks her (unseen) visitant up and down and screams... She runs to the bathroom and locks herself in; from a POV outside the glass door, she can now be seen struggling with an invisible assailant. A moment later, she falls dead, blood on her lips. The showerhead has sprung into life, spraying her body with water. The camera closes in, *Psycho*-style, on the plughole of the shower as the water swirls down... and the title of the film ripples into view. We then cut to Asakawa in a cab, exchanging pleasantries with the driver. They halt at a red light and a motorcyclist draws up alongside of them. Asakawa glances towards him; without warning, he jerks his head back as though he is struggling for breath. He topples from his bike and appears to be fighting to remove his helmet. Asakawa and the driver try to help, but it is too late — the biker is dead, blood smeared on his cheek and a look of terror on his face. (In the novel, this second death is reported in the third-party; Asakawa is not present in the taxi.) Asakawa notices the time on the boy's wristwatch: it is 12.48am.

When Asakawa returns home, his wife tells him that her niece has been found dead. (This is Tomoko, the girl in the bathroom.) When later they visit the house to pay their respects, Asakawa's suspicions are aroused and he checks in the bathroom. He spots a clock on a shelf which seems to have been stopped by the effects of the water: it shows a time of 12.48am. At the newspaper office where Asakawa works as a proof-reader, he next comes upon a story about a young couple who inexplicably were found dead in their locked car. From the condition of the bodies, it appears that they were *in flagrante* at the time. Asakawa queries the time of death. 12.48am...

Thus the intrigue is set in motion, and before long Asakawa has arrived at the rental villa and original scene of the crime. He quickly procures the videotape which the four had watched prior to their deaths and settles down to view it.

One of the most interesting aspects of *Kanzenban* is that it contains the first attempt by film-makers to capture the potency of Suzuki's 'cursed' video onscreen, and there is a significant difference in the approach taken in this version of the story to that in later readings of *Ring*. Not so much in the content of the tape itself, as in the depiction of its viewer's reaction to it.

In *Kanzenban*, the video plays almost entirely as its creator decreed.

The screen fills with static... a red dot swims into view to preface a montage of shots depicting an erupting volcano... a prism of faces are overlaid by three dice, showing six, two, one... more static, then an old woman's face as she talks to camera... another group of faces converge on the viewer... a new-born baby cries... the word 'sada'... then the old woman again... amid the sea of faces, a young boy clutches his throat and falls dead... a new face leers at the screen; the man reels back suddenly, a bite on his shoulder... blood splashes into view... finally, the ominous

Above: Ring:
Kanzenban:
*Sadako (Ayane
Miura).*

prophecy of doom: "*You* who have watched this
— you have seven days remaining. In seven days,
at this time, you will die. If you do not want to
die, the way to save yourself is…"

And a last flash-frame of an eye in huge
close-up.

While all these images are unfolding,
Asakawa is shown to be profoundly affected by
them, exactly as he is in the novel. Unlike the
subsequent adaptations, it is not the images
themselves which disturb but the fact that he
feels himself being drawn in to the events on the
tape, as though he were party to its tale of woe.
The figures on the video loom up behind him in
the room… When the shot of the baby appears, he senses himself holding the self-
same infant; he looks at his hands, but they are empty. The old woman sits momentarily to his right while she speaks to him on the video… In the end, he keels over
from sheer exhaustion at the resultant drain on his emotional resources.

It should be apparent from this that *Kanzenban* chooses to depict the *effects* of
fear rather than attempts to engender it and, from this point on, it settles into the
unravelling of the mystery with only occasional nods in the direction of the odd.
Asakawa now has until eight minutes past ten on the evening of the seventh day to
save his life. He enlists the aid of a saturnine college professor, the enigmatic Ryuji
Takayama, and the two set out to solve the puzzle as before. (A sidebar elaborates the
murky element from the novel in relation to Ryuji's character to give him more of an
aura of mystique: in *Ring*, Ryuji is characterised as a self-confessed rapist [although the
claim is recanted at the end], but in *Kanzenban*, he is suspected of having murdered
his wife by occult means. Asakawa believes Ryuji's version of events, that he merely
had a premonition of his wife's death at the hands of another.)

One especially effective scene occurs when Ryuji notices Asakawa blinking as he
scours the tape for clues, which leads him to the conclusion that the 'blackouts' are
the product of *nen*-telegraphy. This clever use of cinematic shorthand obviates the
lengthy exposition in which Suzuki has to indulge in print to arrive at the same conclusion. The ending of *Kanzenban* is more apocalyptic in tone than Suzuki allows himself to be in the novel: Asakawa is shown wandering the bustling streets of Tokyo in
search of an unsuspecting victim to whom he can pass the curse in order to save the
lives of his wife and unborn child. Implicit in the scene is that he unwittingly has
become the harbinger of an exterminating plague. Suzuki intimated much the same

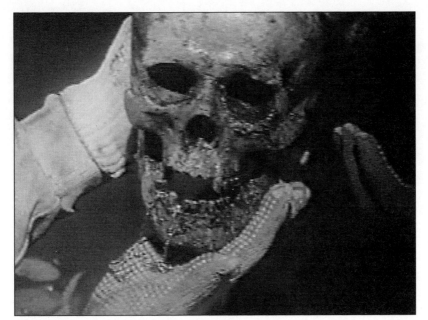

thing, but he left the way open for the further experimentation to defeat the threat which would be the main focus of his sequel, *Rasen (Spiral)*.

Having followed the trail to Oshima and sourced the video to Sadako, the script for *Kanzenban* now introduces its one curious digression from Suzuki's original. Sadako is shown in flashback indulging in an incestuous affair with her father. (The alert reader might have noticed the incongruous presence of a 'young boy' in the video; he is Shigemori, who stumbles upon the twosome in his desire to have Sadako for himself and pays for his impetuosity with his life.)

The part of Sadako was played by twenty-year-old nude model and sometime actress, Ayane Miura, who was chosen for the same reason that Hammer would fill its films with bosomy starlets like Veronica Carlson, Valerie Leon and Stephanie Beacham. The screenplay not only required Sadako to appear nude, but she had to engage in a graphic rape scene with Tomorowo Taguchi's Dr Nagao. Miura's acting abilities are patently limited, but she manages to make a reasonable distinction between the demure young girl of the earlier part of the film and the malevolent harpy who appears increasingly at intervals towards the close. This would have been a difficult balance for any actress to strike, and subsequent adaptations were to circumvent the problem in another way. The infamous well into which Sadako is hurled by her murderer in *Kanzenban* is of *square* construction, pointing up the fact that Suzuki's use of *Ring* as

Ring: Kanzenban:
*Sadako appears
to Ryuji.*

his title was originally intended to indicate the literal ringing of the telephone after the video has been viewed, as well as the collective nature of the curse in action; only later would the term come to be symbolised by the well itself.

Sadako's transition from unburied corpse (whose wilful malignance has managed to transcend death) to full-fledged ghost was also begun in *Kanzenban*. Screenwriters Joji Iida and Taizo Soshiya had been presented with a story which lacked a visual climax: Asakawa merely recovers the remains, sees to it that they receive proper burial, and the spell is broken — for him, at least. Ryuji's subsequent death is anticlimactic, and much in accordance with those in the prologue. It fell to Iida and Soshiya to come up with a finale which would better accommodate the dramatic needs of the different medium; it was therefore a logical move to have Sadako actually *appear*, in order to literalise the otherwise invisible threat.

(An analogy of sorts can be found in Robert Wise's 1971 production of Michael Crichton's *The Andromeda Strain*, which also focussed on the threat posed by an alien 'virus'. Towards the end of the film, the bacteriological enemy has effectively been defeated by purely scientific means, so Wise played up the 'false' climax of the book to provide a more cinematic resolution, in which James Olson's Dr Hall has to race against time — and laser cannon! — to prevent the Wildfire underground decontamination lab from self-destructing.)

Ring: Kanzenban:
the rape.

Not only the threat was literalised, however; a passage from the novel which Suzuki had written to imply *sensation* on the part of Asakawa as he recovers the skull from the well is translated to the screen as an actual occurrence: 'Sadako Yamamura blinked her melancholy eyes two or three times to shake the water from her eyelashes… She smiled at Asakawa, then narrowed her eyes as if to focus her vision. *I've been waiting to meet you…*' This flight of fancy by his protagonist in relation to the skull is preceded by the qualification that Asakawa's imagination 'clothed it with flesh'. But no such subtlety is allowed to permeate *Kanzenban*. Having opted to personify the spirit of Sadako in the buxom form of Ayane Miura, the film then goes the whole hog and shows her dealing death to her one on-screen victim by clutching at his throat with mud-caked hands.

To make good on the implication of her relationship with her father and indulge in a little horror film cliché at the same time, Sadako appears to Ryuji clutching a baby to her breast: "Sadako-san — that's your child, isn't it?" he affirms, before surrendering to his fate. Suzuki's sequel to his original novel had not yet been published at the time of *Kanzenban*'s production, so the presence of a baby posits the possibility of a different story development (either that, or its writers simply overlooked the fact that the baby in the novel was Sadako's *brother*). However, *Kanzenban*'s most shocking scene, true to the book, shows Nagao discovering the truth of Sadako's physiological make-up during his attempt at rape; having seen fit to assert that she suffers from testicular feminisation syndrome, the film seemingly is blind to the consequence that persons thus afflicted are biologically unable to conceive, as they have no womb. How then has Sadako managed to bear a child? The inclusion of this ingredient of incestuous conception is a matter of pure contrivance and it tarnishes an otherwise praiseworthy and honourable adaptation. But in the killing of the boy, and later of Ryuji, a different precedent was established. In the novel, it is not Sadako herself who is responsible for the various deaths, it is the product of her rage as she lay dying in the well. *Kanzenban* not only turned Suzuki's murdered innocent into a 'ghost', it turned her into a monster as well.

Director Takagawa succumbs to horror convention in his adoption of a first-person camera when the spirit of Sadako is intimated to be approaching (or receding from) her victims, *a la* Sam Raimi's *Evil Dead* series, while angled shots of air-conditioning fans are straight out of Alan Parker's *Angel Heart* (1987), but the film is otherwise competently and efficiently handled. As a made-for-TV movie, it puts most Western offerings in the same vein in the shade. It is not, however, the least bit scary; interesting and involving, yes, but scary — no. *Kanzenban* had converted Suzuki's paranormal thriller into one of *supernatural* mystery, with an *Exorcist*-style incidental score, but the next version of *Ring* was to complete its transformation into an all-time classic ghost story.

Advertised with the tag-line 'Accident, or unnatural death? A young girl's hatred that steals four lives' (*Jiko ka! Henshi ka! Yottsu no inochi o ubau shojo no onnen*), *Ring: Kanzenban* was transmitted on 11 August, two days before the start of the annual Obon ('Festival of the Dead') holiday, which in many ways is a Japanese variant of the Western tradition of Halloween. Its première on television was timed to coincide with the publication of *Rasen*, the sequel to *Ring*, which Kadokawa Shoten had put out in hardback the month before. In the meantime, Suzuki had written other books, but on the topic of fatherhood: *Fusei no Tanjo* (*Birth of Paternity*), *Kazoku no Kizuna* (*Bonds of Family*) and *Papa-ism*. He had also translated crime writer and one-time BBC radio producer Simon Brett's 'Little Sod' Diaries into his native tongue, as well as producing a children's book of his own — *Namida* (*Tears*) — and he was recognised as something of an authority on the subject as a result. "I believe I'm an American type of man," he gleefully declared. "American fathers work for their children; Japanese fathers work for their companies. Japanese don't naturally go against anything or anyone, whereas Americans naturally feel the need to overcome difficulties. I feel that I'm this type of man. I believe my stories have more of an American mindset." His 'American mindset' was much in evidence in *Rasen*, which picked up the story of Sadako's curse precisely at the point where *Ring* had left off.

Despite a sleeve blurb in the English edition which suggests that it can be read as a stand-alone work, *Rasen* not only follows on from events in *Ring* but also imitates the stylistic approach of its predecessor, splitting the narrative into five parts: *Dissecting*, *Vanishing*, *Decoding*, *Evolving* and *Foreshadowing*, plus a Prologue and Epilogue.

If Suzuki's intention was to turn his original story on its head, he largely succeeds, but it is a brave — or foolhardy — author who sets out consciously to produce a sequel to a novel that negates much of what went to pass in the parent. For those who expected a more conventional follow-up, things quickly go awry. Whereas *Ring* was predicated on a viral contagion which produced a coincidence of corpses, no such coincidence appears to exist for the characters in *Rasen* who, when presented with a series of equally strange deaths (namely several of the protagonists from the previous book), have to investigate the circumstances afresh but from a different perspective. This sounds very clever in principle, but it is a blatant betrayal of devotees of *Ring*. And that is only the beginning. In fact, *Rasen* reads like a book that was written to succeed an *unsuccessful* novel, where continuity and consistency matter less than the tricks which an author can play on his own creation. The idea of elaborating on the 'science' of *Ring* while toning down its supernatural element is almost acknowledgement of the fact that the first book enjoyed relatively little notoriety when its notional sequel was written, and *Rasen* was Suzuki's attempt to use the same plot but potentially to better effect. Subsequent events obviated the need. "When I wrote *Rasen*, *Ring* wasn't selling at all," Suzuki confirmed. "The book sales came about after the success of the movie." Had the screen version of *Ring* been released before the novel of *Rasen*, however, it is debatable whether Suzuki would ever have contemplated this sequel at all.

He spread the photos out on the table once more. One in particular held his attention. In it, a stocky man sat with his head resting on the edge of a bed, the position he'd been in when he stopped breathing. There were no evident external wounds. The next photo was a close-up of his face. No evidence of blood congestion, no signs of strangulation. In none of the photos could Ando find anything to establish a cause of death. Which was why, even though there was nothing to indicate a crime, the body had been sent to the ME's office for a post-mortem. It looked to be a sudden death, an unnatural one at that, and under the circumstances the body couldn't legally be cremated until the cause of death was discovered.

The corpse was found with both arms and both legs spread wide. Ando knew the man, knew him well — an old friend from college, whom Ando had never dreamed of having to dissect. Ryuji Takayama, who'd been alive up until a mere twelve hours ago, had been a classmate of Ando's through six years of medical school...

- **Koji Suzuki**, *Rasen* (1995)

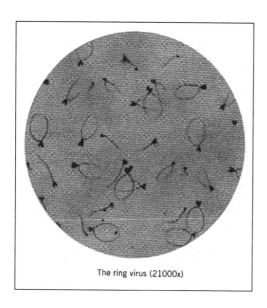

The ring virus (21000x)

Above:

Illustration taken

from the Vertical

edition of Spiral

(1995).

Pathologist Mitsuo Ando, still pining over the death of his young son Takanori in a drowning accident, is given the unenviable task of conducting a post-mortem on old medical school classmate Ryuji Takayama. Having dissected the corpse and stuffed the gutted torso with newspaper prior to sewing it up again, he notices a piece of the paper idly jutting out from the suture: on it are six numbers which he conjectures to be some kind of cypher. Decoded, they spell 'RING'.

Ryuji's girlfriend Mai Takano is also on the case, desirous to find out what she can about the untimely death of her erstwhile lover. While Ando and she start to probe for clues (literally, in his case), another example of 'sudden death' syndrome is brought to his notice: an automobile accident near the entrance to the Tokyo Harbour Tunnel has turned up two more bodies, those of Shizu Asakawa and her daughter Yoko. Kazuyuki Asakawa was driving the car at the time and his wife and child were seated in the back. But an examination at the scene revealed that both of them had died an hour *before* the actual accident, and that Asakawa's eventual discovery of this had probably led to the crash. Furthermore, it transpires that Asakawa was an acquaintance of Ryuji's and that there was a VCR in the vehicle. Curiouser and curiouser.

While searching among Ryuji's effects, Takano feels compelled to watch the video. Meanwhile, Ando's fellow pathologist Miyashita establishes that all of the victims are infected with a virus similar to smallpox. Ando is no longer able to contact Takano and he tries to discover her whereabouts. *Daily News* reporter Yoshino arrives on the scene to reveal to Ando that Asakawa was investigating a story about a cursed videotape; he is looking for Asakawa's notes on the case, which he feels sure that a seasoned reporter like Asakawa would have compiled along the way, but he has so far turned up no trace of either word processor or disk. (It takes a full 100 pages before Yoshino appraises Ando of the broad facts in relation to *Ring*.) The virus is discovered to be mutating.

Ando traces the word processor to Asakawa's effects, which had since been passed on to his brother Junichiro; he retrieves the floppy disk with the 'Ring' report on it and figures out that of the two videotapes which were known to exist, one was destroyed in the accident that put Asakawa into a coma, while the copy must now be in the hands of Mai Takano. Asakawa's minutely detailed report brings Ando up to speed on the video, the virus and the baleful influence of Sadako Yamamura.

It is at this point that the first nagging doubts start to creep in about the veracity of Suzuki's narrative. When exactly did Asakawa have time to compile his 'Ring' report? According to the plot of *Rasen*, he did it after the curse was lifted, when Ryuji had left Oshima for Tokyo but before his subsequent death. But would *sleep* not have beckoned instead? Be that as it may, Ando and Miyashita construct a theoretical model between them of how the Ring virus must operate: the images on the videotape induce a neurological reaction in the viewer's brain that causes a virus already embedded in human DNA to mutate and form the fatal strain. Mind over matter. In this, they are helped by a *second* code which Ryuji had neatly managed to implant into his own DNA at the moment of his death (or before), and which deciphered spells 'mutation'.

Returning to the still-absent Takano's apartment in his search for more clues, Ando is surprised to see an unknown woman exiting. She joins him in the lift but says nothing. 'Riding in the same elevator with her had shaken Ando to the depths of his soul. She didn't seem to be of this world, and yet, she didn't look like a ghost, either. She'd definitely been there with him in the flesh. But Ando thought he would have had an easier time accepting her if she had been a ghost.'

Following this encounter, Ando hears that Asakawa has died in his hospital bed and that Takano's body has been found inside a ventilation shaft on the roof of a building nearby. A post-mortem reveals that she had recently given birth — an unlikely event, in Ando's opinion, as she did not appear to be pregnant when last they met. And if she had watched Ryuji's video on the date that he suspected, her death was a week overdue.

What has still to be solved is the mystery of how some who had watched the video died, while others did not. Miyashita comes up with an ingenious solution: viruses are genetically pre-programmed to replicate themselves, he reasons, and so it was with the video. But when the 'charm' — the instruction to *copy* the tape — was erased by the four teenagers in the cabin, an error was introduced into the tape's make-up which created a mutant strain. The error would also be replicated along with the images, so anyone who watched the video would die without creating the necessary copies and the virus itself would die. Those who watched the mutated 'copy' simply died on cue, including Asakawa's wife and child. Viruses are programmed to survive, however, and the Ring virus must therefore have looked for another way to propagate itself. In the case of Asakawa, it went to his brain and infected the Ring *report* that it inspired him to write; it subsequently disposed of its host. But what of Mai Takano, who had watched the 'copy' tape but had died a week later than she was due? (Not all of the anomalies which have now been created in Suzuki's revision to the basic plot of *Ring* are addressed by this theory, but we press on regardless.)

Ando and Miyashita travel to cabin B4 at the Pacific Land resort to see the well and its environs for themselves. It now occurs to them that they might also be infected with the Ring virus through some means presently unknown to them. On returning to Tokyo, Ando again spots the strange tenant of the empty apartment on a station platform.

The woman tells him that she is Mai Takano's sister Masako. They share a cocktail and a night of passion, about which Ando has only vague memories the following day. He senses that something is not quite right — something that relates to Masako…

She has semi-transparent skin and broken fingernails, hypnotic eyes and an ethereal air, and she is immune to the cold of a Japanese December; still Ando's curiosity as to her real identity is not sufficiently piqued. He takes her to see Luc Besson's *Nikita*, and she mouths the dialogue in synch with its cast and ahead of the subtitles, as though she can read their thoughts. And she deflects all questions and reacts to food as though she has not tasted any in, say, twenty-five years…

While Masako showers, Ando receives a fax from Miyashita which shows the face of Sadako Yamamura from her days with the rep company in Tokyo. It is the same face into which he has been staring, doe-eyed, for the past twenty-four hours…

Ando screams and races from the apartment.

Plying his shaken colleague with brandy, it is again left to Miyashita to explain all: as with Asakawa, the virus had looked for an alternative route to survival. Takano had been in the middle of her menstrual cycle at the very moment that she had watched the video, and the virus fertilised her egg with its own DNA. The result: a new Sadako was gestated and born in a week, who then matured to adulthood in another week after that. The host was again discarded, for the new Sadako is a fully-formed hermaphrodite who quite literally can inseminate herself. Thus, the world is now threatened by two strains of the Ring virus — the one infecting the report (which Junichiro, in the meanwhile, has prepared as a novel ready for publication as a 'blood-curdling cult horror'), and Sadako herself, who is able to propagate at will.

When they return to Ando's apartment, Sadako is gone. Obligingly, she has left him a letter confirming Miyashita's hypothesis. And asking for a favour. In return, she will grant him his dearest wish; she has the power.

Without wishing to stretch the reader's patience to breaking point, 'one detail shall be added' (as M R James wrote in 'Casting the Runes'): where do Ryuji's cryptic clues fit into this scheme of things, given that they were key to Ando and Miyashita setting off in the right direction to begin with? Ryuji, it transpires, has been part of the plan all along. He is Sadako's silent partner — the real power behind the Ring… 'The only thing left for Ando to do was to join his voice with Ryuji's, with the chuckling in the dark.'

(Part of the climax to *Rasen* is predicated upon the fact that Ryuji and Takano had been lovers, and thus Ryuji had knowledge of Takano's menstrual cycle before willing her to watch the video in order that she be impregnated by the virus, but this claim was specifically denied by Takano herself at the end of *Ring*.)

An Epilogue finds Ando on a beach, six months later, watching his reborn son play at the water's edge. He is joined by Ryuji, who obliges him with a partial (and it has to be said wholly unsatisfactory) explanation of what it was all about. In effect, Ando has sold the human race down the proverbial river so that he could be reunited with his lost Takanori. Sadako has become a movie star to spread her rage through the mass media. And Ryuji? Well, Ryuji merely desires to be present at the destruction of mankind as a bemused observer, like Satan after the Fall.

In contrast to the sweeping breadth of narrative that was exhibited in *Ring*, *Rasen* is an internal dialogue on the part of Ando for much of its length, interspersed only by an external exchange of ideas with fellow pathologist Miyashita as the story nears the first of its multiple climaxes. This makes for a rather turgid first half, as an investigation of circumstances already familiar to readers of the first book is undertaken *again*, and its various plot points are examined in clinical detail. In place of the foot-slogging of the traditional detective novel, Ando manages to work out most of what he needs to know to further his researches by theoretical analysis prior to embarking on the next stage of his quest; most of his surmises prove to be correct, which tends to take the edge off any tension which might otherwise have been encouraged by particular events. *Rasen* bears all the hallmarks of an adventure dreamed up at a study desk and constructed from city maps and scientific pamphlets. It totally lacks the feel of the real, as though it were an intricate computer game complete with detailed sidebars full of important-seeming but ultimately unnecessary data. Worst of all, it lacks the passion for pure storytelling that was such a vital ingredient of *Ring*.

To those familiar with J Sheridan le Fanu's 1871 novella *Carmilla*, which Hammer Films famously adapted as *The Vampire Lovers* in 1970, the penultimate twist in *Rasen* will come as no surprise, despite its author's elaborate attempts to conceal it. Takano's 'sister' goes under the name of Masako; substitute a 'D' for the 'M' and the answer to the riddle of the mysterious woman in Takano's apartment, and later Ando's bed, soon stares one in the face — unless that one happens to be Matsuo Ando — just as Le Fanu's vampiress went variously under the pseudonyms of Mircalla and Marcilla.

The revelatory last third of *Rasen* bears more than a passing resemblance to Arthur Machen's 1894 short story 'The Great God Pan', the plot of which already owed much to Stevenson's *Strange Case of Dr Jekyll and Mr Hyde* which had been published eight years before it. Before it postulates its fantastical climax — part surrealism, part science fiction — *Rasen* once more descends into the Gothic territory that was so much a feature of *Ring*, with the alchemical creation of an homunculus which is destined to grow into a devil-god. Suzuki tries to blind the reader to this black magical scenario by infesting his narrative with the minutiae of code-breaking techniques and lectures about DNA, but Machen's similarly half-human anti-heroine Helen Vaughan was also sired through the pseudo-science of a supposed 'experiment', and another reading of the same theme is to be found in Dennis Wheatley's *To the Devil – A Daughter* (1953). All Suzuki has done to ring the changes on the Gothic staple of unholy union is to render the means of impregnation necessary to produce the Antichrist as a virus which, in *Ring*, he already suggested might have emanated from the devil himself: "'The devil always appears in the world in a different form,'" Ryuji is moved to speculate at one point. "'Maybe the devil's behind this whole thing after all.'" So for all its technological profundities and determined air of deconstructionism, *Rasen* remains mired in the preoccupations of the Gothic. It presents a view of the world which is at once detached and analytical, while at the same time heavily susceptible to superstition and the anxieties of nightmare.

Whereas *Ring* was a mystery of detection, *Rasen* is one of intellectual conceit. Such is the needless complexity of Suzuki's diversion into code-breaking that it seems by the end of the process that Ando could have constructed *any* word combination out of the sequence of letters encased in Ryuji's DNA: 'futile exercise', for example. Despite the 'evidence' ostensibly proliferating throughout the story, most of the deductions arrived at by Ando and Miyashita are entirely theoretical in nature. The reader has to take their word for things, in effect. This gives a hollow ring to much of the narrative, whose myriad preposterous assumptions are vindicated by an equally pulp fictional conclusion. There is some philosophical debate towards the end of the book which tries to draw a parallel between the spontaneous appearance of the Ring virus and the birth of life itself, in that both reflect a conscious act of will on the part of a super-being, but this is too weighty a metaphysical proposition for the tale that undertakes to sustain it.

The title *Rasen* translated into English as *Spiral*, though 'Tangent' might have been more appropriate. Suzuki nevertheless was unrepentant about the curious direction in which he had decided to channel his story. "Actually, I boldly predicted my success in *Spiral*," he observed.

> "A million-seller, huh?" Ando already knew this. He'd seen it in newspapers. The book had already been through several reprints, a fact that was trumpeted in its marketing. But every time Ando saw the word 'reprint' it made him think of 'replication'. *Ring* had been able to effect a near-instantaneous mass reproduction of itself. There were now more than a million

people carrying the virus.

"They're even making it into a movie."

"A movie? *Ring*?"

With his tongue planted firmly in his cheek, Suzuki has Ryuji further reveal that the Sadako of the movie is to be played by Sadako herself! Remember, dear reader (a wink and a nod), she did once train to be an *actress*. Yes, very amusing. Though it has to be said that it all smacks just a little too much of a literal version of video feedback. "As it happens, my prediction became a reality, but on a much, much bigger scale," Suzuki was tickled to note.

The finale of *Rasen* is pure literary conceit — a hokey attempt to blur the distinction between the fictional and the factual by cheekily positing a version of reality where the original *novel* is now a conduit for the viral curse which features in its pages. *Rasen* is a con trick on the reader, a self-conscious play on ideas. By extending his thesis to the power of infinity and populating the planet with an infinite number of Sadakos, Suzuki merely over-extends *himself*. The plot of *Rasen* is simply preposterous — an intellectual mind-game for an anally-retentive elite. Fortunately for the remainder who require only to be thrilled and entertained, a wholly different take on *Ring* was about to ensure that *Rasen* would instead be swept under Sadako's tatami mat.

In 1996, *Rasen* won for Suzuki the Eiji Yoshikawa Young Writer Award and *Ring: Kanzenban* was released as an unrated feature for the V-cinema market. Things were moving up a gear. A *manga* version of *Ring* by Koujirou Nagai had already been issued by Kodansha Comics in February, and now there were plans for a movie. Sales of the original novel had increased markedly in conjunction with the release of *Rasen*, so Suzuki decided to embark on *another* sequel to his awakening success story.

Koji Suzuki's second sequel to *Ring* was *Rupu* (*Loop*), in which the future world is plagued by a new threat in the form of the Metastatic Human Cancer Virus. A medical student named Kaoru Futami embarks on a quest to eradicate it, and he stumbles upon a sophisticated computer programme which has recreated life on Earth through a virtual reality simulation. In the much-accelerated course of its evolutionary development, this 'Loop' world had become infected with the Ring virus, resulting in all life on the simulated Earth dying out. Kaoru wonders if there is a relationship between what is currently happening on Earth and the prediction from the Loop world.

In exploring his thesis further, Kaoru hones in on the events of the first two books, which he can replay from Loop's backup memory. Eventually, this puts him in contact with Ryuji Takayama — at the moment of his death in *Ring*. It transpires that an escape route was made available to Ryuji by the creators of Loop, which involved cloning him out of their virtual world and into the real one. The resultant clone is none other than Kaoru Futami, which was why he always felt himself drawn towards the 'loop' to begin with. But in cloning Ryuji, they inadvertently cloned the Ring virus along with him: it mutated into the Metastatic Human Cancer Virus which is now decimating the globe.

Kaoru is immune, however, and so his body holds the key to mankind's survival. A deal is struck whereby he relinquishes his body to scientific research for an alternative consciousness inside of Loop. He sacrifices his physical form so that humanity can be given hope, and when he stares at the night sky in his new persona, he knows for sure that there are gods out there…

Rupu — *Loop* in English — is not so much science fiction as science fantasy. It takes the theme of *Ring* as far away from that of the original novel as it is possible to go. It also abandons Sadako in favour of the further adventures of Ryuji Takayama, clearly Suzuki's favourite protagonist of the two (as insinuated at the end of *Rasen*).

"*Loop* totally denies the paranormal horrors employed in the first two instalments," Suzuki explained to Akemi Yokoyama. "It gives people hope. I didn't want to end it by giving readers the creeps. You can't call it a horror. It's a story about a self-replicating life form that lives in a computer environment. It's like an extraordinarily advanced simulation. A hero appears and tries to deal with it. At the beginning, you don't know how it's connected to *Ring*; the cast is different. Then halfway through, you realise that there's a connection, and there's an unexpected development at the end. *Loop* is based on modern science. I really don't like horror stories…"

The novel was published on 31 January 1998, again to coincide with the release of a screen adaptation of *Ring*. But this time was different. This time, *Ring* was to sweep all else before it. And while the publication of *Loop* on the back of *Ring* the movie was to result in another multi-million-selling earner for Suzuki, his narrative variations on his own theme were soon to become as forgotten in the wake of the new film's success as was Sadako herself after she was thrown down the well.

"Novels are different from movies," Suzuki conceded in interview. "If a man reads a line of text, his instinct, his imagination, his circumstance shapes the image in his brain of the hero or heroine. This is the nature of the novel. But movies are a direct experience. Movies go straight into the eyes and ears, so imagination is not necessary. It goes straight into the head."

"Sadako's going to breed with the media," Ryuji had said at the end of *Rasen*, in reference to her fictional career in the movies. Her real appearance on film came on the very same day that Suzuki's second sequel was published.

The claim that Koji Suzuki had put into the mouth of his character proved to be more than prophetic. After Sadako was seen by the cinema-goers of Japan in a feature version of *Ring*, she and the media were to be found breeding like rabbits.

Genre cinema operates to yet another demographic from either books or television: the horror film requires a villain — preferably one who is larger and more ghastly than life. So it was left to the film's screenwriters to turn Sadako into a supernatural villain in line with the cultural preoccupations of J-horror. Those preoccupations were specifically with ghosts and monsters.

There were no ghosts or monsters in Koji Suzuki's *Ring*, or were there? Beneath its author's determined attempt to write a postmodern horror story, are there not traces of something older, more atavistic, more elemental? "I imagined the video not as a concise story, but rather as a series of nonsensical scenes. Letting my imagination take over, I wrote down images as they flashed in my mind. When I'd finished writing, I saw that I had twelve scenes in total. After this, I sat down to analyse them. I found that I could split them into two categories. One group was something that could be seen through the eyes, while the others were things that could only be imagined in the mind."

The video is the key: Suzuki confessed it to be a product of the subconscious, not only of Sadako's but of his own, as well. "In some ways, it was like composing music. I was listening to a story in my head and I wrote it down. It was kind of like Mozart — it was said that symphonies and concertos went through his brain and Mozart wrote down the notes. He didn't know where the music came from; I didn't either. It just came."

But what was it that had come? Suzuki's mind had conjured images of volcanic eruption, blood, mystic voices, leering faces, and a circle of light. To these, he added a girl in white, somehow born from the sea...

To find out more, we have first to follow Asakawa's lead, dig into the cultural past of Japan itself, and begin at the beginning... ⦿

Day Two: The Investigation

NAME: Sadako Yamamura

MOTHER: Shizuko Yamamura

FATHER: Unknown — probably Heihachiro Ikuma, assistant professor of psychiatry at Taido University

DATE OF BIRTH: late 1947

PLACE OF BIRTH: Sashikiji, Izu-Oshima Island, 110km south-west of Tokyo

If you spend all your time playing in the water, monsters are bound to get you.

- Koji Suzuki, *Ring* (1991)

What is it about Japan and ghosts?

"Most Japanese ghost stories seem to reflect the modesty of Japanese people," Koji Suzuki explained to Andrew Osmond of *SFX* magazine. "If someone dies in hate, his resentment persists, but slightly. It does not appear directly, but stays in the air like an odour. It is interesting that in Japan, many ghosts are women. One of the most famous ghosts in Japan is Oiwa-san, a sad woman in *Yotsuya kaidan*. So is the Snow Lady, from another traditional Japanese ghost story and, of course, Sadako is there too. There is no Dracula or Frankenstein in Japan. I have no idea why, but I, too, cannot write male ghosts."

The *Tokaido Yotsuya kaidan* to give it its full title, or 'Ghost Story of Yotsuya', is a blood-spattered Japanese *Macbeth* — a kind of oriental Jacobean tragedy — which was written in the early eighteenth century and based on a real incident. In the fictional version, a faithless and ambitious husband arranges the disfigurement of his wife Oiwa so that he can marry another. After Oiwa's subsequent suicide, her ghost persecutes him until he, too, is dead, but not before he has mistakenly murdered all those around him. So what is it about Japan and *female* ghosts, as illustrated by the *Noh* mask of the *Hannya*, a hideous female demon?

First, a word about Japan itself. Japan is an ancient island nation that is situated in the North Pacific, to the east of the Korean peninsula, and separated from the Asian mainland by the Sea of Japan. It consists of four large islands — Honshu (in the middle of which is the Japanese capital, Tokyo), Hokkaido, Kyushu and Shikoku — which in turn are surrounded by some 3,000 smaller ones; the four main islands of Japan are largely mountainous, and the most rugged area is that of the Japanese Alps on Honshu, the jewel in whose crown is the 12,390 foot Fujiyama (Mount Fuji), a dormant volcano lying sixty miles south-west of Tokyo, which was last seen to erupt in 1707. More than 160 such volcanoes are to be found in Japan, of which fifty-four remain active. Earthquakes are common, with anything up to 1,500 occurring each year, though most of them cause relatively little damage. Japan has a monsoon climate and typhoons are also common, as are tidal waves, or *tsunamis*, which themselves are caused by offshore earthquakes. Due to the volatile nature of its terrain, only twenty percent of the country is capable of agricultural development; as a result, the Japanese economy is industry-based. Until the 1990s, Japan was Asia's most prosperous industrialised nation.

Japan, like Britain, is a monarchical state, the origins of which supposedly date back to 660 BC. Buddhism was introduced to replace Shintoism as the official religion of the country in 552 AD. Imperial rule held sway in Japan until a warrior class known as Shoguns ('great generals') rose to power during the twelfth century; with the Shoguns came the Samurai — the Knights Templar of the East — warriors who swore allegiance to *daimyo* (provincial overlords) and maintained order through their harsh martial code of Bushido. Shogun rule continued for seven centuries until Emperor Meiji regained power in 1868. The policy of isolationism from the outside world, which had begun in 1637, was ended in 1854 when the American Commodore Perry forced Japan to sign a treaty with the United States. Notwithstanding this, Japan's imperial ambitions began in the 1880s: in 1894-5, it fought a war against China; in 1904-5, it defeated Russia in a war over Korea; in 1931, it occupied neighbouring Manchuria; and, in 1937, fought a second war with China. In 1942, the Japanese air force attacked the American Pacific Fleet at its base in Pearl Harbor, Hawaii, which precipitated America's entry into World War Two. After the atomic bombings of Hiroshima and Nagasaki on the island of Kyushu, the Imperial army surrendered and the American military then occupied the country until 1952. The 1947 American-imposed Constitution reduced Japan to a constitutional monarchy, under a national parliament that is composed of a House of Representatives and a House of Chancellors — which is where we came in. The country today is a modern, Westernised, liberal democracy.

Throughout its 3,000 year history, Japanese society has been male-dominated. The history of Japan is one of centuries-long internal strife, culminating in a brief period of external imperial ambition. The Japanese male has been at war — with himself and with those around him — for a thousand years, and the Japanese female traditionally has been posted to keep the home fires burning. As their men were constantly engaged in battle, it fell to the womenfolk to take care of the household and raise the children; with such a schism so often in play, it is hardly surprising that Japanese women, like much else in the national culture, developed two very distinct sides to their character. To the outside world — and to Western eyes in particular — they were passive, subservient and humble, but in the domestic environment, it was they who had learned to rule the roost. Men in war are not always faithful to wives who are left behind, and guilt over sins committed *in absentia* is the engine that drives many a Japanese folk-tale and ghost story. In no other society in the world is *woman* so often seen as an object of fear, but in no other society have male and female roles been so comprehensively polarised. If Dracula was representative to the English of the threat from without, then the vengeful female ghost of Japan was a literary manifestation of the potency of the threat from *within*.

So powerful did Shoguns become that feudalism in Japan extended several hundred years beyond similar periods of cultural development in Western Europe (and provided fertile if somewhat restrictive ground for later Japanese film-makers in the process). The combination of Buddhism and Chinese Confucianism, which informed the macho code of Bushido, did not even accord women second-class status; to the contrary, they were not allowed to own property, had no legal rights, and entry into heaven was forbidden them. In addition, they could write only in *hiragana*, whereas literary works and formal documents were transcribed in the pictogrammatical *kanji*. Not only were women deemed to be less than men, they invariably were treated as though they were less than human: as one writer on Japanese affairs put it, they were thought to 'generate a karma of evil and impropriety.' The 'modern' or emancipated woman (*moga*) did not appear in Japanese society until the 1920s, with the coming of a new middle class, though she still was not granted the vote until 1946. Small wonder that the pejoration of Japanese womanhood impressed itself so forcefully on the popular culture.

In a way, the Japanese woman is partially responsible for the demonic image of her sex which exists in her own country. What is commonly considered to be the world's first novel was written in Japan in 1002 by Shikibu Murasaki, a lady-in-waiting at the Heian court, and among the myriad characters in the epic *The Tale of Genji* is the Lady Rokujo, an aristocratic seductress so besotted with the royal prince of the title that her spirit lingers on after death to haunt the dreams of Genji's subsequent lovers. The next most famous literary harpy is the Oiwa of whom Suzuki spoke, another wronged wife who exacts revenge in the form of a shape-shifting spectre. And there is Okiku,

The Ghost of
Okiku *(1890) by*
Tsukioka
Yoshitoshi.

from a Kabuki play called *Bancho sarayashiki* ('*The Dish Mansion of Bancho*'), who is killed and disposed of in a *well* by her spurned samurai master, only for her shade to return at evening and send him insane with its melancholy wailing. Females also feature among the many traditional species of Japanese 'ghost', such as the long-necked *rokurokubi*: a normal woman by day, but a life-draining succubus by night.

The Japanese *obake*, or ghost, is a less focussed concept than its counterpart in the West. The Concise Oxford Dictionary defines a ghost as a 'spectre esp. of dead person appearing to the living,' while the Universal English Dictionary more helpfully describes it as an 'apparition, wraith, disembodied spirit of the dead' which manifests itself to the '*senses*' of the living. Encyclopaedia Britannica qualifies this by adding a footnote to the effect that the disembodied spirit concerned is 'believed to be an inhabitant of the unseen world.' In all cases, the traditional figure of the Gothic ghost is perceived as a *revenant* — one who *returns* — rather than the revelation of another form of reality.

In Japan, a ghost is *any* manifestation of the extraordinary in an otherwise ordinary object or mundane situation, the word *obake* having been derived from the verb *bakeru*, which means 'to undergo change'. As Japanese cultural historian Tim Screech outlined in the now-defunct American *Mangajin* magazine, 'Myths about Japanese ghosts do not talk of the ghoul on the frozen staircase, the skeleton in the musty closet, or the draughty bell-tower, but of the tangled bedclothes or the broken fan... A discarded umbrella may enter the world of the strange as an umbrella obake — steam seeming to rise oddly from the waxed paper brim and forming a leering face... Obake,' he summarised, 'undermine the certainties of life as we usually understand (them).' Within this broad genus, *obake* subdivides into various other species, of which the *yurei* — 'faint spirit' — comes closest to the Western concept of the melancholy shade.

The two traditions therefore are distinctly different in their approach to the subject of the ghostly. The English ghost story of the ninteenth century — not surprisingly, given its flowering at the very height of Empire — conformed to rules and patterns familiar to the knowing reader: even the dead were required to behave in a certain way, their clammy embraces somehow comforting in their predictability to those whose spines they sought to chill. But as the century neared its end, a less respectful type of ghost made its initial appearance in a short story called 'Canon Alberic's Scrap-Book'. It was one which was more in tune with the increasingly troubled times, and coincidentally more in sympathy with the kind of ghost to which Japanese culture had always been subject.

Pulp Terror*maester* H P Lovecraft, in his famous essay entitled 'Supernatural Horror in Literature', wrote: 'The oldest and strongest emotion of mankind is fear, and the oldest and strongest kind of fear is fear of the unknown.' Fear of the supernatural unknown is precisely what M R James, antiquarian, scholar and author of 'Canon Alberic', introduced into the stately English ghost story in 1895. In doing so, he rang a change in the tale of Terror which was to conform more closely to the Japanese ideal, and whose influence on the cinema of the supernatural reverberates all the way down to *Ring*.

> Yet this was only the beginning of the horror.
> - **Lafcadio Hearn**, 'Ingwa-banashi' *In Ghostly Japan* (1899)

Japanese history is divided into different periods or eras (*jidai*), in much the same way as British history is compartmentalised under the name of the monarch at the time, such as Victorian or Edwardian. The roots of modern civilisation in Japan were laid in the Nara and Heian periods, which stretched from 710 to 1185 AD. Thereafter, our own thirteenth century is represented by the Kamakura period (1185-1333), the fourteenth to the sixteenth by the Muromachi (1333-1568) and Azuchimomoya Ma (1568-1600), the seventeenth to nineteenth by the Edo (or Tokugaya, 1600-1868) and Meiji (1868-1912), and the twentieth century by the Taisho (1912-1926) and Showa (1926-1989) periods. The present era in Japan is known as the Heisei. The setting for most of the samurai films which are familiar in the West is either the late Muromachi period, during which the country was ravaged by a ten year civil war (the Onin no Ran), or the Edo Shogunate period, when Japan adopted a policy of national isolation and experienced two centuries of cultural and commercial renaissance as a result.

Buddhism was mandated as the official religion of Japan by the Emperor Shomu in the eighth century, when it replaced the more tribal Shinto faith — although both religions continued to coexist in real terms, and do so to this day. In many respects, Buddhism and Shintoism share a common philosophical base, and this is particularly true when it comes to beliefs in relation to the world of spirits. Both have combined in the popular mind to propagate a widespread acceptance of all manner of occult phenomena, as well as a multitudinous variety of 'ghosts'. In contrast to Judaeo-Christian notions that any manifestation of the supernatural is fundamentally evil, the Japanese 'ghost' not only is seen to be an integral part of the earthly realm but is actively encouraged to participate in human affairs. Sharing a dance with one's ancestors during the Obon festival is one thing, however; sharing a taxicab with a *yurei* from Tokyo's Aoyama cemetery is quite something else.

It can be taken from this that not all Japanese ghosts are benign *shugorei* watching over the day-to-day activities of living relatives. To the contrary, three of Buddhism's six realms of existence are inhabited by the kind of ghost whom no one would desire to meet on a Bon Odori dance-floor, while Shinto tradition has it that the world is populated by eight million *kami* (spirit-beings), among which are numerous *oni*, or demons. Of these multifarious phantoms, *yurei* are universally the most feared and also the most terrifying. Predominantly female, *yurei* are the ghosts of rage invoked from a lifetime of suffering and sorrow, who return from the land of the dead to seek revenge on those whom they consider to be responsible for their earthly misfortunes. Invariably clad in white and hovering perceptibly above the ground, *yurei* are the vengeful female ghosts of Japanese literature and film.

The Japanese ghost story really came into its own during the relatively tranquil Edo period, when art and commerce flourished, and advances in printing and the growth of the Kabuki and Bunraku theatres brought about 'a heightened interest in the grotesque and supernatural,' according to literary scholar Hiromi Tsuchiya. Medievalist writers like Akinari Ueda drew on history and myth to inaugurate a new form of literature — in effect, Japanese 'Gothic' — coincidentally at the very time when the Gothic movement was taking hold in England following the publication in 1764 of Horace Walpole's *The Castle of Otranto*.

Japan's self-imposed isolationism inhibited any cross-cultural currents however, at least until after 1868 and the restoration of the Emperor Meiji, when trade links were once more established with the outside world. The English Gothic Revival of the late 1800s had reawakened interest in all things bloody and demonic but, by the turn of the century, the full-blown Gothic horror of Robert Louis Stevenson's *Strange Case of Dr Jekyll and Mr Hyde* (1886) and Bram Stoker's *Dracula* (1897) had been distilled into the less visceral chills of the increasingly popular 'ghost story', whose flowering in the more genteel Edwardian era would prove an apotheosis in the Literature of Terror. The spectres of Japan previously had operated to their own coda and within the confines of their natural habitat, but with the country's rulers having agreed to open the floodgates to cultural diversity after more than two-and-a-half centuries of navel-gazing, Western influence gradually began to bear on the traditional Japanese ghost.

At first, it was the other way around. In 1890, an Irish author of Greek birth named Patrick Lafcadio Hearn decided, at the age of thirty-nine, to emigrate to Japan. Having trained as a journalist in Cincinnati and New Orleans, Hearn previously had been working as a translator with Harper Publishing Company, during which term of employment he had added novelist to his credentials. After settling in Japan he took up teaching positions at schools in Matsue and Kumamoto, married into a samurai family, and went on to be a professor of English Literature at Tokyo's Imperial University, where he remained until 1903. He died the following year of a heart attack. In the relatively short space of time which was allotted him, Lafcadio Hearn embraced the native culture of Japan like a man reborn, and it was he who first introduced Western readers to the ghostly folklore of his newly-adopted homeland.

Hearn's Celtic background naturally inclined him towards the weird and wondrous in Japanese life, and though he absorbed himself in translating many tangential aspects of Japanese society, it was his abiding passion for all things supernatural which was to bring him lasting fame. He collected and anthologised numerous strange tales from the literature of the past, which he published in volumes such as *In Ghostly Japan* (1899), *Shadowings* (1900) and, perhaps his best-known work, *Kwaidan* (1904). He had taken up Japanese citizenship in 1895 under the name of Yakumo Koizumi, but his training in journalism and prior success as a novelist introduced a Western narrative sensibility and distinctly occidental flavour into the traditional Japanese ghost tale. H P Lovecraft wrote of *Kwaidan* that it 'crystallises with matchless skill and delicacy the eerie lore and whispered legends of that richly colourful nation.'

Above: Patrick Lafcadio Hearn.

The 'golden age' of the English ghost story was from the 1890s to the 1930s, and in terms of practitioners of the form, none were more golden than Dr Montague Rhodes James, Provost of Eton and King's College, Cambridge. As Hearn set about translating Japanese folk-tales into English for the benefit of Western readers, 'Monty' James was transmuting the Gothic ghosts of Dickens and Wilkie Collins into spectres which were more befitting a modern age of spiritual uncertainty and non-specific dreads.

Like many of his fellow writers of supernatural fiction, James had been subject to a strict religious upbringing: Joseph Sheridan Le Fanu was born into a family descended from Huegenots; Robert Louis Stevenson, one of staunch Christian Covenanters; Bram Stoker was tutored for much of his youth by the Reverend William Woods; Montague James was the son of an Evangelical clergyman. Reflections at eventide on the eternal damnations which had been promised in childhood as reward for transgressions of the flesh were never far from the minds of the Gothicists, and the lessons that they learned in impressionable youth remained with them throughout their lives to be mirrored, as in a glass darkly, in the literature that they left behind them. By the time the young James attended Temple Grove preparatory school at East Sheen in Surrey, his head was filled with the apocalyptic visions which to the devout Victorian were part and parcel of the 'devotional' life. The third son and fourth child

*Montague
Rhodes James.*

of a minister of the cloth, Monty James had passed his early years in a caring home, but under a daily regime of prayers, hymns and Bible studies. As a result, he lay awake at night contemplating the trumpet-call to Judgement: "I thought… I should run to the window and look out and see the whole sky split across and lit up with glaring flame: and next moment I and everyone else in the house would be caught up into the air and made to stand with countless other people before a judge seated on a throne with great books open before him…"

The ghost stories of M R James were firmly rooted in the Gothic tradition. In 1882, a scholarship from Eton had sent James up to Cambridge University where, five years later, he was awarded a Fellowship of his undergraduate college of King's; in 1889, he became Dean of that same royal college. At Eton he had assured his popularity among his peers by the performances which he put on when engaged in what he termed 'dark séances' — the telling of ghost stories after lights out. The extramural activities at Cambridge, where James ultimately would spend more than half his life, offered ample opportunity for this adolescent pursuit to continue in adulthood: the Gothic cloisters of King's (where Horace Walpole had also been tutored after going to Eton) afforded an evocative venue for the storyteller, while winter light and the approach of Candlemass nurtured the appropriate mood.

It was in this rather rarefied atmosphere, during convivial gatherings of the Chitchat Society, that James' abiding passion for the supernatural bore fruit. His first rendition to the society came in October 1893, and was a tale entitled 'A Curious Book'. When it had served its purpose as a ghost story for Christmas, James was persuaded to send it to Leo Maxse, who was both a friend and publisher of a periodical called the *National Review*. This was in 1894, when James was thirty-one; the same year that Bram Stoker began work in earnest on *Dracula*. 'A Curious Book' saw print a year later, under the title of 'The Scrap-Book of Canon Alberic' (later amended to 'Canon Alberic's Scrap-Book'), and Montague James' second-string career as a writer of supernatural fiction was thus set falteringly in train.

Out of a total of thirty-three short stories written at a rate of approximately one a year until 1935 (he died in 1936), James penned two tales about vampires ('Count Magnus' and 'An Episode of Cathedral History'), three that dabbled in black magic ('Lost Hearts', 'Casting the Runes' and 'Two Doctors'), two that involved witchcraft ('The Ash-Tree' and 'Martin's Close'), three that invoked demons ('Canon Alberic's Scrap-Book', 'The Treasure of Abbot Thomas' and 'The Diary of Mr Poynter'), two conventional tales of the supernatural ('The Haunted Doll's House' and 'A View From a Hill') and two that basically were whimsical ('An Evening's Entertainment' and 'The Malice of Inanimate Objects'); the remaining eighteen were pure ghost stories.

Ghost stories were not the *sine qua non* of M R James; to the contrary, they merely filled some quiet hours in a prodigious schedule of scholastic endeavour. But they held for him a lifelong fascination — both in reading and contributing to that curious corpus which drifts like a melancholy residue over the landscape of English letters.

The typical James ghost story was to be recognised as having two main ingredients: a half-glimpsed apparition of some kind, and the motif of nemesis-retribution visited upon the living by the dead. James' unique contribution to the field was the idea of the *extra*ordinary intruding into the over-ordinariness of everyday experience. His

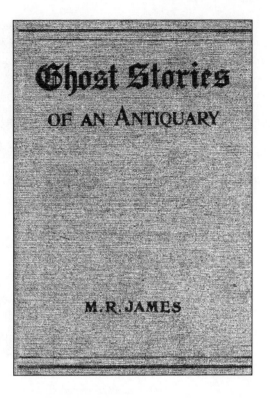

Above: Ghost Stories of an Antiquary *(Edward Arnold, 1904).*

James McBryde's illustration for 'Oh, Whistle, and I'll Come To You, My Lad' from Ghost Stories of an Antiquary.

spectral beings provided the extraordinary, while his academic background and obsession with the minutiae of verisimilitude provided the ordinary. But the fact that the vast majority of James' phantoms are vengeful, and act with an independent intelligence of sorts, is what gives his tales their power and distinction. James invariably refused to specify the exact nature of his terrors, but he was specific about their purpose, and it was in this regard that he was to initiate a new mood in the Literature of Terror.

The ghosts of M R James were *self-determining*. They were active in the pursuit of their preordained goals and not passive, as many of their kind had been in the past. James' ghosts could choose their own moment to make their presence felt (usually their teeth and talons, as well); they could chart their own paths, in terms of when to intervene and bring an end to the prying of inquisitive venturers into their domain. And they operated to a single injunction: no trespassing.

The change which James wrought on the persona of the ghost was significant. His spectres were neither real, nor wholly unreal; they could *interact* with man (often in the most unpleasant manner) and, in so doing, they seemed to occupy some weird halfway house between life and death — between the world of the visible and the invisible. They still possessed many of the traditional attributes of ghosts, in that they could traverse material barriers and the like, but they could also introduce themselves into the earthly plane at will, to mutilate and murder their chosen prey as the occasion demanded.

In James' hands, the ineffectual ghosts of old became highly effective participants in a well-organised web of tease, treachery and violent death. Of course, the visitants in the ghost stories of M R James and others who ploughed the same furrow in the wake of the Gothic Revival were not ghosts in the true sense at all, but demonic entities from another dimension coexistent with our own. The pretence was finally stripped away in 'Casting the Runes' (1911), when James recast his typical ghost in the non-human form to which it really had always belonged, as the goblin agent of a malevolent devil-God; an albino imp of the perverse, whose sole purpose was to terrify the story's unfortunate protagonist into shimmying up a tree from which he then falls and breaks his neck and, climactically, to lob a fatal brick onto the head of the diabolist Karswell.

Lovecraft was entirely in concert with James' approach to ghosts: 'The true weird tale has something more than secret murder, bloody bones, or a sheeted form clanking chains according to rule,' he said in his essay. 'A certain atmosphere of breathless and unexplainable dread of outer, unknown forces must be present; and there must be a hint, expressed with a seriousness and a portentousness becoming its subject of that most terrible conception of the human brain — a malign and particular suspension or defeat of those fixed laws of Nature which are our only safeguard against the assaults of chaos and the daemons of unplumbed space.'

> Late on Monday night a toad came into my study: and, though nothing has so far seemed to link itself with this appearance, I feel that it may not be quite prudent to brood over topics which may open the interior eye to the presence of more formidable visitants.
> - **M R James**, 'Stories I Have Tried to Write' *The Touchstone* (1929)

James' tales were certainly antidotal to the vogue for a more benign view of ghosts which concurrently was being fostered by the table-rapping antics of the new 'science' of spiritualism. With spiritualism came such exotic philosophies as Rosicrucianism and Theosophism, even returns to the older religions of Magick and nature worship. (Algernon Blackwood, a contemporary of James' and his nearest rival in the popular mind, was a professed mystic and shrewd self-publicist; he was to claim intimate knowledge of his supernatural subject-matter and thus become one of the originators of the cult of the writer as media personality, intrinsically more interesting in themselves than the books they put their names to.) The impact of this literal (and literary) fascination with things ghostly was felt around the globe, but while Tomokichi

Fukurai was enabled to indulge his experiments in telepathy at Tokyo University as a result of it, Japanese storytellers remained tied by tradition to a thousand-year heritage of *kaibyo* (ghost-cats) and *kappa* (river-monsters). Despite the proliferation of terror-tales from foreign lands in the early years of the twentieth century, other forces were now to intrude which would ensure that the ghost story took a back seat to the detective mystery instead.

By the end of World War One, Japan had been fully integrated into the international network and Japanese culture came increasingly to parallel that of the West. In twenty years, newspaper circulation had risen fourfold to more than six million copies and, by the mid-1920s, the increasing literacy of the population at large had generated a boom in mass-produced paperbacks and monthly magazines, as well as the development and growth of popular fiction. English literature already was taught at university level, but the appetite for modernity did not stop at translations of Shakespeare, Marx, Kafka and Dostoevsky; alongside these had come populist works from the likes of Arthur Conan Doyle and Edgar Allan Poe. In 1922, in response to an upsurge in demand for mystery stories laced with a hint of the supernatural or macabre, a young writer and adherent of Poe called Taro Hairo adopted as his pseudonym a phonetic rendition of his American mentor's name, and 'Edogawa Rampo' went on to carve a successful career in his own right, eventually being acknowledged as the Father of the Japanese mystery genre.

No sooner had these new-found freedoms been granted, however, than they started to be eroded from within. Under the Meiji restoration, education was used to instil into Japanese youth a new sense of national identity and loyalty to the emperor. Traditional ideas of self-sacrifice and obedience were revived and consolidated, and the stage was set for a servile populace to be manipulated by authoritarian rule. Economic problems, strained relations with the West, and a powerful and increasingly independent military coalesced in 1927, with the ascendancy of Emperor Hirohito, to lead Japan on the road to wars, totalitarianism and the censorship trappings of the fascist state. By the 1930s, so-called security police had acquired wide-ranging powers to stifle dissent in all of its mass media forms; the extinguishing of free speech and free expression in the arts was the predictable consequence. Lafcadio Hearn had been alerted to the dangers inherent in nationalistic fervour more than twenty years before, though he never lived to despair at their outcome.

Western influence was systematically expunged in a new wave of ultra-nationalism, though some forms of mass entertainment proved more resistant to the interventions of state censorship than others: detective mysteries survived intact and were revived in the 1940s by the likes of Seishi Yokomizo (*Murders at the Inn/Honjin*, 1947; *The Village of Eight Tombs*, 1950). But the Gothic was morally subversive, and morals are always high on the agenda for demagogues. While the ghost story blossomed and developed in the West in tandem with the murder mystery (and in answer to the resurgent interest in spiritualism), Japanese Gothic moved on from the reverential embalmings of Lafcadio Hearn only so far as the psycho-sexual makeovers of Kyoka Izumi (*The Holy Man of Mount Koya/Koya hijiri*, 1900) and troubled Ryunosuke Akutagawa (*Rashomon*, 1915; *Hell Screen/Jigokuhen*, 1918), both of whom had also depended on folk-tales from the *Konjaku monogatari* (*Tales of Times Now Past*, 1120) for their inspiration. The artists and writers who regularly had patronised Maruzen, Tokyo's leading foreign bookseller since its opening in 1869, now had nowhere to go but into the arms of propaganda and national glorification as dictatorship brought an end to cultural eclecticism.

The kindling flame of democracy that had been lit during the Meiji era was snuffed out ruthlessly in the Showa, as Japan embarked on a programme of imperial expansion which began with the invasion of Manchuria, and was followed up by withdrawal from the League of Nations, war with China, and the eventual forming of a coalition with the Axis powers of Germany and Italy which culminated in the disastrous defeat of World War Two. The rise of militarism, which had been set in motion as early as the 1880s when disenfranchised samurai banded together into secret societies like the Black Ocean and Black Dragon sects, set the country's cultural development back by at least a quarter of a century. (Japan was still producing silent films well into the 1930s.)

Lovecraft credited James in 1927 with inventing 'a new kind of ghost', but it would take another *three*-quarters of a century before its influence was finally to be felt in Japan, through the medium of the Japanese horror film. ○

Day Three: Brine and Goblins

Men really need sea-monsters in their personal oceans. An ocean without its unnamed monsters would be like a completely dreamless sleep.

- **John Steinbeck**, *The Log from the Sea of Cortez* (1951)

This is Tokyo — once a city of six million people. What has happened here was caused by a force which up until a few days ago was entirely beyond the scope of man's imagination. Tokyo — a smoldering memorial to the unknown; an unknown which at this very moment still prevails and could, at any time, lash out with its terrible destruction anywhere else in the world. There were once many people here who could have told of what they saw. Now, there are only a few…

- **Steve Martin (Raymond Burr)**, *Godzilla* (1956)

In the aftermath of World War Two, the Japanese as a nation were more likely to be the subject of a horror film than the producers of one. Newsreel footage of the atrocious conditions experienced by Allied prisoners of war in Japanese labour camps vied with that from Nazi concentration camps such as Belsen and Auschwitz for the attention of Western audiences and led to best-selling books like Lord Russell of Liverpool's *The Knights of Bushido*, which served up details of the atrocities that film and television editors had been prohibited from imparting to the viewing public in their own media. These, in turn, inspired popular and highly successful films, like David Lean's sombre and respectful *The Bridge on the River Kwai* (1957) and Val Guest's livelier and more rousing *The Camp on Blood Island* (1958) for Britain's Hammer Films; the first received eight Oscar nominations and won seven awards, while the second was castigated by the same critics as sickening exploitation. For a time, in the 1950s, the term 'Japanese' was considered a byword for inhuman cruelty and degradation.

Of course, Japan had paid the price for its failure to observe the Geneva accords during the hostilities: by March 1945, Japanese cities were being fire-bombed by the

United States Air Force; one raid on Tokyo killed and injured almost 125,000 people, and left a million more homeless. In the closing days of the war, a B-29 Superfortress called Enola Gay had taken off from the Marianas with a twelve-man crew and headed for Hiroshima, a strategically unimportant naval base on the island of Honshu. The aircraft had been modified to carry a ten-foot, 9,700lb, uranium-based 'atomic' bomb, which had been code-named 'Little Boy'. The device exploded 1,800 feet above the Aioi Bridge, destroying two-thirds of the city and killing 70,000 people in an instant. Three days later, a second plutonium bomb of greater destructive power and code-named 'Fat Man' was dropped on Nagasaki, the site of a Mitsubishi torpedo factory on the island of Kyushu; yet another bomb had been earmarked for Tokyo, the nation's capital. Five days after the detonation at Nagasaki, Emperor Hirohito signed the declaration of surrender and stripped himself of monarchical power and claims to divinity in the process. The war in the Pacific was at an end. So, too, was a thousand years of Japanese history and tradition. 1945 was Year Zero for Japan in more ways than one, but in more ways than one was the Phoenix to rise inexorably from the radioactive ashes.

After the war, the reconstituted Japanese film industry had taken refuge in the country's medieval past and forcibly-placated present. Domestic production devolved to five major players: Toei, Shochiku, Daiei (all three of which were based in Kyoto, the film capital of Japan during the golden age of post-war production), Nikkatsu and Toho — which eventually was to be viewed by fantasy fans in the West with the kind of affection that they usually reserved for Hammer or Universal-International. These five not only divided the home audience into constituent parts based on the specific genres of film in which each one specialised, but between them owned all of the studios and the distribution outlets, as well.

In the highly controlled and well-ordered society that was the new Japan, corporate identity was king, and corporate identity extended to include the product of individual film companies and their docile legions of loyal followers. Thus Toei concentrated on the general entertainment of historical spectacles and detective thrillers, Nikkatsu dealt in films pertaining to social problems, Schochiku pandered to a predominately female audience with its romantic melodramas, Daiei made sex-comedies for mature viewers and Toho's appeal was to the juvenile trade, which came to encompass science fiction and (later) horror. Much of this product — at least in terms of the popular cinema — was anodyne in the extreme.

If, at this stage, a foreigner's eye-view of Japan — as exemplified by its films — was one of inscrutable courteousness, seemingly at odds with the militaristic nation which only a few years before had to be dissuaded from its aggression by the threat of atomic annihilation, then it was intentional. Part of the reason for the traditionalistic nature of immediate post-war cinema in Japan lay with the strict codes of censorship which had been levied on the film industry by the Civil Information and Education Section of the Supreme Command for the Allied Powers. Based on studies of the Japanese character which had been conducted during the conflict, a list of thirteen 'forbidden' themes had been drawn up; these included revenge, militarism, and elements of nationalism and feudal loyalty — this last being by far the most serious offender. In the early years of the Allied occupation, sword fights had also been banned from historical films (*jidai-geki*); their return in the fifties transformed the genre into *chanbara*.

Japan is one of the most densely populated countries in the world, with 126 million souls presently occupying a land mass no bigger than the state of California. In 1945, the population was just over 70 million, but this had risen to 90 million in the 'baby boom' years to 1955 and to nearly 100 million by the middle of the 1960s. With a domestic audience almost half the size of that of the United States — and twice the size of Britain — the Japanese industry felt no requirement to 'internationalise' its films. As the companies involved owned the means of both production and distribution, Japanese films effectively were self-financing and the Big Five remained content, artistically and commercially, to pander to the home market. This insular approach within the domestic industry severely restricted the commercial viability of Japanese product in the West, as well as making much of it culturally and aesthetically impenetrable.

By the early 1950s, the Japanese film industry had become one of the largest in the world, merely through the supply of product to its internal market, though epics such as *Rashomon* (1950) and *The Seven Samurai* (*Shichinin no samurai*, 1954), both from the fiercely independent Akira Kurosawa, had provided some notable 'breakout' successes on the international art-house circuit. The supernatural tradition in Japanese literature featured rarely in films of the period and when it did, it tended to come in the form of classic folk-tales and legends told, then retold again, for the modern movie audience. One of the greatest examples of this cultural regeneration is Kenji Mizoguchi's *Ugetsu*, which was based on three of the stories in a collection of weird tales written in 1776 by Akinari Ueda (real name Senjiro Ueda), entitled *Tales of Moonlight and Rain* (*Ugetsu monogatari*). The film was made by Daiei and released in Japan on 25 March 1953.

> As a priest, I must warn you I see death on your face. Haven't you come across a ghost, or something?
>
> **- Old Priest (Sugisaku Aoyama)**, *Ugetsu* (1953)

The main narrative thread in *Ugetsu* is drawn from Ueda's 'The House Amidst the

Thickets', whilst woven into it are elements of two more tales from his original nine: 'The Lust of the White Serpent' and 'The Caldron of Kibitsu'. The film takes place in the war-torn sixteenth century and the protagonists of the piece are Genjuro and Tobei, two brothers-in-law who are drawn to the rich pickings of the city of Omizu by greed and ambition respectively: Genjuro sees a profit to be made from the sale of ceramic pots, while Tobei desires to become a mighty samurai, and both of them leave their wives to the mercy of the marauding Hashiba army while they go off in

Above: Ugetsu Monogatari *(1953): Genjuro (Masayuki Mori).*

search of material gain. Tobei succeeds in his quest, but finds that his wife has been gang-raped in his absence and reduced to selling her favours in a geisha house. The main focus of the film is on Genjuro (Masayuki Mori), however, who finds himself subject to the attentions of the mysterious Lady Wakasa (Machiko Kyo). After being encouraged to marry her by her maid, he discovers to his horror that she is a ghost and that the Kutsuki mansion-scene of their tryst has been a burnt-out shell all along. Guilt-ridden and confused, he returns to his village home to be greeted by a forgiving wife — but after a night's rest, he wakes to find that she, too, was a ghost, his real wife having been killed trying to protect their son from bandits soon after he left for Omizu.

Ugetsu was awarded the Silver Lion at the 1953 Venice Film Festival and later was nominated for an Oscar for Best Costume Design at the 1956 Academy Awards; that same year, Machiko Kyo acted opposite Marlon Brando in *The Teahouse of the August Moon*. American critics in particular were smitten by Mizoguchi's poetic fable, sensing a rediscovery of the art of pictorial storytelling in its sedate visual style and thematic evocation of F W Murnau's silent classic *Sunrise* (1927); haunting and beautiful as it is, it nevertheless is overrated in purely dramatic terms. Despite the rapturous reception which the likes of *Ugetsu* and *The Seven Samurai* were often accorded on foreign soil, Japanese producers and directors still saw little requirement to extend their imaginative horizons beyond the boundaries of their own shoreline.

The Japanese movie moguls exhibited many of the same autocratic tendencies as their American counterparts, and a studio system similar to that of pre-war Hollywood predominated. According to a paper written by Dudley Andrew and Michael Raine for Yale University, 'The spread of cinema as a key element in mass culture during the Taisho and Showa eras (1912 to 1989) resulted not from Japanese traditions but from vernacular modifications of industrial and textual practices developed by Hollywood studios in the 1910s.' The Japanese had merely adopted methods of movie-making that had originated in America, in other words. The product of this industrial espionage was no more free from foreign influence than were the means of its achievement — far from it. But a sociological divide nevertheless pertained, and Japanese films invariably were no more welcome abroad than those from India, that other competitor to Hollywood in terms of sheer scale of output. Indigenous product might not have travelled far from Japan in consequence, but Japan itself was a sponge for product from beyond its own shores — a process that escalated during the American occupation of the country, which lasted until 1952. Andrew and Raine again: 'The vast majority of the hundreds of films Japan produces each year betray a massive importation of elements and conventions from Hollywood, Europe, and other Asian cinemas. In fact Japanese cinema was international before it was national. The first films to be exhibited there had been produced abroad while the first Japanese productions depended on foreign-made equipment and advisers.' The stranglehold operated by the major studios ensured that independent production was rare; original programming rarer still. If the American-Japanese cultural collision was also to be felt in American films like *Sayonara*, *Stopover Tokyo* and *Escapade in Japan* (all 1957), the impact of Hollywood on the domestic Japanese industry was to surface more clearly in a film that reflected the global cataclysm which had brought these two diverse nations together in the first place.

Ugetsu
Monogatari.

During 1952-3, RKO's legendary *King Kong* (1933), arguably the greatest monster film of all time, had been theatrically re-released to the tune of $3 million at the world box-office. Kong was a monster from a simpler era, when Africa was still the 'dark continent', and he had been born out of the mystic Imperial fantasies of Rider Haggard and Edgar Rice Burroughs, rather than from the techno-freakery of the atomic age. But his reappearance coincided with the beginnings of a sci-fi boom in fantasy cinema, itself inspired by the docudrama *Destination Moon* (1950). Old fears soon resurfaced to haunt new dimensions, and the wonders of voyaging through the uncharted oceans of the cosmos were quickly supplanted by bleaker visions, as planets became the new dark continents of the modern age, on which were harboured alien monstrosities intent on devouring the Earth. The 'super-science' — in the ominous words of the narrator of George Pal's *The War of the Worlds* (1953) — which was laying mankind open to such mind-boggling threats itself became an object of fear and apprehension: the splitting of the atom had been akin in the popular mind to the mythic opening of Pandora's Box (literally so,

in Robert Aldrich's 1955 *Kiss Me Deadly*) and no one knew what horrors might be unleashed as a consequence. It was left to the film-makers to imagine them.

The successful reissue of *King Kong* had inspired Kong creator Willis O'Brien's stop-motion successor Ray Harryhausen (who already had one giant ape variant to his credit in *Mighty Joe Young*, 1949) to update the allegory for the nuclear age. In 1953, Harryhausen was given the opportunity by Warners to unleash *The Beast From 20,000 Fathoms*, in which a fictitious rhedosaur is thawed from its Arctic slumber to trample over New York, before being cornered on Coney Island and despatched by means of a bullet tipped with a radioactive isotope; this, in turn, was elaborated from a short story by sci-fi author Ray Bradbury entitled 'The Foghorn', in which a lovelorn sea-beast is attracted to the warning siren of a lighthouse. The film was a runaway success, taking a total of $5 million, and it turned out to be "the surprise money grosser of the year," its young effects-designer recalled. 'The construction of the monster is amazingly lifelike,' *Picture Show*'s reviewer remarked. 'I shudder to think of the effect on cinemagoers (myself included) if this film had been made in 3-D...'

> In the folklore of Odo island, the monster is known as Godzilla.
> **- Dr Yamane (Takashi Shimura)**, *Godzilla* (1954)

Only one nation on Earth had experienced the potential horrors of the atomic age at first hand, however, and tensions between the United States and the Soviet Union over the ongoing Korean War (with its ever-present threat of a nuclear strike on the North, like those on Hiroshima and Nagasaki in 1945) now saw Japan caught geographically in the middle. H-bomb testing in the Pacific by the American military only added to the air of anxiety in the country, which almost begged for a means of expression through which it might be assuaged. Taking his cue from *King Kong*, but using Harryhausen's *Beast* as his model, Toho house-producer Tomoyuki Tanaka decided to attempt a home-grown version of the Warners' hit, in which a prehistoric monster is awakened from millennia of sleep by the unpredictable side-effects of nuclear radiation. The result was *Godzilla* (*Gojira*), and no more vivid metaphor for the awesome destruction that could be meted out by atomic holocaust was imagined by anyone in the 1950s than that of the gigantic fire-breathing dragon which, in 1954, rose up out of a boiling sea and brought about on celluloid the death and devastation to the newly reconstituted city of Tokyo which once had been threatened for real, and which still plagued the fevered dreams of Japanese society eight years on. Why Tokyo in particular — and why a monster from the deep?

Japanese history and myth are inextricably intertwined. Leaving aside the impact of war, Tokyo was also prone to natural disasters, the most famous of which had been the Kanto earthquake of 1923. When Westerners think of earthquakes, they tend to conjure up an image of that which struck San Francisco on 18 April 1906. The sixty-second San Francisco quake resulted in a prodigious fire, and it was this which claimed the lives of some 700 to 2,000 residents of the city (estimates vary). But the earthquake which hit the Kanto region of Honshu on 1 September 1923, specifically in the areas of Tokyo and Yokohama, brought about a firestorm which left 100,000 dead and another 40,000 missing, believed dead. The epicentre of the quake was close to Oshima island.

To the far south-west of Tokyo Bay is the Ryukyu island chain, wherein is situated the port city of Okinawa. According to legend, the Ryukyu islands are home to Ryujin, or Ryu-o, the great 'dragon-king' of the sea. Ryujin is the keeper of the Tidal Jewels, by which he exerts controls over the ebb and flow of the waves. Tsunamis, or 'harbour waves' to give them their literal translation, are nothing to do with tides and everything to do with earthquakes, but not every Japanese is a seismologist and terror from the sea has a strong superstitious connotation. Since the earliest recorded tsunami in 684 AD, the islands of Japan have been struck by these monstrous waves more than sixty-eight times, the highest rate of occurrence anywhere in the world; 6,000 people lost their lives as a result of six major tsunamis in the twentieth century alone. On 3 March 1933, a tsunami in the Sanriku area of north-eastern Honshu reached a height of thirty metres, killed 3,000 people, and destroyed 9,000 homes and 8,000 coastal craft. Other equally devastating tsunamis have thundered in on Japan in 1944 and 1946 — though all pale in comparison to that which hit Indonesia and Sri Lanka on Boxing Day, 2004, as this book was being written. Fear of the sea; fear of sudden and terrifying destruction; fear of radiation and its after-effects of disease, sickness and death — all these conspired to create a monster whose mythology was unique to the Japanese psyche, and whose omnipotent attributes would continue to be felt in a tale of a murdered girl who returns from a watery grave to wreak havoc on the world at large, four decades later...

Tanaka had hit upon the idea of making *Godzilla* after an Indonesian co-production called *Behind the Glory* (*Eako Kaje-ni*) was abandoned at short notice. A replacement film had been sought, and rather than look inward like so many of his contemporaries, Tanaka looked across the ocean at what was happening in the wider film community beyond. What he saw were monsters, and he knew instinctively that any monster worth the name in Japanese terms would have to come from the sea — a source of wonder and terror for his own countrymen since time immemorial. Adopting as his starting-point a real-life nuclear accident in which the crew of a tuna boat named 'Lucky Dragon' had accidentally been contaminated with radiation from an American H-bomb test at Bikini Atoll, Tanaka, science fiction novelist Shigeru Kayama, screenwriter Takeo Murata and director I(no)shiro Honda set about crafting the giant monster movie to end all giant monster movies. To aid them in realising the project, they called upon the forty years of expertise which had been racked up by Toho in-house effects maestro Eiji Tsuburaya, who had seen *Kong* during its initial run in 1933: "When I worked for Nikkatsu, *King Kong* came to Kyoto and I never forgot it," Tsuburaya recalled. "I thought that some day, I will make a monster movie like that."

Between these five, the Japanese horror film was born.

The phonetic *Godzilla* began life variously as a whale, a giant fire-breathing simian (the name Gojira being a conflation of the Japanese words for gorilla and whale) and a similarly Cyclopean octopus — Tsuburaya's preferred design — before emerging in his final saurian form. He was played, in this first film and most subsequent adventures, by Haruo Nakajima. In the original script, he was also to have toppled a lighthouse, as did Harryhausen's rhedosaur, but that was considered too slavish a copy for comfort; in the final draft, he first clambers onto land at Odo Island, where he

Above: Godzilla *(1956).*   flattens some mud huts and their inhabitants.

To capitalise on old myths rather than try to create one anew, the monster is given a natural history which predates his appearance in the film. When two trawlers disappear at sea off the coast of Honshu, hackles are raised among the Odo islanders. "Something terrible's happening," a fisherman mutters; "It must be Godzilla," another opines, when the fish catch is suddenly depleted. "When he cannot find any fish in the sea, he comes to land to prey on men." The islander goes on to explain that they used to sacrifice a young girl to appease this monster, in the same way that the Skull islanders sacrificed a maiden to Kong. In a sequence which was to find itself imitated in every giant monster film thereafter, an island home is demolished during a storm by some inexplicable (but mostly unseen) force.

A research party led by palaeontologist Dr Yamane (the role benignly sketched by Toho contract-player and Kurosawa veteran Takashi Shimura) is promptly dispatched to the island to carry out a scientific survey, and it finds traces of radioactivity as well as a trilobite — a crustacean supposed to have been extinct for millions of years. As they investigate further, the 'Big G' makes his first proper appearance, in puppet form and standing behind a hilltop. Yamane reports his findings: "The H-bomb explosions must have disrupted his peace," he conjectures. "He couldn't stay there any longer so he started moving, looking for a secure place where he would be safe from the H-bombs." He further reasons that the monster itself is radioactive. An 'Anti-Godzilla' headquarters is set up in Tokyo and stock footage depth-charges are detonated out to sea to try to force the awesome amphibian to the surface. These efforts fail. The nation holds its breath as it awaits the inevitable assault. Night falls, and Godzilla rises from the waters of Tokyo Bay at Kannon-point. A wave of destruction follows swiftly, as the monster reduces the city to rubble and incinerates what remains of it with blasts of his radioactive breath.

In the meantime, physicist Dr Serizawa (Akihiko Harata) has invented a potent new weapon in his very own mad lab — the 'Oxygen Destroyer', which does exactly what it says on the label and depletes the sea of life-giving oxygen. Initially, he is unwilling to allow his device to be deployed in anger, but that soon changes after Godzilla struts his stuff. Serizawa sacrifices himself during the irreversible destruction of Godzilla on the ocean floor — irreversible in the context of *this* film, that is! — partly so that the secret of the Oxygen Destroyer will die with him and partly in 'honourable' suicide for being cuckolded by the hero (his weapon of choice is the ritual knife, but here it is employed to slit the air hose to his diving suit rather than his stomach). "I can't believe that what we destroyed was the only Godzilla," Yamane intones grimly at the fade-out. "If they keep experimenting with deadly weapons again and again, another Godzilla is sure to surface somewhere in the world." The doctor's words were solely devised to impart the appropriate Awesome Warning, but they doubled conveniently as a trailer in the wake of the film's success.

Godzilla's illustrious place in the horror hall of fame rests principally on the scenes of destruction as the monster ravages Tokyo, and their now-legendary status is for once justifiable. Honda was a personal friend of the famed Kurosawa, and when his beastie finally rears its pock-marked head, he delivers a dark and doomy nightmare spectacle, perfectly pitched to capture the atomic anxieties which were so prevalent in the fifties. The sequence where the monster bears down on Tokyo as screaming crowds flee from it in panic is primally powerful in its vision of apocalypse. And few tricks are missed in conveying the sheer terror that the onslaught of such a biblical dragon would inspire: a mother widowed in war whispers to her frightened daughter that she will "soon see" her father, as they huddle in the street to await their fate at the feet of the titan. Despite its melodramatic inadequacies, Honda's film sent a genuine shiver of fear through all who saw it, and a new myth entered into Japanese culture in consequence.

Above: Ramond Burr in Godzilla.

Godzilla was released in Japan (as *Gojira*) on 3 November 1954, to much acclaim and more ticket sales, and its commercial impact was such that enterprising American showman Joseph E Levine picked up the rights to the film for distribution in the West. Levine was a new post-war breed of exhibitor-turned-distributor, who had switched to specialising in the importation of foreign art-house movies, such as Roberto Rosselini's *Rome, Open City* (*Roma, città aperta*, 1945) and Vittorio De Sica's *The Bicycle Thief* (*Ladri de biciclette*, 1948). His novel idea in respect of *Godzilla* was not to release the original but to cut, dub and refine it in tune with domestic taste. To that end, he needed an indigenous star, and he settled on Raymond Burr.

Canadian-born Burr was experiencing something of a career hiatus, having suffered from a whispering campaign orchestrated by Senator Joseph McCarthy and his House Un-American Activities Committee. Before 1954, Burr had been making a name for himself as a heavy in films like *Horizons West* (1952), *The Blue Gardenia* (1953) and, most famously, Hitchcock's *Rear Window* (1954), but with the HUAC putting the brakes on, he was up for grabs to the highest bidder; it did not take much of a bid to have him shoot some footage for a Japanese monster movie in the role of Steve Martin, foreign correspondent to United World News. (The year after *Godzilla* was released in America, Burr turned his back on films in favour of television, and a long-running series as Erle Stanley Gardner's *Perry Mason*.)

With Burr on tap, Levine decided to pare Honda's film down to its bare essentials: the giant fire-breathing monster. This meant that much of substance in the original had now to go. Composer Akira Ifukube's rousing martial music for *Godzilla*, once heard, was not easily forgotten — except by Levine, who 'forgot' to include all but the briefest of extracts from it during the Tokyo attack scene in the American version.

George — here in Tokyo, time has been turned back two million years. Here is my report as it happens… A prehistoric monster the Japanese call Godzilla has just walked out of Tokyo Bay. He's as tall as a thirty-storey

American poster

for Godzilla.

building, and now he's making his way towards the city's main line of
defence — 300,000 volts of electricity strung around the city as a barrier:
a barrier against Godzilla...

- **Steve Martin (Raymond Burr)**, *Godzilla* (1956)

The Americanised version of *Godzilla*, subtitled *King of the Monsters*, begins with a hospital sequence which comes *after* Tokyo has been demolished in the original and
relates the bulk of the story in flashback. Burr's integration into the extant film is well
thought out if often crudely executed (by Terry Morse): some curious cutting takes
him from a reception desk at an airport into the chartroom of the Nankai Shipping
company by means of a single corridor(!). "I'm afraid my Japanese is a little rusty," he
remarks, enabling the motley group of Japanese-American actors hired alongside him
for the occasion to explain what is going on in the non-subtitled sequences in which
he is now supposed to be participating. Martin is naturally required to *observe* much
of the action, popping up like a jack-in-the-box at opportune moments, although his
insertion into the episode at Odo Island is accomplished with some ingenuity. Other
authorities have claimed that Burr's scenes were shot in a day, but given the number
of complicated set-ups in which he appears, not to mention his numerous costume
changes, this hardly seems credible. His *narration* is likely to have been recorded in a
day; his scenes in a week. For all its valiant efforts in the art of deceit, much of
Godzilla's editing is clumsy in the extreme: Martin is often shown conversing with
obvious stand-ins who present only the backs of their heads to camera.

(An example of the inadequacies of the dubbing in the American print can be
found when stalwart young hero Ogata [Akira Takarada] makes his call-to-arms. "If we
don't defend ourselves from Godzilla now, what will become of us?" he bleats.
Compare this to the more impassioned appeal of the subtitled version: "If we don't
destroy Godzilla, Godzilla will destroy us all!")

The same palaeontological mistake of a mere 'two million years' for the duration of
the Jurassic period which featured in *Gojira* is transferred intact into the remix, but the
height of the monster is exaggerated in the dubbing from the more feasible 168 feet to a
wholly unbelievable 400. Most of the footage deleted to make way for Burr involved the
romantic triangle between the three Japanese leads, though the American version also lost
Godzilla's inaugural assault on a family of Odo islanders. Other sequences are trimmed
along the way, with only the Tokyo assault left intact, but even that is embellished with
footage that comes *before* the attack in the original. Critically, the contrast of the print was
reduced through forced-exposure, so that the monster could more easily be seen.

Nevertheless, *Godzilla* turned into a huge international hit for Joe E Levine, and
the repercussions on Japanese cinema were profound. Tsuburaya's dragon turned out

to be much more than a titan of technological terror: he became the front-runner for an entire monster industry. In the years that followed this first release, *Godzilla* was to be joined by a whole pantheon of like-minded creatures, as Dr Yamane had predicted in the film, and all of them bent on similar levels of mass-destruction.

Sure enough, 'another' Godzilla surfaced a mere six months later, on 24 April 1955, in *Godzilla Raids Again* (*Gojira no gyakushu*) — and *literally* so, in the case of the American version. Much of Dr Yamane's fleeting return to postulate the appearance of a second monster in the Godzilla family was deleted in the translation, along with his portentous warnings about the hydrogen bomb. The film was disseminated to American audiences in 1959, under the aegis of Toho lawyer and accredited producer Paul Schriebman and the misleading title of *Gigantis, The Fire Monster*, after Joe Levine refused distributor Warner Brothers the use of the name Godzilla. With the need for explanation as to the first beast's supposed recovery from the effects of the Oxygen Destroyer thus obviated, Godzilla/Gigantis is discovered on a different island, locked in combat with a monster named Angilas. In due course, he turns his radioactive attentions to Osaka before being 'destroyed' again in an avalanche of ice. Despite offering up two monsters for the price of one, the film was catchpenny, a situation compounded in the crass American re-edit which incorporated footage shot by Hugo Grimaldi. Its commercial motivation was too transparent even for the loyal Japanese audience, and Motoyoshi Oda's muddled and perfunctory direction of the eighty-two minute feature (cut to seventy-eight in America) was a poor substitute for that of Ishiro Honda; on his second outing, Gojira/Godzilla/Gigantis raided all but the box office. Honda, however, was already hard at work on his own sequel of sorts.

(An interesting footnote on the differing attitudes to censorship in the fifties can be gleaned from pilot Kobayashi (Minoru Chiaki) and his use of the word 'bastard' in the subtitled print of the film; in *Gigantis*, the expletive is either ignored or he is dubbed as exclaiming to the monster, "And now, you must die!" A more explicable excision is the protracted bout of bonhomie involving the principals and set at an eatery in Hokkaido, ostensibly to celebrate their imminent nuptials. This was nothing more than padding in the original, designed to allow Tsuburaya's effects technicians time to gird the loins of their monsters.)

The success of *Godzilla* in international markets encouraged Toho to abandon its planned production schedule (as Hammer was also to do in the mid-fifties, and for the same reason) and indulge in more monster mayhem. Dr Yamane having alluded to him in front of the Diet committee in *Godzilla*, it was perhaps inevitable that Toho's next outing for Honda was *The Abominable Snowman* (*Jujin yuki otoko*, 1955), which did not see release in America until 1958, as *Half Human*, with horror star John Carradine turning the Burr trick of stapling together inserted American footage. The

Above: Rodan –
The Flying
Monster *(1956)*.

film unspooled in this version at a mere sixty-three of its original's ninety-eight minutes, half of which was then comprised of Carradine discoursing with colleagues about
events in the other half, while B-movie stalwart Morris Ankrum conducted an autopsy in an adjoining room. Honda had taken Akira Takarada and Momoko Kochi, his
romantic leads in *Godzilla*, with him into the film, leaving Toho pin-up Hiroshi
Koizumi to the mercy of *Godzilla Raids Again*, but their presence went largely unnoticed in the abridged version.

　　While Ray Harryhausen returned the compliment which Toho had paid his
Beast by topping the ocean-liner attack in *Godzilla* with one of his own for a giant octopus opus called *It Came From Beneath the Sea* (1955), the Tokyo-based studio, with one
eye on Warner's *Them!* (1954), was cloning the commercial success of the original film
into a repeat performance with a new monster: *Rodan*.

　　…But what have these tests done to Mother Earth? Can the human race continue to deliver these staggering blows without arousing, somewhere in the depths of earth, a reaction — a counter-attack — a horror still undreamed of? There are persons in the Japanese islands who believe that the horror has already been seen. What is the aftermath? This is the story of such an aftermath…

- **Narrator (Les Tremayne)** *Rodan - The Flying Monster* (1956)

Steeped in the Kabuki tradition and unwilling to spend two years on special effects, it seemed more natural to the creators of Japan's monsters to realise their scenarios by kitting out an actor in a rubber suit and have him crash through miniature sets. The sets themselves brought praise from reviewers for their attention to detail, but the technique fooled no one except for those willing to suspend disbelief in the face of the 'awesome' destruction that this ploy was able to facilitate. *Godzilla* had managed to disguise such obvious fakery by the fast clip of its editing and the often impenetrable night-shooting which gave the piece much of its power. It also had utilised extensive superimpositions of fleeing crowds of people in the foreground of the monster shots. But *Rodan*, filmed in Eastmancolour, quickly gave the game away as speed and papiermâché stood in for *Godzilla's* hordes of extras.

In its original form, *Rodan* (*Sora no daikaiju Radon*) took its lead from the 'UFO' scare that was prevalent at the time and played heavily upon the unidentified nature of the object that was to be seen flying at supersonic speed above the skies of Japan; one early scene in which a fighter pilot chases the creature with fatal consequences apes the real-life incident of USAF Captain Thomas Mantell, whose F-51 crashed after tailing a supposed UFO above Godman Airfield in Kentucky on 7 January 1948: "Captain John Hughes, United States Air Force, was killed this morning while engaged in the pursuit of an unidentified flying object," a news broadcast in *Rodan* declares. "His supersonic pursuit-ship, caught in a slipstream of hurricane proportions, disintegrated in mid-air."

Rodan was no alien, however, rather a titanic pteranodon hatched from man-eating larvae unearthed by mining. The film opened in Japan on 26 December 1956, and American rights were snapped up by the King Brothers, Frank and Maurice, who produced a giant monster movie of their own four years later, with *Gorgo*. The Kings chose not to follow the lead of Levine and merely dubbed *Rodan* throughout, using the voice talents of George Takei and Paul Frees. Screenwriter David Duncan, who would go on to pen *The Monster That Challenged the World* (1957), *Monster on the Campus* (1958) and *The Time Machine* (1960) among others, redrafted the American version to tie the beast more closely to the mutant effects of nuclear radiation: "I realise now, that by the narrowest of margins, Man had proved himself the stronger. But will it always be so? May not other and more terrible monsters even now be stirring in the darkness?" Frees' voice intones at the close. "And when at last they spring upon us, can we be certain we shall beat them back a second time? The answer lies in the future..." Maybe so, but the 1950s were an age of monsters, and the next towering threat to Man was not long in coming.

Rodan paid its way in international markets on the strength of colour and spectacle alone. It was a more conventional film than *Godzilla* in every way, but a new genre of Japanese cinema had been born and Toho was anything but slow in making the most of it after the runaway success of its first three giant monsters.

Godzilla had whetted the public's appetite for *kaiju eiga*, or 'monster movies', and the years that followed produced a whole slew of similar beasts — from King Ghidorah to Ebirah, 'Horror of the Deep'. Eventually Daiei, Nikkatsu and Schochiku abandoned their traditional territorial splits and joined with Toho in the science fiction fray: Daiei with *Gamera* (*Daikaiju Gamera*, 1965, and sequels) and *Majin* (*Daimajin*, 1966, and sequels), Nikkatsu with *Gappa, The Triphibian Monster* (*Daikyoju Gappa*, 1967 and *no* sequels — the company folded after the film's release!) and Schochiku with *Gilala*, or *The X From Outer Space* (*Uchu daikaiju guilala*, 1967), and *Goke - Bodysnatcher From Hell* (*Kyuketsuki Gokemidoro*, 1968). Inside a decade, there were more monsters stomping around the islands of Japan than there were inhabitants to stomp on. Of these increasingly fantastical creatures — Mothra, Baragon, Gigan, Megalon and hybrids like Mecha-Godzilla — only Honda's *Varan the Unbelievable*, shot in Tohoscope and murky monochrome late in 1958, managed to recapture something of the horror and intensity of the movie that started it all.

Varan advertises its debt to *King Kong* by having a team of scientists stumble upon a remote island village whose denizens worship the God Baradagi; they put this down to native superstition until they explore deeper into the fog-shrouded jungle and Varan, or Baran (dubbing and/or subtitling made the names of Toho's monsters user-variable), emerges out of a primeval lake. Next stop, Tokyo — but only as far as the bay. Varan's assault is restricted to some tail-lashing at Henada Airport, before he is sent to a watery grave by 'light' bombs.

For a quadruped with wings, *Varan the Unbelievable* was a more convincing beast than some (until the viewer becomes alert to the actor on his hands and knees), and the film benefited from an evocative score and the unusually sombre mood evoked by the extensive night shooting. But even by this time, the residents of Tokyo must have been used to having to evacuate their city at short notice, as it was now being annihilated at almost annual intervals. 'Hackneyed, uninspired carbon-copy,' was *Variety's* epitaph.

As science-horror films became more graphic towards the end of the fifties,

Toho's contribution was *The H-Man* (*Bijo to Ekitainingen*), in which Tokyo is menaced not by a giant dinosaur but by a green protoplasmic ooze from a deserted fishing trawler that dissolves everyone with whom it comes into contact, before turning them into 'H' (for Hydrogen) men. With a plot that was drawn both from *X The Unknown* (1956) and the same incident which had inspired *Godzilla* (that of the Lucky Dragon [Fukuryu Maru], a tuna boat which had found itself showered with radioactive fall-out when it sailed too close to an H-bomb test at Bikini Atoll on 1 March 1954 — a reference in the film to the ship's *twenty-three* crew members confirming its source), *The H-Man* was an attempt by Toho to combine several of its genre staples in a single film. The result was patchy at best, with some effectively spooky scenes aboard a ghost ship replete with liquid monsters vying for attention with a funereally-paced *yakuza* sub-plot which climaxes in what must be one of the worst car chases ever filmed: passers-by can be seen meandering *in front* of the vehicles during the pursuit! The more adult nature of the material was emphasised by a bevy of scantily-clad nightclub dancers — one of whom dissolves to leave only her G-string behind (a scene cut in American and English prints) — and a heroine who is forced at the climax to flee from the title-being in her underwear.

Above: The H-Man *(1958).*

The H-Man was released domestically in June 1958, but the addition of Tohoscope saw it picked up by Columbia for distribution overseas a year later, where it was paired with either *The Woman Eater* (1957) or *Terror in the Midnight Sun* (1959). In Britain it further benefited from the cachet of the obligatory X certificate. And in a reversal of what had become the *status quo* for Japanese science fiction, the plot of *The H-Man* was quickly plagiarised to provide *The Blob*, a first starring vehicle for the young Steve McQueen, which opened in America in September 1958, three months after the release of Honda's film in Japan.

After his *H-Man*, Honda moved swiftly on to a predictable 'G-man' (remember that the Japanese read the opposite way to occidentals). *The Human Vapor* (*Gasu ningen dai ichigo*, 1960) was better acted and directed than its predecessor, but its stilted pace and overly melodramatic storyline relegated it to the level of a novelty item. A cross between *The Invisible Man* (1933) and *The Phantom of the Opera*, *The Human Vapor* involved a 'gaseous superman' engineered by an experimental physicist. His madness comes in pedestrian form, however, and he spends most of the film robbing banks in order to fund the farewell performance of his classical dancer girlfriend. (The garishly grinning *Noh* mask worn by Kaoru Yachigusa in her routine was to find a more satisfying outlet in Kaneto Shinto's *Onibaba* four years later.) *The Human Vapor* was too quaintly Japanese in theme to find itself a distributor in Britain, where its 'Gasman' might have been confused by the general audience for a utilities inspector, though it did surface briefly in America.

Toho also extended Tsuburaya's talent for miniatures into the field of space opera. Notable in this regard was *The Mysterians* (*Chikyu boeigun*, 1957), in which colonists from the planet Mysteroid, a satellite lying between Mars and Saturn, plot to take over the earth and much battling ensues, but the film as a whole is conducted on the level of a Flash Gordon serial of the 1930s. *The Mysterians* was a Japanese version of *The War of the Worlds*, just as the earlier *Mysterious Satellite* (*Uchujin Tokyo ni arawaru*, 1956) had performed a similar duty for *The Day the Earth Stood Still* (1951). They were the first of a number of juvenile space adventures — such as *Battle in Outer Space* (*Uchu daisenso*, 1959), *The Green Slime* (*Gamma sango uchu daisakusen*, 1968) and *Latitude Zero* (*Ido zero daisakusen*, 1969) — that Toho was to produce intermittently throughout the sixties, but offerings like these brought little or no return for the company in the West: most were released as second features if they saw release at all. By the time of the last of them, *Thunderbirds* creator Gerry Anderson was aping their plots and bettering their model-work on a weekly basis on television.

> O, the fury of a woman maddened… is truly like unto… the greatest horror there is.
>
>   - **Screen caption,** *The Ghost of Yotsuya* (1959)

At the end of the 1950s, the Japanese could fairly claim to have carved a niche for themselves with a highly specific take on the science-fantasy genre, largely inspired by atomic anxiety and heavily imbued with *mea culpa*, but out-and-out horror had thus far passed them by. In the West, however, the sci-fi boom of the past half-dozen years had already come to an end, and a new and more graphic fantasy cycle had been set in train by a small and relatively unknown British exploitation company called Hammer Films, whose *The Curse of Frankenstein* (1957) had breathed a new and bloody life into the horror film by infusing the Gothic with a welter of sex, sadism and secret taboos.

The Hammer product, with its strict Christian menagerie of vampires, werewolves and mummies, did not offer Japanese film-makers the same richness of pickings which previously they had enjoyed from the giant monster cycle. So-called Japanese 'Gothic' having stalled in development in the 1920s, those with a bent to plough the furrow that Hammer had inaugurated were left with little choice but to revive yet again the ghostly fables of the Edo period and literally infuse them with fresh blood. A prime example of the curious hybrid which resulted from trying to cross-fertilise a Kabuki play with the mechanics of Hammer Horror was provided in director Nobua Nakagawa's adaptation of *The Ghost of Yotsuya* (*Tokaido Yotsuya kaidan*, 1959). Produced by the low-budget Shintoho Studios (originally an off-shoot of Toho itself), for whom Nakagawa had shot *Black Cat Mansion* (*Borei kaibyo yashiki*) in 1958, while fellow directors like Akira Miwa, Tervo Ishii and Koreyoshi Akasawa churned out a more typical *Supergiant* series for television (episodes of which were re-edited to feature-length during the sixties, such as 1964's *Evil Brain from Outer Space* [*Supa jaiantsu uchukaijin no shutsugen*]), *The Ghost of Yotsuya* is a film in which the two traditions can clearly be seen to collide onscreen.

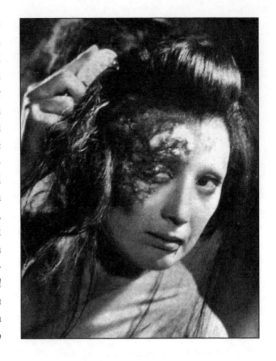

Above: The Ghost of Yotsuya *(1959).*

The oft-told tale of Oiwa (herein named Iwa) is played out initially in conventional fashion: she is deceived into the bed of the unscrupulous Iemon, then cruelly poisoned in order to clear the path for another. Along the way, there is much murder and intrigue. Nakagawa even begins this version by lifting a stage curtain, to remind the audience of the film's theatrical origins — a device which he honours by capturing much of the early action in single takes, to emphasise the formal nature of the proceedings in the manner of Olivier's *Henry V* (1944). With the poisoning and consequent disfigurement of Iwa, however, as well as her death and subsequent reappearance in various phantom forms, *The Ghost of Yotsuya* plummets headlong into a series of *guignol*esque images which owe more to the highly-coloured horror films of the day than they do to the 1813 play by Nanboku Tsuruya on which this and previous versions of the story were based.

Tsuruya himself had been a Kabuki moderniser, employing elements such as suave villains and imperilled heroines in his reworkings (*naimaze*) of tales from the *Konjaku monogatari* which already had become familiar to Western readers of Gothic romance, and Nakagawa followed his lead in borrowing from Hammer to paint the scope-screen blood-red as Iwa (Kazuko Wakasugi) surfaces in a fetid swamp amid a pool of gore, or looms up out of the ground to threaten Iemon (Shigeru Amachi) in a

Above: UK poster *for* The Split *(1961).*

graveyard, her scarred face prefiguring that of Herbert Lom in Hammer's upcoming *The Phantom of the Opera* (1962). *The Ghost of Yotsuya* was released in Japan on 11 July 1959, but its slow pace, static dialogue — "Do you think I will leave you with this debt unpaid?" she vows before dying; "I will visit my hatred on you. Be sure of that" — and traditional theme were too dated to set any new trend in Japanese horror as the sixties beckoned.

(In the early 1960s, exploitation film-maker Mitsugu Okura's Okura Films imported director Roger Corman's Poe series into Japan, with its own stable of vengeful female ghosts, such as that of Elizabeth Medina in *Pit and the Pendulum* [1961] and Morella in *Tales of Terror* [1962].)

Like its genre counterparts in the West, Toho rotated the same actors through each and every film, and when they were not working for Toho, they were working for other companies in a similar capacity: Tetsu Nakamura, who had played a small role as the gangster Chin in *The H-Man*, turned up in *The Split* (*Kyofu* [*The Manster* in America], 1959) as a mad scientist with a laboratory on the slopes of a volcano: Dr Suzuki injects foreign correspondent Larry Stanford (British-born Peter Dyneley, better known as the voice of Jeff Tracy in television's *Thunderbirds*) with a serum which brings out the beast in him, in an eye-poppingly literal translation of Jekyll and Hyde. Stanford splits into two, man and ape-man. Not so much a Japanese film as a American-Japanese co-production shot in Japan, a budgetary convenience of which exploitation producer George Breakston had previous experience, *The Split* was garish and grim, silly and shocking by turns. Fondly remembered by genre fans for the scene in which its protagonist discovers an eyeball emerging from his shoulder-blade, the film is a genuine oddity. Despite the staginess of its settings, crude lap-dissolve transformation effects and hokey monster-on-the-loose finale, the sequence in which Stanford births a *second* head in a psychiatrist's office still packs a punch, and its sombre approach to predictable pulp material engenders a curious air of charnel horror. *The Split* was released in Britain to the kind of curiosity crowd that was likely to be attracted by the more salacious title of its voodoo-inspired running-mate, *Macumba Love* (1960). Both received X certificates.

'A pathetic pot-boiler,' was the opinion of *The Split* voiced by the same *Monthly Film Bulletin* which thought *Rodan* expounded 'a serious moral concerning the use of atom and hydrogen bombs' but that the later *Onibaba* was 'impossible to take seriously'.

He was an average sort of guy, the image of us all. How can I say this? There was good in Larry and there was evil; the evil part broke through — took hold. Call it an accident or… call it a warning.

- **Ian Matthews (Norman Van Hawley)**, *The Split* (1959)

Above: The Split: *Larry Stanford (Peter Dyneley; right).*

The collapse of Shintoho in 1961 paralleled a backlash against the graphic excesses of the new horror cinema in the West, and the horror film went into turnaround for the remainder of the sixties. With the heavy hand of increased censorship being brought to bear even on examples of the *kaiju eiga* genre as innocuous as the King Brothers' own production of *Gorgo* (which was accorded an X certificate in 1961 because of the volume of its soundtrack!), the emphasis in Japan swung away from antediluvian monsters as villains and onto the same creatures as unlikely heroes.

The trend was begun with *Mothra* (*Mosura*, 1961), in which a giant, er, *moth* wins audience sympathy by pitting its colossal wits against the unscrupulous showman who dares to kidnap the tiny twin priestesses of its exotic island cult. Godzilla experienced

Above: UK poster for King Kong vs Godzilla *(1963).*

the same subtle modification over the course of a half-dozen ancillary features, until he no longer was recognisable as the atomic Asmodeus who had spewed terror on Tokyo in 1954; instead, he began to be seen as a kind of perverse national mascot.

The low point was reached in 1963, when a distinctly porridgy-looking King Kong was put into the ring against Japan's national champion in *King Kong vs Godzilla*; erroneous rumour had it that so as not to offend national sensibilities on either side of the Pacific divide, two alternative endings to the film were shot: in one, Godzilla won, while in the other, Kong did likewise. In the event, *both* survived to die another day. In Britain, the film got by at the box-office on the strength of the obligatory X certificate which was being given to such innocuous fare because reactionary ex-Labour cabinet minister Lord Morrison of Lambeth was the puritanical president of the British Board of Film Censors at the time.

Two years later, the same treatment was meted out to the Frankenstein monster, and as the writers of these movies could conceptualise in no terms other than the super-tall, Mary Shelley's famous creature suffers the indignity of growing to a height of 100 feet after his newly transplanted heart is accidentally irradiated. Deprived of the subliminal effect of a rubber suit, the only thing that the humanoid hero of *Frankenstein Conquers the World* (*Furankenshutain tai Baragon*) managed to achieve was to make even more transparent the obvious trickery of a normal-sized actor wading through papier mâché sets in slow motion, as trade magazine *Kine Weekly* appeared to appreciate: 'This will appeal to the more simple-minded echelon of monster-fanciers.'

After New York, Paris, Tokyo and more had variously been destroyed by Godzilla, Rodan, Mothra, Baragon and King Ghidorah among others, the self-fulfilling prophecy of *Destroy All Monsters* (*Kaiju soshingeki*, 1968) pitted beast against predictable beast and effectively brought the cycle to an end, although its death throes were to last for a further few years and increasingly desperate attempts at resuscitation: Mecha-Godzilla vied with Mechani-Kong for the dwindling attentions of a diminishing band of patrons in all territories outside of Japan, where local indulgence continued to assure the series of reasonable returns. In the 1990s, Toho took advantage of the digital magic of CGI to launch a new generation of more spectacular Godzilla films, though speed of delivery was still of the essence and the rubber suit remained the *sine qua non* of the genre.

The seemingly infinite varieties of monster which the back-room boys at Toho had dreamed up across forty years found a more suitable outlet for their kind from 1997 on, when *Pokémon* ('Pocket monsters') hit both the television networks and the toy stores of the world. With the honourable exception of Godzilla, all of them were always the product of a child-like imagination and a super-simplistic, even ritualistic, view of the universal battle between good and evil.

> Turning quickly, I saw that there was movement among an extraordinarily shaped mass of fungus, close to my elbow. It was swaying uneasily, as though it possessed life of its own. Abruptly, as I stared, the thought came to me that the thing had a grotesque resemblance to the figure of a distorted human creature. Even as the fancy flashed into my brain, there was a slight, sickening noise of tearing, and I saw that one of the branch-like arms was detaching itself from the surrounding grey masses, and coming towards me.
>
> - **William Hope Hodgson**, *The Voice in the Night* (1907)

As the giant monsters began to run out of steam (and cities to reduce to rubble), so Japanese studios turned to other sources of the fantastic. Adaptations of works outside of Japan's own rich literary heritage were few and far between, but an exception to the rule came in 1963 with *Matango - Fungus of Terror* (*Matango*).

Matango was taken from 'The Voice in the Night', a William Hope Hodgson

"Exotic, torrid . . . a witches' blend of terror and death."
New York Times

ONIBABA

a film by **KANETO SHINDO**
with **NOBUKO OTOWA** **JITSUKO YOSHIMURA**
PRODUCED BY TOKYO EIGA CO. LTD. / KINDAI EIKYO RELEASED BY EAST WEST CLASSICS © 1987
EAST WEST CLASSICS WES

Above: American poster for Onibaba *(1964).*

short story from 1907, in which a seven-strong group of survivors from a shipwrecked schooner fall foul of mutant mushrooms on a mysterious isle. Hodgson's story had been adapted by Stirling Silliphant five years before, for an NBC television series called 'Suspicion' and executive-produced by Alfred Hitchcock. As though to acknowledge the fact, or to comment on Japanese fantasy cinema in general, one of the group remarks in passing, "Civilisation has progressed by borrowing. Each generation takes an idea and improves it." The film is often genuinely suspenseful, and the ever-dependable Honda's direction tries to recapture something of the mood of *The H-Man* in a sequence where the seven go walkabout in the eerie, deserted hulk of an abandoned trawler.

Matango eventually degenerates into the usual clutch of fantastic creatures running amok in richly-hued undergrowth, and it was held up in release in both America and Britain until 1965 and 1969 respectively, by which time its theme of 'magic mushrooms' had a different connotation for some audiences. But if the Japan of the 1950s had offered up timeless classics of the samurai genre, the 1960s were still to provide three outstanding examples of the supernatural in the Japanese film: *Onibaba*, *Kwaidan* and *Kuroneko*.

Deep and dark… its darkness has endured since ancient times.
                               - Screen caption, *Onibaba* (1964)

November 1964 saw the release in Japan of Hiroshima-born writer-director Kaneto Shindo's *Onibaba*, whose title translated into English as 'devil-mother' but in Britain was given as 'The Hole'. Shindo's stark and dark tale of survival is set during the Onin Civil War of 1467-77, a period of turmoil which ended the Muromachi shogunate and during which Kyoto, ancient capital of Japan, was razed to the ground. Two women, a mother and daughter-in-law, have been left to live on their wits. This they do by luring unsuspecting samurai to their deaths in a deep pit amid the reed-beds and stripping the bodies of their saleable armour. All is going swimmingly until the arrival of Hachi (Kei

Onibaba.

Sato), an army deserter who sets his sights on the younger of the two to the chagrin and frustration of the elder. The mother leads a high-ranking samurai to his death and dons a white robe and his demonic *Noh* mask in order to frighten away the daughter-in-law from her nightly trysts with Hachi. For a time, her plan works — but the ruse is revealed when she finds that the mask has adhered to her face: "I'm not a demon. I'm a human being!" she screams, as jealousy corrupts and ultimately destroys the trio.

Shindo's elegant moral fable displayed a rawness (not to mention raunchiness) that was perfectly in tune with the times. He extends the metaphor of 'the hole' just a little too far on occasion, as Hachi peers into it and exclaims, "I want a woman!" (an overtly symbolic use of landscape which is later complemented by the mother wrapping herself around a phallic tree in a similar display of sexual need). The film's graphic sex scenes and prevalent nudity denied it a certificate of exhibition in Britain until 1968, although it was granted an X in the capital by the review board of the Greater London Council on its initial application in 1965. Aside from the vivid brutalities of war and horrors of the psychological kind, superstition and terror are deployed in *Onibaba* to advance the age-old tale of the eternal triangle, as mother torments daughter-in-law with visions of Hell and warnings about the price of sin being damnation.

Kiyomi Kuroda's exquisite studio lensing and Hikaru Hayashi's strident percussive score evoke a genuine sense of foreboding and unease, while the tempo of the swaying reeds is used to modulate the pace and reflect the emotions in play. *Onibaba* was, and is, an eye-opener, though the hard-nosed *Variety* critic was unimpressed: 'Too often, it turns out to be a potpourri of ravenous eating and blatant sex,' he wrote.

The film's demonic 'ghost', which looms menacingly over the reeds, was strictly

Above: Kwaidan
(1964): 'Black
Hair' (top) and
'Snow Woman'
(Keiko Kishi).

of the human variety — but Shindo's next outing into the same territory was to discard the psychological reading of *Onibaba* in favour of a purely supernatural one.

In old Kyoto lived a young samurai…
- **Screen caption**, *Kwaidan* (1964)

At a time when American horror cinema was churning out anthology films adapted from the works of indigenous authors like Edgar Allan Poe (*Tales of Terror*) and Nathaniel Hawthorne (*Twice Told Tales*, 1963), the Japanese thought naturally to turn their backs on the sea-borne terrors of London-born William Hope Hodgson and look instead to a naturalised one of their own for similar inspiration. Thus, hot on the heels of *Onibaba* came *Kwaidan* (*Kaidan*), which opened in Japan on 29 December 1964.

This loving and leisurely tribute to the writings of Lafcadio Hearn and the Japanese supernatural tradition in general was choreographed by Masaki Kobayashi, a painter by training and director of 1962's *Harikiri*. *Kwaidan* — or 'Stories and Studies of Strange Things' as Hearn subtitled his work — consists of four separate stories, the last of which is used to link back to the first and thus complete the circle of fate. The four are 'Black Hair', 'Snow Woman', 'Hoichi the Earless' and 'In a Cup of Tea', only two of which actually feature in *Kwaidan*. 'In a Cup of Tea' was drawn from Hearn's *Shadowings* of 1902, while 'Black Hair', or 'The Reconciliation' as Hearn called it, comes from *Kotto* (1902). The last tale was itself a variant on the tale of 'The House Amidst the Thickets' in Ueda's *Ugetsu*, which in turn had utilised themes that were common currency in the *zhiguai* (strange records) of China's Tang dynasty, more than a millennium before. In its original form, *Kwaidan* ran a marathon 164 minutes, but it was reduced to 125 for distribution outside of Japan by the removal of the more surrealistic second episode of the 'Snow Woman'.

The inaugural episode, 'Black Hair', is the most iconic Japanese ghost story of the four: an ambitious samurai abandons his devoted wife to better his status elsewhere. He remarries into money and class and, for a time, enjoys the fruits of success. But, as the marriage palls, he finds himself haunted increasingly by memories of the woman he left behind. The years pass, till finally he decides to leave his present life and return to that of the past. He reaches his former home to find his first wife as he had left her, engaged in tapestry-weaving. In a plaintive scene, he begs her forgiveness — readily given — and they spend the night in each others' arms. When he awakes the next morning, however, he finds that he has slept with a *corpse*, whose long, black hair snakes in tendrils about its skull, driving him to the edge of insanity: he gazes into a pool of water and sees that he is now an old man... There is more to this elegiac fable than meets the eye. The past cannot that easily be recaptured, so the wise man will pursue a course where regret and recrimination do not become a feature of the future. (The same folk-tale from which Hearn derived 'The Reconciliation' was used by Oliver Onions as the basis for a short story of his own entitled 'The Cigarette Case' [1911] — Onions was an occasional writer of ghostly fiction who is best-known for 'The Beckoning Fair One', another classic tale of a vengeful female spirit.)

'Snow Woman' finds two travellers caught in a blizzard who encounter the female demon of the title — she drains the very life from one of them but leaves the other with a promise that should he ever tell what he has seen, she will return and kill him also. The man marries, sires children, and eventually forgets about his ordeal in the snow, till one evening, the image of his wife seated by the fire calls to mind the face of the succubus who murdered his companion long ago. He is moved to recount the strange tale: 'It was a snow woman seeking blood or human warmth... or a dream,' he proposes. 'It wasn't a dream,' his wife contradicts; *she* is the Snow Woman, but she allows to him to live for the sake of their children before vanishing into the night... The elegant Keiko Kishi was an actress of long standing before she was called upon to work for Kobayashi, but her portrait of the chill, shape-shifting vampire in the 'Snow Woman' segment of *Kwaidan* is the archetypal visualisation of the pale-faced, raven-haired female spirit of Japanese myth and legend.

The third tale is that of 'Hoichi the Earless', in which a blind *biwa*-playing minstrel is summoned by the ghosts of an ancient tribal feud to sing to them of their exploits in battle during the Genpai War. Hoichi recounts the naval engagement at Dan-no-ura, in the Shimonoseki Strait off the southern tip of Honshu, in which the Genji clan defeated that of the Heike on 25 April 1185. In this risky endeavour, he is protected against the potential ravages of the life-sapping samurai spirits by a Buddhist holy man (played by *Godzilla's* Takashi Shimura), who transcribes the sutra over his entire body. But as in the Greek tale of Achilles' heel, he forgets about Hoichi's ears — the ghosts extract their revenge in the manner dictated by the title fifty minutes earlier. 'Hoichi the Earless' is the longest and least successful episode of the quartet. It is epic in scale and ravishing to look at but ultimately unsatisfactory in execution: its occasional lapses of light relief saw it retained in the film over the more downbeat

'Snow Woman', which was a better adaptation of Hearn altogether.

The final episode, in which an anonymous author mysteriously disappears halfway through narrating an unfinished tale entitled 'In a Cup of Tea', owes more to the fiction of Lovecraft than Lafcadio Hearn, and its unsettling mood and surprising denouement were to impact significantly on the many similar portmanteau productions of Britain's Amicus Films which were to follow in the wake of *Kwaidan*.

Kobayashi's background in art can be evidenced in the vivid cyclorama skies which are a prominent feature of his film, and which were created on the vast sound stages of the Toho studio in the Setagaya suburb of western Tokyo. At times, *Kwaidan* is almost *too* reverential and funereally paced. It is a film which is rooted in the formal traditions and visual splendour of Kabuki theatre — stately, measured and precise, and quite often a wonder to behold. It weaves its magic through stagecraft, forced perspective, lighting and floor effects, and employs little in the way of conventional cinematic trickery. For all its considerable length, *Kwaidan* exerts a hypnotic spell on the viewer and, like any true, timeless classic, it improves immeasurably with age.

Kobayashi's ghostly epic won the Jury Prize at the 1965 Cannes Film Festival, and it was nominated for (and received) the Oscar in 1966 for Best Foreign Film. However, trade magazine *Variety* still was not won over to the subtleties of Japanese storytelling: 'Film is visually and physically stunning but its three tales of the supernatural are more intellectual than visceral,' it commented.

Kaneto Shindo returned to the field of the Terror film in February 1968, along with the striking and prolific Nobuko Otawa, his star from *Onibaba* and spouse in real life. *Kuroneko* (*Yabu no naka no kuroneko*), commercially subtitled 'The Black Cat', opens with the brutal gang rape of another mother and daughter combo by a wandering band of samurai. A black cat drinks the blood of the dead women and they return to the land of the living as *bakeneko* (cat-monsters); in the guise of their former selves, they entice the offending samurai to their doom. The son of the house returns from the wars and is allocated the task of seeking out and slaying the seductresses: "Get rid of the monster that kills samurai by biting necks!" his master demands. But this proves to be more of a dilemma than he imagined when he discovers the real identity of the female fiends.

Whereas Shindo's *Onibaba* was a timeless parable set in the metaphorical milieu of medieval Japan, *Kuroneko* is a modern take on the ancient folk-tales of shapeshifting spirits and flying ghosts. It is no *Ugetsu* or 'Ghost of Yotsuya' — its design is informed by the horror films of the sixties with their tense chords and shock cuts, and its plot has much in common with the American revenge western; indeed, its first reel was to serve as the template for the Patrick Curtis-produced, Raquel Welch-starrer *Hannie Caulder* in 1971. But the moonlight rides through the bamboo grove by which

Kuroneko *(1968)*.

the pair ensnare their willing victims are chilling in their classical simplicity. There are several effective shocks, such as when the daughter's hand transforms briefly into the paw of a cat while she serves saké to an unsuspecting samurai, or when Yone's son spies the reflection of his mother's feline self in a pool of water, but the film meanders into melancholy at the halfway point and never quite regains the Lewtonesque edge with which it began.

The radical mood of the time of its production is evinced in its strident anti-samurai tone, in which the 'knights' of Bushido are depicted not only as rapists and murderers but shallow, deceitful, corrupt and glory-seeking. *Kuroneko* recovers some of the grim poise of its opening encounters in a tense climactic stand-off between mother and son, each one knowing that their own lives depend upon the death or defeat of the other, but it nevertheless defers to *Onibaba* in the longer run. Shindo's film was well-received in the West, though. 'It's a pleasure to be frightened again by ghosts,' was the welcoming declaration of New York's *Herald Tribune*.

As was the case in so many other spheres in the late sixties, *Kuroneko* represent-ed the last gasp of the thoughtful, thought-provoking, Japanese horror film. The end of the cycle of *kaiju eiga* — at least as far as foreign markets were concerned — coin-cided with an hiatus in low-budget horror in the seventies that had resulted from over-exploitation of second-rate material. Japanese producers switched to making variants of Hammer's already exhausted output, with films like *Night of the Vampire* (*Yureiyashiki no Kyofu: Chi o suu Ningyoo*, 1970), *Lake of Dracula* (*Noroi no yakata: Chi o suu me*, 1971) and *Evil of Dracula* (*Chi o suu bara*, 1974), before giving up the ghost altogether in the wake of the *Exorcist* and *Omen* franchises, whose Judaeo-Christian themes did not translate easily into a Buddhist ethic with no obvious tradition of an all-powerful Satan figure or Biblical prediction of apocalypse.

With the effective collapse of the Big Five studio system in the seventies, independent Japanese producers turned to the youth market for inspiration, as the genre itself took a temporary leave of absence from British and American shores and looked to European film-makers like Dario Argento and Lucio Fulci (and Canadian David Cronenberg) to inject the fresh blood which was now required to see it through its crisis of confidence. In the cases of Argento and Fulci, 'fresh blood' turned out to be no metaphor, as Italian *giallo* thrillers began to foist a veritable plague of fiendishly sadistic serial killers onto the jaded sensibilities of international audiences. In light of this mood shift, violent and sexually explicit adult *manga* adaptations became the next source of genre offerings in the domestic theatre, in sensational but fast-forgotten gore-fests like Toshiharu Ikeda's *Angel Guts* franchise (*Tenshi no Harawata* and sequels, 1978 on), a Japanese response to the vacuous and nihilistic excesses of Clive Barker's *Hellraiser* series.

(Ikeda went on, Wes Craven fashion, to craft a second franchise in the later eighties which was to have a bearing on *Ring: Evil Dead Trap* (*Shiryo no Wana*, 1988) took as its starting-point for the predictable bloodbath a late night television presenter who receives a 'snuff' video in the mail. Deciding to investigate the truth of the tape, she and her team of reporters end up in an abandoned research plant where the deranged killer sets about eliminating them in an inventive variety of gut-wrenching ways.)

For the remainder of the 1970s — and much of the eighties and nineties as well — the Japanese horror film descended into the murky depths of giant monster nostalgia trips, soft porn, sado-masochistic excess, 'school' ghost stories and gratuitous slasher films, in even starker emulation of the lack of original thinking which was being exemplified by their counterparts in the West. These films represented another cycle, but it was one without direction or purpose that was content merely to imitate the graphic violence of the genre during the Reagan era, and the only difference between the product of either country lay in their respective quotas of entrails. The majority of Japanese offerings in this period disappeared completely from Western screens and found a home of sorts in the video underground, where they naturally acquired the kind of cult following which usually attaches to anything anti-establishment or morally questionable in terms of the mainstream. Japanese horror cinema had been unashamedly derivative from the outset, but after *Kuroneko*, and in the self-satisfaction of their post-war economic miracle, the Japanese were content to churn out ever more jaded and lazy copies of American imports for a largely lethargic home audience. (1999's *Godzilla 2000* was the first Toho film to be granted a wide North American release in more than fifteen years.)

A parallel might be drawn between the publication of Mary Shelley's *Frankenstein* in 1818 and that of Charles Dickens' *A Christmas Carol* in 1843. Gothic horror did not vanish from the stage between times; to the contrary, it continued to flourish in literally thousands of cheaply printed chap-books and 'penny dreadfuls', each of them intent on out-grossing the other, though few are now remembered. There were exceptions which proved the rule, such as Reverend Charles Maturin's *Melmoth, the Wanderer* of 1820, but graphic excess and originality of ideas rarely share a platform. The same situation arose in respect of the horror film in Japan during the 1970s and 1980s — and in much of the rest of the world, as well.

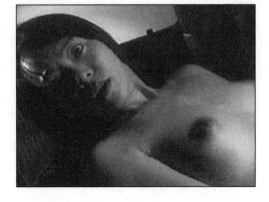

Above: V-cinema version of Ring: Kanzenban *(1995), with added sauce.*

Things did not change drastically until the late 1980s, with the inevitable economic crash, the beginning of the end of runaway Japanese capitalism and the commencement of a period of enforced austerity and re-evaluation; slowly but surely, original elements began to creep back into Japanese fantasy. Troubled times create troubled art (with the emphasis on the 'art'), and Japan as a nation unarguably was headed towards some very troubled and unpredictable times indeed.

So it was that a middle class teacher-cum-writer, with no great success to his name, and in a reversal of the traditional male-female roles, opted to remain at home with his children while his professional wife went out into the increasingly competitive world of new model Japan to earn their living. His efforts to craft a novel which reflected upon the empty legacy of hi-tech materialism created the prototype for a generation of horror films which were to return the genre to its roots in *fear*.

Ring had been published with no fanfare and to only moderate success, while Fuji's functional adaptation of it had come out looking like any other made-for-TV movie. A slightly expanded version of *Kanzenban*, with more nudity and stronger sex scenes had been released into the lucrative V-cinema (straight-to-video) market the same year, and that, in truth, should have been that. But something about *Ring* resonated deeper within the Japanese psyche than tales of apparitions in schoolhouses, or forlorn wives wasting away to skeletons while awaiting the return of errant husbands. As forty years of post-war economic boom crashed and burned, and increasing numbers of Japanese women took to the workplace as a result of the social upheavals which followed, so the reassertive figure of Sadako inexorably began to take hold in the minds of those who had read the novel, or seen the TV movie, or both. All she needed to make the transition from minor cult figure to mass media icon was for her character to be invested with a more tragic grandeur — and for her supernatural pedigree to be enhanced. The key was not so much in what Fuji's version had left out, but what it had seen fit to *include*: Sadako was too solid, too real, too much of a figure in the landscape of *Kanzenban*; she required to be more enigmatic, more ethereal, more... spectral. The television special having generated interest in Kadokawa to produce a feature film version of *Ring*, it was left to Koji Suzuki himself to suggest how such subtle embellishments might now be achieved.

The answer that he came up with was Hideo Nakata.

Despite its various digressions into splatter cinema during the eighties and nineties, the Japanese horror film nevertheless has been unable to rid itself of its obsession with its own metaphorical demon: Godzilla. The great sea dragon had been reinvigorated by Toho for its remake of *Gojira* in 1985, from which he embarked on a whole new series of monster-tackling adventures, and he was afforded yet another makeover in 1999 for *Godzilla 2000: Millennium* (*Gojira nisen mireniamu*). So emblematic is this sea beast in the mythic iconography of Japan that any reading of *Ring* which sought to heighten resonance in the figure of Sadako was almost duty-bound to allude to it. The novel had done so literally *and* elliptically, in its reference to the statue of En no Ozunu, and *Ring* screenwriter and Lovecraft aficionado Hiroshi Takahashi tapped into this ripple in the dark waters of Suzuki's story. Godzilla was the sea, while Sadako was a ghost, but like the half-human offspring in Lovecraft's tales of Dunwich and Innsmouth, the evil that lurked in Sadako was now to be sourced in the deeps of the ocean. (The episode in the novel concerning the recovery of the statue of En no Ozunu from the waters of the bay echoes of Daiei's Majin mythology, in which an effigy of the golem-like giant is blown up and deposited in a lake.)

"We Japanese still have a tradition that the sea itself, the water-like floods, or the recent tsunami, can take many people's lives, as in natural disasters. Because Japan is such a small island country, people have been killed in the sea over many, many years. So there's an almost subconscious level of fear towards the sea," Nakata explained to Javier Lopez. "That's what the scriptwriter and I discussed: Sadako's father could be a non-human existence from the sea. A real person was the model for Sadako's mother in the novel; she used to go to the sea every day and just stare at it. Of course, she was not saying 'I got pregnant' as a result, but we thought the fact that she was going to the sea every day and looking at it every day for no obvious reason was significant."

We do not want to see the bones of their theory about the supernatural.
- **M R James**, 'Some Remarks on Ghost Stories' *The Bookman* (1929)

H P Lovecraft gave his own concise run-down of the informal rules by which M R James thought a ghost story should play: 'a ghost story... should have a familiar setting in the modern period, in order to approach closely the reader's sphere of experience. Its spectral phenomena, moreover, should be malevolent rather than beneficent; since fear is the emotion primarily to be excited. And finally, the technical patois of 'occultism' or pseudo-science ought carefully to be avoided; lest the charm of casual verisimilitude be smothered in unconvincing pedantry.' James himself put it with less verbosity: 'Two ingredients most valuable in the concocting of a ghost story are, to me, the atmosphere and the nicely managed crescendo. Let us, then, be introduced to the actors in a placid way; let us see them going about their ordinary business, undisturbed by forebodings, pleased with their surroundings; and into this calm environment let the ominous thing put out its head, unobtrusively at first, and then more insistently until it holds the stage' (from his Introduction to *Ghosts and Marvels*, 1924).

Adhering to these principles meant that two important changes had to be enacted on Suzuki's source novel for it to translate more effectively to the screen: Sadako had to be made consciously malevolent, and all of the pseudo-scientific philosophising which accompanies Asakawa's and Ryuji's investigation of the mystery had rigorously to be excluded from the narrative.

Ring director Hideo Nakata confessed to both the cinematic and literary influences which bore upon him in the making of the film: 'I can see many influences from Robert Wise's *The Haunting* (1963), or the Henry James novella *The Turn of the Screw*, which was made into a film by a British director (Jack Clayton's *The Innocents*). I've been influenced by many directors outside of Japan, and my scriptwriter advised me strongly that I see these films.' Yet the strongest influence on *Ring* was not that of Henry James, but of *Monty* James, who disdained the psychological contrivances which his namesake had enacted in *The Turn of the Screw*.

Ring, the movie, owes as much of its power and narrative dynamic to a film made four decades before as it does to Koji Suzuki. That is not to diminish it in any way. To the contrary: in Nakata's hands, *Ring* became a perfect blend of Eastern mysticism and Western tale of Terror, and the best exemplar of the Jamesian technique — as delineated by Lovecraft — that cinema had offered since the 1950s.

With its timeless Gothic allusions to predestination and the consequences of hubris, Nakata's screen version was to elevate Suzuki's tale to the level of myth and open up a new and vibrant chapter in the history of the Japanese horror film in the process. ○

Day Four: Eruption

The only thing he knew for sure was that Godzilla, no matter how you looked at it, was an imaginary monster. *So what about demons…? And are demons unique to Japan?* No, other cultures have the same type of thing. Devils…

— **Koji Suzuki**, *Ring* (1991)

'Frolic in brine, goblins be thine'.

— *Ring* (1998)

'Sleeper' is the term employed by the film industry to denote a low-budget independent production which slowly gathers momentum and ultimately attains commercial success through word of mouth, rather than as a consequence of careful marketing. The most notable sleeper of the 1990s was Daniel Myrick and Eduardo Sánchez's *The Blair Witch Project*, a semi-professional scare-fest whose clever pre-release employment of the relatively new promotional medium of the World Wide Web enabled it to rake in a staggering $138 million in ticket sales within three months of its official opening on 30 July 1999, against a petty-cash budget of $22,000 for the mostly amateur shoot. To date, the film has taken more than $240 million.

The Blair Witch Project follows the trail of a trio of amateur film-makers as they set out to make a documentary about the so-called 'Blair Witch'. The film begins *after* the events with which most of its running time is occupied, as various interested parties try to piece together a scenario to account for the fact that in true Lovecraftian fashion, the three now appear to have vanished. But in line with the literary device of the discarded notebook, a camcorder has been found, and the viewer is then treated to a first person account of exactly what happened in the Blair woods… The phenomenal success of the film caused many in the industry to sit up and take notice; the techniques which Myrick and Sánchez had employed on the Internet to encourage interest in (and notoriety for) their film could not easily be repeated, so inventive and audacious had they been. But the genre into which the film naturally disposed itself was

old and venerated — albeit one which had lain dormant since the 1960s. *The Blair Witch Project* was a pure tale of Terror, whose premise was the possibility of supernatural events. In other words, it was a ghost story.

Above: Ring *(1998).*

In the event, no ghostly apparition or supernatural manifestation made its presence felt in *The Blair Witch Project*, but the threat of such had hovered tantalisingly on the edge of the narrative throughout in the same way that the threat of violence had hung over Tobe Hooper's *The Texas Chain Saw Massacre* (1974), even though little actual violence ever materialised on screen. Film-makers desperate to cash in on the success of *Blair Witch* could no more repeat its formula of a film-within-a-film than they could its unique marketing technique, but they could certainly capitalise on its theme. Thus, *The Blair Witch Project* was instrumental in rekindling a global appetite for filmed ghost stories, and as the more traditional horror film headed into a period of decline inspired by the knowing winks of Wes Craven's self-referencing *Scream* franchise and its more cartoonish *Scary Movie* spin-offs, and culminating in the tired monster-fests of *Freddy Vs Jason* (2003) and *Alien Vs Predator* (2004), the cinematic tale of Terror was creeping insidiously to the forefront to take its place.

The Blair Witch Project did more than redefine the genre for the moviegoers of the new millennium: it also offered a first glimpse of an alternative cinematic reality to the formulaic, market-tested, factory-produced fodder that the major studios churned out in increasingly homogeneous fashion to feed the maws of their money-making multiplex empires. This semi-professional, self-financed labour of love represented a return to a cinema of inspiration and inventiveness, free of the leaden constraints imposed by the big corporations which have run the industry for the last quarter century, and for whom creativity matters less than low-common-denominator predictability in order to ensure the widest-possible product acceptance. With the World Wide Web offering a gateway for independents to connect with a mass audience for the first time in history, without the need to compromise their concepts in the cattle-market of commercial production, *Blair Witch* signalled the arrival of a more eclectic supernatural cinema for the coming century; a cinema once again open to the challenges of original thought and individual vision. If anything was unambiguously clear about *The Blair Witch Project*, it was that despite post-release accusations of partial plagiarism, the 'thing' that mattered most in the film was the *idea*.

While the success of *The Blair Witch Project* sparked off a whole series of 'ghost' thrillers ranging from the ridiculous (*The Haunting*, 1999) to the commercially sublime (*The Sixth Sense*, also 1999), word began to spread among the more dedicated fans of the genre about a sleeper of a different kind. The film in question was no low-budget shocker which just happened to find appeal among the faithful, despite having cost only a modest $1.2 million to produce; to the contrary, it had turned out to be a spectacular success when it was released in its home territory in January 1998. The difference was that its home territory was on the other side of the world.

In *The Blair Witch Project*, the object of dread upon which the story was predicated was left purposefully unspecified. But word on the Japanese supernatural horror *Ringu*, as Nakata's film soon came to be known in international circles, had it that exactly the opposite was the case with this unheralded foreign horror, to the degree that allegedly it delivered the biggest fright of any movie since *The Exorcist*.

Fans of Far Eastern horror cinema already were aware of the existence of *Ring* — a super-shocker which apparently had sprung from nowhere but which had provided the lynch-pin for the revitalisation of the entire Asian horror industry. The impact of *Ring* had been profound: by the time the film surfaced in the West, officially at the Brussels International Festival of Fantasy Films in 1999, it had set in motion a cinematic cycle which was soon designated as New Asian Horror and later more clumsily regionalised to 'J(apanese)-horror', despite the inclusion of Korean, Thai and Hong Kong product in subsequent critical appraisals.

In Japan, the genesis of the film had been unremarkable. *Ring: Kanzenban*, the first screen version of Suzuki's novel, had premièred on television one month ahead of the publication of *Rasen*, or *Spiral*, the better-promoted sequel to *Ring*. Adapting the story for the cinema was now a logical move, and a consortium headed by production outfits Asmik Ace Entertainment and Omega Project took out option rights on both books and began to cast about for a director. Executive producer Masato Hara decided to seek the opinion of *Ring*'s author who, by chance, had seen a feature by a young director named Hideo Nakata which had struck a chord of recognition in him. "I was approached by the producers," Nakata told Donato Totaro. "And the writer of *Ring*, Koji Suzuki, liked the way I worked and asked me to direct the film version."

Nakata was thirty-five years old at the time. Born in Okayama (which lies in the Chugoku region of Honshu, eighty miles to the east of Hiroshima) on 19 July 1961, he had studied journalism at the University of Tokyo, where he also developed an interest in films and filming. "Initially, my favourite directors were David Lean and François Truffaut," he said. "Later, I began to appreciate American cinema, and the films of Clint Eastwood, Sam Peckinpah and Don Siegel. I discovered Japanese movies by attending the class of Shigeriko Asumi; he fed my cultural hunger by showing me many Japanese and foreign classics." And horror? "I can remember watching *The Exorcist* during my high school days." After graduating from university, Nakata was hired as an assistant director at the studios of Nikkatsu, where he was apprenticed to Masaru Konuma, himself a one-time assistant director on *Gappa, The Triphibian Monster* and veteran of the 'pink *eiga*' and softcore 'roman porno' films in which Nikkatsu then specialised. "I was treated almost like a slave," he told Jasper Sharp. "We worked very long hours on very low budgets, shooting sixty-seventy minute films in just seven or eight days. We often didn't sleep for thirty-six hours. Sometimes, we had to lie to people who owned the properties in which we shot. One time, we shot some sex scenes in an amusement park, so we had to pretend that it was for a TV production and carry different scripts! In one film, we shot a scene in a car very near to Shinjuku station, and we had to put a black cloth up so that passers-by couldn't see what was going on…"

The set up at Nikkatsu was similar to that at Roger Corman's New World Pictures, or other exploitation companies of the same ilk, in that, provided the regulation number of erotic/violent encounters were delivered per film, their directors were pretty much at liberty to do as they pleased. Nakata had been thrown in at the deep end, but it proved to be an excellent training ground and he stayed with Nikkatsu for seven years.

A stint in television in the early 1990s had brought Nakata into contact with Hiroshi Takahashi, an avid horror fan and the screenwriter of Konuma's *Beautiful Hunter* (*XX: Utsukushiki karyuudo*, 1994), and the two decided to look for a project on which they might collaborate. Nakata, meanwhile, transferred to London on an artistic scholarship, to research the British 'Free Cinema' movement of the early 1960s. In the course of his studies, he determined to make a documentary about director Joseph

Above: Don't Look Up/Ghost Actress *(1996): the victim (top) and the ghost.*

Losey but lacked the necessary capital. Returning to Tokyo in 1994, he called up his prospective partner and by the following year, he and Takahashi had embarked on a film of their own — but not about Losey; instead, it was a horror thriller. "I worked at the idea with the notion of making some money to shoot the documentary on Losey," Nakata said.

Hideo Nakata's directorial début had come in *Don't Look Up*, known alternately as *Ghost Actress (Joyu-rei*, 1996), for which he also wrote the original story. When a film crew set out to shoot a TV drama set in the war years, a sequence from a previous film from 1971 appears on the rushes, ostensibly as a consequence of their having using old and undeveloped stock. Thinking the footage to be part of a feature that he remembers from his youth, director Toshio Murai (Yurei Yanagi) decides to investigate further, and he notices the presence of a second figure standing behind the actress in the clips. Strange things start to occur on set, culminating in the death of starlet Saori Murakami (Kei Ishibashi) when she falls — or was she pushed? — from the catwalk high above the sound stage. It eventually transpires that the original feature was never completed, and therefore not transmitted, due to the death of *its* lead actress in similar circumstances, so Murai must be subject to some kind of false-memory syndrome. His editor believes that the piece of film itself is the cause of the manifestations of evil by which the crew now seem to be plagued and suggests that it be burned, but Murai is not to be deflected from trying to solve the mystery. Arriving on set late one night, he is startled to hear lead actress Hitomi (Yasuro Shiroshima) calling to him from the catwalk; he joins her there, but as he walks towards her, another figure suddenly appears behind her...

The similarities with *Ring* are obvious but superficial, and *Don't Look Up* is by no means a template for Nakata's better-known follow-up (although, conceivably, he could have read Suzuki's novel or seen *Kanzenban* before writing his original story). Central to the plot is a strange piece of film which itself has a tale to tell that appears to parallel events in the present day, and behind it all is another vengeful spirit. But

Nakata uses this premise to comment on confu-
sions between perception and reality; between
the real world and the world of illusion. For
much of its length, *Don't Look Up* has more in
common with Antonioni's *Blowup* (1966), and
when its proprietary ghost does finally appear, he
finds that he has nowhere to go but towards a
swift fade-out. "The initial reaction to *Ghost
Actress* was not very good," Nakata recalled. "We
were on the late show for six weeks and we
counted only 800 people in that six weeks who
came to see the film."

*Above: Hiroshi
Takahashi.*

Nakata's handling of mood, and of the film's several unsettling interludes, no
doubt endeared him to Suzuki when it came to the latter suggesting him for *Ring*;
however, it was his understated approach to an unusual ghost story, rather than the
theme of *Don't Look Up*, which surely put him into the frame. He fails to make enough
of the hints and allusions in relation to the director in the film who, we are informed,
was scared of the television tube as a boy, and no explanation is offered as to why this
ghost *cackles*, like Grace Poole in *Jane Eyre*. But the climax provides an indicator to the
influence of M R James on Nakata and his screenwriter Hiroshi Takahashi, which
would come to feature more prominently in *Ring*: having followed Hitomi to the catwalk, Murai is confronted not by the actress for whom he secretly pines, but by the
malignant spirit of his dreams, who pursues him into a stockroom and there (presumably) frightens him to death... This payoff is strongly resonant of James' 'A Warning
to the Curious', in which an amateur archaeologist named Paxton is deceived by a
shape-shifting spectre into thinking that he is being beckoned by two friends on
Seaburgh sands, until he turns the corner of the harbour wall and walks straight into
the arms of the waiting ghost.

Don't Look Up ultimately remains unsatisfactory in resolution — a tyro piece
whose storyline poses more questions than its director finds himself capable of
answering. But Nakata has since made a virtue out of the obliquities with which his
films are suffused and despite its flaws, his début feature carried with it a mood which
Koji Suzuki felt by then was better suited to a prospective feature version of *Ring* than
the treatment it was afforded in *Kanzenban*. By 1998, Suzuki had published *Rasen*, his
first sequel to *Ring*, and was working on a third volume in the series; both were help-
ing to revise his (and his readers') view of the events in the original novel. *Kanzenban*
had been an accurate representation of that novel taken in isolation, but the screen
version was to reflect the feel of what had since become almost a *mythology*, which was

still evolving through the re-evaluations of continuing instalments.

The most noticeable thing about Nakata and Takahashi's feature version of *Ring* is its ominous 'mood music'. After the regulatory credits, the film's title swims into view out of a swirling, primordial sea — as though it were formed from the luminous eyes of some awesome, underwater beast. Immediately, the viewer is plunged into the mystical aquatic realm of Godzilla, of Cthulhu's R'lyeh, of the discarded statue of En no Ozunu, as it beckons Sadako's mother from where it slumbers submerged in the bay: 'She said that the Ascetic's eyes had called her to the ocean floor. The green eyes of the statue, master of gods and demons, had glowed at the bottom of the deep, dark sea...'

Like all great Terror films — *The Exorcist* included — *Ring* is invested with a mythic history that resonates far beyond the incidents from which its story is culled.

> It has been written, since the beginning of time — even unto these ancient
> stones — that evil, supernatural creatures exist in a world of darkness...
> - **Opening narration**, *Night of the Demon* (1957)

A prologue depicts the events which lead to an inexplicable death, apparently as the result of a curse... an interested party decides to investigate further, only to find that he, too, has now become subject to the same curse… along the way, he discovers that to lift the enchantment, he has to pass the source of it on to someone else… this he eventually does, and a third party dies in his place at the predicted hour. The plot of *Ring*? No. The protagonist's change of sex ought to have given it away, if nothing else. This is the plot of Lewton alumnus Jacques Tourneur's *Night of the Demon*, a masterpiece of the macabre from 1957, which was based on 'Casting the Runes' by M R James.

'Casting the Runes' was first published in James' *Ghost Stories of an Antiquary* in 1904, and the tale revolves around a 'hex' that is cast upon academic Edward Dunning by a vengeful alchemist named Karswell, after Dunning rejects a paper which Karswell has submitted for publication. (Karswell's literary aspirations in the story parallel the real-life efforts of 'Great Beast' and self-styled black magician Aleister Crowley, who was known to James as a student at Cambridge University — though their paths did not cross directly; Crowley also served as the model for the character of Mocata in Dennis Wheatley's *The Devil Rides Out*.) The recipient of the hex is 'allowed' three months to live, and a similar curse levied on a previous critic of Karswell's work did indeed result in an untimely demise for the hapless man — John Harrington in James' story — at the predicted hour. Aided by John's brother Henry, Dunning eventually unravels the mechanics of the curse and succeeds in turning the tables on his tormentor, saving his life at the cost of Karswell's own.

Above: Night of the Demon: *Julian Karswell (Niall MacGinnis) and John Holden (Dana Andrews).*

Tourneur turned this story into a memorable supernatural thriller thanks in part to a literate script by former Hitchcock collaborator Charles Bennett. In the screen version, parapsychologist John Holden (Dana Andrews) is conducting a scientific investigation into the alleged activities of a devil-cult headed by Julian Karswell (Niall MacGinnis). Antagonised by the interest, Karswell casts a death curse on Holden by secreting about his person a parchment containing runic symbols; a victim is allowed three *days*. When he uncovers the subterfuge, Holden initially laughs off the threat until he starts to sense the presence of *another*, in the form of the invisible entity which has been conjured by the runes. Inveigling the secret of the parchment out of a former disciple of Karswell's, Holden effects to pass the parchment back. After a climactic confrontation, the wizard is torn to pieces by the very demon that he had called forth to deal with Holden.

Night (*Curse* in America) *of the Demon* is atmospheric to a fault, as befits a director of Tourneur's experience with *noir* subjects. The result is a work of real power, and key scenes linger in the memory: Karswell victim Henry Harrington's frantic first reel drive through the benighted countryside in a last-ditch attempt to have the curse lifted; Holden's own terrified flight through a dark wood (a vivid visual metaphor for the film's, and James', trenchant use of a quote from Coleridge's *Rime of the Ancient Mariner*, paraphrased in the film as 'Like one, that on a lonesome road/Doth walk in fear and dread… Because he knows, a frightful fiend/Doth close behind him tread.'); the climactic showdown with the demon, when Karswell is himself torn to shreds by his horrific emissary.

Poor box-office on release meant that no other tale from James' pen found its way onto the big screen after *Night of the Demon* (though Michele Soavi's *The Church*, [*La Chiesa, Demons 3*, 1989] is credited as being based in part on James' 'The Treasure of Abbot Thomas'), and other adaptations were confined to BBC Television's series of 'A Ghost Story for Christmas' in the 1970s. If *Night of the Demon* was too subtle and intelligent a film by half for the sensation-seeking audiences of the fifties, its reputation has grown steadily ever since. "I guess we were *The Exorcist* of our day," star Andrews remarked some twenty years on, after the themes addressed by *Night of the Demon* had been afforded more colourful bluff-and-bluster in that notorious makeover, while a line from the film might have served equally well in *Ring*: "What is this twilight — this half world of the mind that you profess to know so much about?" Karswell asks of Holden as they walk in the grounds of the magician's stately home. "How can we differentiate between the powers of darkness and the powers of the mind?"

Hideo Nakata has made no mention in interview of having seen this film, let alone having been influenced by it, but the similarities between the narrative structures of the two are striking in the extreme. Unlike the more detached approach taken by the novel, or the way that the story is unfolded in *Kanzenban*, *Ring* builds suspense by having its protagonists become aware of the *presence* of Sadako as their investigation progresses. Nakata's sly visual hints — from Reiko imagining that she has glimpsed her in the glass of the television screen after watching the video for the first time, to the subtle *advance* of the video's last scene at each successive screening — are what separate this film from its source and align it with Tourneur's. *Night of the Demon* posited a scenario in which the truth about its supernatural monster gradually began to encroach on the incredulity of the sceptical scientist to whom it was attached; *Ring* does the same. It goes out of its way, on a sensory level, progressively to weaken the intellectual arguments that can be lodged against its fantastical premise. This is where its power to terrify lies, and this is what makes the fatally inevitable appearance of its own monster such a nerve-jangling cinematic sensation. Teasing hints, a creeping sense of unease, vague intimations of the horror to come; the paraphernalia of paranoia, strategically deployed to inspire fear in the onlooker. This is what M R James was all about — the curtain of the rational, swept suddenly aside by the irrational. Its appeal is directly to the emotions, bypassing logic and reason in the classic Hitchcockian manner, and it is what made *The Exorcist* work. It is also what makes *Ring* work.

James' trick was to set his frights against the recognisable background of ordinary, every-day life — in his case, the dull and dusty world of Oxbridge academia — and not in some Gothic hinterland, where the existence of vampires and werewolves can be taken as read and their ability to terrify reduced in consequence. The Jamesian juxtaposition of the tediously ordinary with the potentially *extra*ordinary is the magic bullet of fear. Most horror films initiate a fantastic premise in which to regurgitate their repertoire of familiar scare-tactics, and if the viewer begins by thinking that anything can happen, he or she is hardly to be surprised when anything *does*. Hitchcock operated to the opposite standpoint of identification with his audience, laboriously establishing mundane chains of events from which to spring his shocks. *Psycho* (1960) is a classic case in point; *The Birds* (1963) is almost an arche-type.

Above: Ring:
Reiko Asakawa
(Nanako
Matsushima).

So not for James or Tourneur or Hitchcock, or Hideo Nakata, the historical remove of Transylvania or the reassuring familiarity of the 'haunted' house; not for them, some strange legend to be explored or mysterious horror to be unearthed. Theirs is the world of the commonplace where, inexplicably, there be Monsters.

Ring

Ring opens in similar fashion to *Night of the Demon* — portentously. Not in the idle chatter of the incidental characters who set the scene, but in the dark swell that seethes behind the titles, in the way that the credits for Tourneur's film were framed against the Cyclopean immensity of Stonehenge. The script then dispenses with Suzuki's elab-orate exposition and cuts straight to the chase. The actual mechanics of the curse matter less to Nakata than they do to Koji Suzuki; all that matters in *Ring* is the fact that it *exists*, a fact confirmed later in the narrative when the telepathic Ryuji also catches a glimpse of someone whom he assumes to be Sadako and inquires obliquely, "Was it you? Did *you* do this?" (The model for this scene is also to be found in *Night of the Demon*, in which the truth about the hexed victim's inexplicable death is revealed to its parapsychologist hero at a *séance*.) From that point on, the hints multiply, along with the growing sense of impending menace…

A screen caption: 'Sunday 5 September'.

In a conscious nod to all the teen slasher flicks from *Halloween* (1978) to *Scream* (1996), the film then diverges from the novel and switches directly to *two* teenage girls, Tomoko (Yuko Takeuchi) and Masami (Hitomi Sato), as they chat idly in a bedroom. "A grade school boy was on holiday down in Izu with his family," Masami says. "He wanted to go out and play… but there was a TV show he didn't want to miss. So he recorded it on the VCR in their room. But the channels down there are different from Tokyo. No station there uses that channel, so it should have been blank. But when he played it back at home, there was a woman on the screen." (She points a finger at Tomoko.) "'You will die in one week,' she said. The kid stopped the tape, and then the phone rang. 'You saw it.' Then a week later, the kid died!"

Incredulities are exchanged, and Masami's tale appears to be no more than another urban legend, of the kind that might be whispered among adolescents trying to frighten the wits out of each other. Then Tomoko looks strangely pensive: '*I saw a weird video the other day…*' she begins.

By the time *Ring* hit theatres, many Japanese teenagers thought that they, too, knew someone who had seen a 'weird' video, such was the word-of-mouth that preceded the film's release. The notion of a death-dealing videotape had already moved beyond the confines of Suzuki's plot and taken on a life of its own — in the same way that the Blair Witch 'legend' was set in train in advance to support the mythology of that film — and Nakata deploys it in his film as a given, thus dispensing with the need to first establish how the teenagers have all come to die. "The fact is that the video rumour about dying within one week of watching the video was already a kind of rumour, an urban legend in certain school groups, like among high school students," Nakata told Donato Totaro. "So maybe the momentum was right to make a film using a rumour that had already existed, with some minor changes in the story itself." Takahashi reflected this cultural sidebar to the plot of Suzuki's novel in his screenplay, where the existence of the 'cursed video' is taken as read from the off.

Among the minor changes which Nakata commented upon, the sex of Asakawa was changed from male to female, in keeping with the new mood of emancipation in Japan (and the fact that females were more often to be found as the protagonists in cinematic ghost stories than males), and thus television reporter *Reiko* Asakawa (Nanako Matsushima) is already investigating the urban legend of the cursed video-tape when the film proper begins. She discovers that her niece, Tomoko, has apparently fallen victim to the very tape that is the object of her inquiries and through her, she is able to track the source to cabin B4 at the Izu Pacific leisure resort. The film is adroit at cutting away all the fat of Suzuki's narrative to focus on the single issue of the tape and, in doing so, it generates a real sense of anticipation about the exact content of the mysterious video. And rather than reveal its effect, the film borrows a trick from Richard Donner's *The Omen* (1976) and merely confirms those who have fallen victim to its curse by distorting their image in photographs. "Takahashi, who wrote the script with me, suggested that we have the idea of the photos, which is actually based on a real life person named Shizuko Mifune, a paranormal," Nakata said. "As a paranormal, this woman Mifune was able to project written words and make them materialise on paper. There is another real story that is related to this. There was this Tokyo University professor who was expelled because of research he was doing into the para-normal. Shizuko Mifune was the actual object of his study. And obviously a Tokyo University professor who was interested in that kind of research was not taken seri-ously. All this is related to the photographs and the image distortion we use in the film, because the writer did do research on that to incorporate it into the film."

By the time that Reiko has laced up the video in the cabin's VCR, night has fall-en and the screen is fairly crackling with tension. At this point, Nakata pulls off the first of *Ring*'s two masterstrokes.

Kanzenban depicted the video according to the description that is given in Suzuki's novel, but *Ring* goes one step further, and produces a cross between what one imagines a genuine *nensha* recording might actually look like and the sort of surreal-istic imagery that Salvador Dali and Luis Buñuel brought to *Un Chien Andalou* (1928). More than anything, it evokes memories of the mental images of the Martian landscape that BBC engineers had to conjure up out of pink string and sealing wax for the 1958-1959 television production of *Quatermass and the Pit*.

Reiko's gaze is glued to the haunting scenes unfolded before her…

Static — through which can be discerned what appears to be a circular image of the night sky, clouds scudding across the moon. No — not the moon, but a figure looking down from on high. A woman stands before a mirror, combing her hair. A jump-cut, and the mirror is displaced to reveal a second figure, smaller and with long, dark locks, standing further back. The woman again; a smile of recognition on her face. The word 'eruption' in a scroll of *kanji* pictograms — all of which wriggle and writhe around, like bacteria under a microscope. More figures scattered across a land-scape, as though they were being pitted against some invincible force of nature. The

Ring: *the*
'cursed' video.

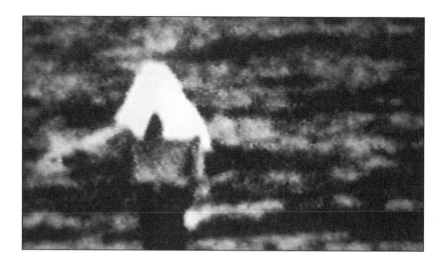

figure of a man stands with arm outstretched against a backdrop of the sea; he is pointing to his right, his head and face shrouded by a towel. The word 'sada', overlaid on
the pupil of an eye. Then a final, lingering shot of an old brick well, standing in a fea-
tureless meadow littered with dead leaves... Static.

"In shooting the cursed video, we didn't want to give to the viewer any reference
points, so there is no reference whatsoever as to where the scene is taking place, or
where the light and dark are coming from," Nakata explained. "We wanted to integrate
into the image the notion that we don't really understand from what point of view we
are watching the scene. We wanted to give it a dreamlike atmosphere, where you're
not able to tell what is what." Nakata also made sure that the tape was available first,
so it could be played by the principals during the shooting of scenes where they were
meant to be watching it, instead of simply cutting away to extracts from it during the
course of action.

The phone rings in the cabin. Reiko picks it up, but all that she can hear is a
sound like the buzzing of flies. She looks at the clock: it is 7.08.

'Tuesday 14 September'.

Reiko turns to Ryuji (Hiroyuki Sanada) for help, but in accordance with the
change of sex of the protagonist in *Ring*, he is reconstituted here into Reiko's ex-
husband and father of her son, Yoichi. To expedite the matter of exposition in relation
the complex back story, screenwriter Takahashi invests Ryuji with more in the way of
the psychic ability that he was shown to possess at the climax of *Kanzenban*; consequently, he has a 'bad feeling' from the moment that he enters Reiko's flat, and he
begins to sense the truth about the curse even before she asks him to snap a Polaroid

picture of her, which typically reveals the same twisted features as those of the four youngsters in the cabin. He asks her for a copy of the tape, so that he can study it more closely.

'Wednesday 15th'. Reiko is back in her office, and watching the tape again. On this occasion, however, the last scene appears to be extended by a fraction of a second: just before the shot cuts to static, there is movement from inside the well... When Ryuji also examines the tape, he detects the faint sound of a voice in the background to one of the clips: "It's something about 'brine' and 'goblins'," he tells Reiko.

By Friday 17th, they have established that the volcano in question is Mihara and have decided to continue the search for answers on Oshima, but not before Yoichi, too, has watched the tape while Reiko slept. "Tomoko told me to," he says to his horrified mother when she catches him in the act. She glances at the television screen as the image fades from view: there is another, almost imperceptible movement from inside the well, as though something were about to clamber out...

On board the ferry, Ryuji confides his fears to his ex-wife. "People feel anxious and rumours start," he states, in a back-reference to Reiko's observation at the beginning of the quest that "these stories start when people die horrible deaths." It is the film's most explicit reference to the mood of change which was sweeping through Japan at the time of *Ring*'s production. Takahashi had elaborated Ryuji's remark in his script: 'This kind of thing... it doesn't start by one person telling a story. It's more like everyone's fear just takes on a life of its own.' He also penned an addendum: 'Or maybe it's not fear at all. Maybe it's what we were secretly hoping for all along.' This last sentence, in which Ryuji appears to desire some kind of apocalyptic salvation from a present predicament, was deleted in the subtitled print; it would have made sense only if *Ring* were to be seen in permanent conjunction with *Rasen*.

The two arrive at Oshima island on Saturday morning and head for the Inn — home of Takashi Yamamura, cousin of Shizuko Yamamura, the woman in the video whom they now suspect of playing a central role in its creation. In a significant departure from the novel, Nakata neatly side-steps all of the scientific analysis in which Suzuki indulges as to how the tape was actually created, preferring instead to let the protagonists' psychic flashbacks tell the story and to leave the audience to fill in the blanks on its own. This was a daring move with which his producers were not entirely in sympathy — any more than they were with his idea of minimising the obvious horror elements: "There was no resistance from the producers, but I did feel some doubt on their part when they asked why there wasn't a sudden death, or why I didn't show any deaths, since the book describes the process of dying," he explained. "Another thing that they were doubtful about was the notion of having a death exactly one week after watching the video. But I persevered in the strategy of a story that doesn't present any deaths directly. And the producers stayed on and supported me."

Ryuji reveals more to Reiko about the history of Shizuko Yamamura, and mentions in closing: "Shizuko had a daughter." At the inn, they find the mirror in which Shizuko can be seen combing her hair in the video; the following day, Ryuji decides to confront Takashi about the girl whose name they now know to be Sadako. He finds the old man on the beach and, as part of his opening gambit, he utters the line of dialect that can be heard on the tape — *"Shoumon bakkari shite'ru to, boukon ga kuru zo"* — followed by a translation of it which approximates to the meaning that Suzuki gave it in the novel: 'If you play in the sea, the goblins will get you.' When the film was eventually subtitled for export, this first sentence was *also* rendered in English, but in a lyrical form that was to become the more familiar, "Frolic in brine, goblins be thine.'

"For us the sea is unlucky," Takashi says. "Every year it swallows some of us." The old man is reluctant to flesh out more of the history of the Yamamuras, but when Ryuji catches hold of him as he stumbles and falls while trying to flee from his inquisitor, he 'sees' Shizuko's psychic demonstration for himself: in both the novel and *Kanzenban*, Shizuko failed this test, but in *Ring*'s flashback to the same incident with the dice, she passes with flying colours. The reporters who are in attendance cry foul regardless, and implicit in Nakata's version of events is that so far as the media is concerned, people in the public eye inevitably find themselves in a 'no win' situation: damned if they do and damned equally if they don't. Somebody shouts "freak!" and, on the instant, one of the pressmen falls dead — a look of terror on his face. Shizuko turns to the daughter who is standing beside her. "Sadako — you did that!" she exclaims. "It was shot on 35mm film, but we did discuss filming it on 8mm or home video," Nakata said of the newsreel feel that he managed to impart in this footage. "The scene was shot on 35mm, then we went to the lab and it was passed through a computer to get the grainy image quality. But the technician at the lab didn't want to give up his secret, so I'm not exactly sure what was done to the image to get that texture! The 35mm was also transferred to video format at some point." (The death of the boy, Shigemori, which *Kanzenban* had employed to illustrate Sadako's lethal gift, was jettisoned in favour of the better-integrated death of the reporter at the demo.)

At last, the truth dawns on Ryuji; he realises why the word 'sada' was imprinted on the videotape. Sadako.

"Sadako killed him?" he asks Takashi. "She can *will* someone dead?"

Takashi looks away. "She was a monster," he replies.

What follows is the film's first and only intimation of the horror to come. Reiko has now caught up with Ryuji and for a moment, she becomes a part of the same

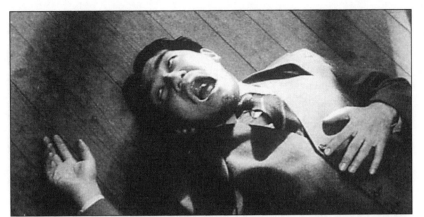

Ring: *the Tokyo experiment.*

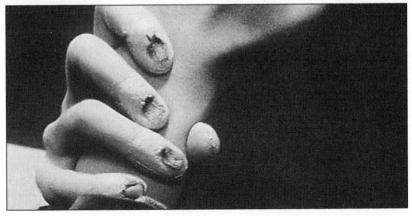

Ring: *the murder of Sadako by Dr Ikuma (Daisuke Ban).*

flashback. Nakata confines himself to the back of Sadako's head as she retreats from her mother's accusation. Reiko looks down as the girl approaches her; suddenly, the unseen Sadako thrusts out her hand and grabs Reiko by the arm. But the hand that grips her is not that of a child: it is a bleached claw, with torn and bloody fingernails...

Storm clouds gather. Wind and rain lash the inn as Ryuji discloses the paranormal nature of the tape to Reiko: "It's a curse," he concedes. "We've been cursed." (In some prints of the film, this line is given as "She's put a curse on us.") Just when it looks as though they might be trapped on the island past the deadline, Takashi offers to take them back to the mainland in his own fishing boat. "Sadako's calling you," he says, by way of explanation.

'Monday 20th...' The last day. The pair make their way to the resort and the site of the well, which they are now convinced is Sadako's burial place. Their intuition proves fortuitous, for Sadako's death at the hands of her stepfather is not revealed to Reiko in one of Nakata's favoured flashbacks until she tunnels into the recess beneath cabin B4 and psychometrically lays her hand on the well itself. *Ring* never wavers in its focus on Sadako as a creature of supernatural evil and, to that end, the film eschews the rape and murder scenario which was central to the novel and which featured in *Kanzenban*. She is invested with no specific human traits in *Ring*, therefore no spurious explorations of her unusual physiology were considered to be appropriate. To the contrary, Takahashi makes overt in his script what Suzuki only nodded towards in passing — that Sadako is actually *half*-human, like Wilbur Whately in Lovecraft's 'The Dunwich Horror'. When Takashi Yamamura reveals more on the boat to Ryuji about Shizuko's background, he relates the tale of how he once hid and listened as she sat on the beach and talked to the sea, but the words that she spoke were '*not* a human

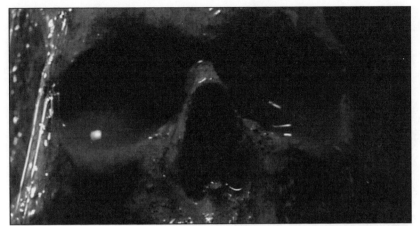

Ring: inside the well.

language'. In consequence, the script turns once more to *The Omen* and has Sadako bludgeoned with an axe and thrown into the well by her own stepfather, Dr Ikuma (who is notionally her father in the story, but no proof of paternal parentage is ever uncovered), for the same reason that Thorn tried to murder his 'son' Damien in Donner's film: Ikuma has come to believe that she is the spawn of the devil. (The translation of Takahashi's screenplay by Javier Lopez renders the line that is spoken by Takashi on the beach as 'She's a devil-spawn', rather than the more prosaic 'She was/is a monster' of the various subtitled prints.) Ikuma assumes the role of saviour, like Jonathan Harker in *Dracula*, and tries to rid the world of a terrible evil. Before *Ring* the movie, Sadako had been a victim; Nakata's film turned her into a *victimiser*, and long

Above: Ring: *the*
virus spreads.

before her untimely death at the foot of the well.

The remainder of the sequence in the well is as before, if somewhat creepier. As the fateful deadline approaches, a swirl of black hair rises to the surface of the rank water in front of Reiko. It coalesces into a shape and starts to emerge. Reiko takes the sodden head in her hands, and the dark tresses and rotten flesh dissolve away to leave the skull of Sadako. She clasps it to her bosom — the spell is broken. Nakata adds the neat touch of the visual stylist: when the skull is revealed, green slime seeps from the eye-sockets, like hideous tears.

As the lights from the summoned patrol cars blink in the background and the police go about the business of removing the body parts, Reiko and Ryuji sit nearby, in quiet contemplation of their release from the curse. "Why did he kill Sadako?" Reiko asks, with regard to Ikuma's motive in hurling Sadako into the well. "She was his daughter." Takahashi grabs a last opportunity to ram home his thesis: "Maybe she wasn't," Ryuji replies. "Maybe her father wasn't... human."

'Tuesday 21st' finds Reiko and Yoichi reunited at home.

A different fate lies in wait for Ryuji, however, as Sadako comes to claim her own.

The film has kept its trump card to the end: with it, Nakata not only plays a winning hand but he also takes the pot which has been accumulating in the field of horror since the high stakes placed on it by William Friedkin's *The Exorcist*. But there is still a trick in store, for Reiko realises with the death of Ryuji that not all of the strange images on the video were explained by the story of Sadako: the shrouded figure of the man, finger pointing, has thus far not figured in the equation. As she ponders the question, she sees the figure of Ryuji reflected in the TV screen — as she did that of Sadako when she first viewed the tape; he is holding the identical pose. He points to the video that she has in her handbag; the one that he watched. It is labeled 'copy'. Reiko understands what she has to do to save her son. She phones her father: "I need a favour. It's for Yoichi…"

With the game just beginning, Nakata cuts to a shot of Reiko driving with Yoichi to the home of her parents. The camera remains high overhead as her Toyota recedes into the distance along an infinite highway, while storm-clouds sweep in towards it. The bombshell impact of *Ring* the movie can fairly be laid at the door of one man: director Hideo Nakata. "Honestly speaking, I don't like horror films," he had revealed in interview to Jasper Sharp, as though to prove the truth of H P Lovecraft's contention that pragmatists are often more effective in delineating 'the spectral and the fantastic', as they see in it 'an absolute and stupendous violation of the natural order'. "But critics and reporters look upon me as a horror film director, so it's almost inescapable for me now," he added ruefully. There are worse things: fantasy cinema has noticeably lacked any genuine 'horror film directors' since the 1970s, other than those to whom the genre represents a source for mockery or an excuse to indulge in gratuitous excess. If Nakata, voluntarily or otherwise, decides to follow in the phantom footsteps of antecedents like Browning, Whale, Tourneur, Corman, Bava and Fisher, then he will be seen as the first of a new breed of (mostly) Asian film-makers who have chosen to retrieve the gauntlet which was set aside by the old masters more than thirty years ago, and the Terror film will be the better for it in the long term. What is unarguable is that as of 31 January 1998, it was given a fresh start, new impetus, a welcome change of direction. It was Nakata's unique vision and his understated handling of Takahashi's more conventional original script that made the difference. And *what* a difference.

From the outset, *Ring* is invested with a palpable atmosphere of dread, where small things build cumulatively to suggest a world at one remove from the perceptive reality that its inhabitants take for granted: a piece of paper flaps towards Reiko in Tomoko's room; her son Yoichi catches sight of a pair of legs, lightly ascending a staircase ahead of him; he turns his head in the street on his way to school, momentarily imagining that he is being followed. In classic Japanese style, the film takes the spectral as a matter of course: ghosts and spirits are part of the fabric of its characters' universe, even if they themselves are not consciously aware of it.

In similar fashion, the script added references to Japanese folklore and tradition to the mix: the shot in the video in which Shizuko Yamamura is shown brushing her hair is reminiscent of the famous set-piece scene in *Tokaido Yotsuya kaidan*, in which Oiwa brushes her hair in front of a mirror after having been poisoned, only to find it coming out in bloody clumps. And Takahashi reinforced the elliptical clip of Nakata's take on the narrative by adding some visual metaphors of his own, such as the 'warping' of the faces of the cursed in photographs, along the same lines as those in *The Omen*.

"The *Yotsuya kaidan* is a classic story that has been told on film for forty years," Nakata confirmed. "The best version is the one by Nobua Nakagawa. It's a story set in the Edo period in Japan, about a poor peasant who wants to be a samurai. He suspects his wife of having an affair with a blind masseur, so he kills them both; he gives poison to his wife, which causes her face to become completely disfigured, as though acid had been thrown at it. The story is about this couple — the wife and masseur — coming back to life to haunt the husband..." He and his screenwriter also borrowed the imagery of the 'hole' from *Onibaba*, as well as quoting the 'Black Hair' episode from *Kwaidan* for their climax. "We tried very hard, as a team, to find the scariest images, and to the Japanese, the long, black hair of a woman has an almost supernatural connotation," he explained to Eric Vespe of Harry Knowles' *Ain't-It-Cool* website. "If you look at *Kwaidan*, there is this kind of subconscious fear of long, black hair... If you were to find an enormous amount of long, black hair on a bed... that's scary by itself."

"The long, black hair... the white dress. Even the well. All of these are faithful to the traditional images associated with ghosts in Japan. There's actually a story with a well, called *Bancho sarayashiki* [the story of Okiku], which relates to this story in the sense that maybe the well is haunted by evil spirits. When I lived in the countryside in Japan I saw a well, only about five metres deep, but it seemed to me as a child like a bottomless Hell," Nakata recalled. "So it's interesting how we can relate the well to some kind of passage to the underworld."

For such a quiet-spoken — albeit *disquieting* — film, *Ring* was a veritable test-bed of audio effects. Its moody incidental music, whose overall tendency towards minimalism is jarringly disrupted by sudden, startling chords at key moments of revelation, was by Kenji Kawai, the same composer who scored Mamoru Oshii's cult *anime*, *Ghost in the Shell* (*Kokaku kidotai*, 1995), and even the everyday electronics of the tale's titular alarm turned out to be multi-layered: "For the sound of the telephone, they mixed four different qualities of phone sounds because they didn't want them to sound like Hollywood phones!" Nakata revealed. "There are fifty tracks for Kenji Kawai's background sounds, and fifty tracks for the effects. It was a huge task, and because [sound technician Yoshiya Obara] wanted a very high quality, he supervised the sound himself. Your ear can't separate the melody from the effects because they're all so well integrated in the overall soundtrack."

Despite her star status as the uncrowned queen of Japanese television commercials, the twenty-four year-old Nanako Matsushima's Reiko is a model of involuntary apprehension as the clock ticks inexorably on, but former action flick regular Hiroyuki Sanada's almost transcendental interpretation of Ryuji remains something of a curiosity in the film as a whole, even after repeated exposure. (*Rasen* better elucidates the anomaly of Sanada's strange turn for much of *Ring*, including the scene where he is confronted by Sadako in the plaza; viewed in isolation, his resentful attitude throughout appears to indicate little more than the surly behaviour of a sore loser after the break-up of a marriage for which he primarily was responsible.)

After some four months of intensive pre-production early in 1997 (which included the writing of Takahashi's screenplay), *Ring* was filmed over five weeks of the summer around the O-bon festival period of July to August. July being one of the wetter months in Japan, its director used this to his advantage when it came to setting the stage for his supernatural scenes. The film was produced by thirty-seven year-old Takashige Ichise, who had collaborated with Nakata on *Don't Look Up* and one of whose earliest excursions into the genre had been the grossest of the three segments in *Necronomicon* (1994), a lively but variable compendium of stories by Lovecraft.

Nakata is adept at isolating his players within architectural or natural landscapes in such a way that their very surroundings seem sentient and strangely threatening, whereas Hollywood film-makers tend to be wed to the star-fixated close-up or mid-shot. Ghost stories are things of ambience and atmosphere, not studies of character (unless they are penned by Henry James!), and Nakata's preparedness to second his actors to the needs of the drama is a significant, if more elusive, element in the success of his film. "I shot scenes in Oshima when there was a very bad and unnatural feeling in the air," he said. "And in rooms which were dark and had an eerie aspect in themselves. This is all part of the supernatural tradition of Japan."

Not since the days of Val Lewton has ambience played such an integral part in the design of a horror film. The evocative RKO mood pieces of Mark Robson (*Isle of the Dead*, 1945), Robert Wise (*The Body Snatcher*, 1945) and Jacques Tourneur himself (*Cat People*, 1942, *I Walked With a Zombie*, 1943) all regarded atmosphere as another member of their casts, though the exemplar of this approach remains Ealing's *Dead of Night* (1945), in which day turns imperceptibly into night outside the cosy confines of the cottage where Mervyn Johns' architect comes increasingly to suspect the terror that fate has in wait for him. By the time Reiko is ready to watch the video in *Ring*, darkness is encroaching both literally and metaphorically, and the onset of twilight sees her switch on the light in the room prior to inserting the tape in the machine. As day turns to night during her stay at the cabin, so the weather also starts to worsen after she has watched the tape: the late summer sunlight which has bathed scenes at the beginning of the film soon gives way to rain and storm-clouds as the allotted seven days wear on.

In the formal rigour of his essentially static set ups, Nakata reveals himself to be a stylist of the old school, and clever editing and precise composition are what give *Ring* its hypnotic power. He keeps the pace deliberately slow; on reaching the cabin, Reiko allows herself a meal break before going off in search of the video. The film is largely devoid of flashy camera angles and the self-conscious intrusions of motion control; for the most part, its director is mercifully invisible. Notwithstanding its lack of effects and unremarkable manner, word soon spread, and *Ring's* Big Bang finale was all the push that was needed to turn an interesting cult item into a phenomenal box-office smash.

Hideo Nakata was as surprised as anyone at the squeals of delight which greeted his film across almost the whole of Asia. "I absolutely did not expect the success of *Ring*," he confessed. "I was very worried when it was released in Japan that it could ever gain enough money to cover its production costs." In fact, *Ring* went on to break box-office records right across Japan, while in Hong Kong alone, it raked in a total of $31 million (approximately four million US dollars) to become the biggest grossing film to play in the territory over the first six months of 1998.

Critical appraisal ranged from the old-as-the-hills tabloid comparative of the video release — 'Makes *The Blair Witch Project* seem like a stroll in the woods' — to the more thoughtful musings of Ian Berriman in *SFX*: 'It takes a special kind of film to make you terrified of not only its images, but also the medium by which they are transmitted. *Ringu* is just such a film. It's possibly the only film ever made which is actually improved by watching it on video — preferably a blank, unmarked videotape — instead of on the big screen. Watched at home, it makes you fear that some unspeakable evil could crawl right out of the set and invade the cosy security of your living room...' To which *Variety* added, 'Genuinely creepy for most of its length, and with an oblique approach to basically genre material, Japanese psycho-chiller *Ring* recalls Kiyoshi Kurosawa's *Cure* in its gradual evocation of evil lying await beneath the surface of normality.' There were the usual dissenting voices, but mostly they were drowned out by a clamour of approval from those to whom Japanese fright flicks suddenly seemed like manna from horror heaven.

Rasen

Such was the reception accorded to *Ring* on release — and subsequently, in the case of its belated arrival in America — that Nakata's symphony of terror overshadowed

anything else which was even remotely connected to it. But a year before, the producers of *Ring* had signed to make *two* films from novels by Koji Suzuki, not one. And the
second had been adapted from Suzuki's own sequel, the idea being that the two extant
parts of the saga would play on a double bill, at least during the first runs. So in the
wake of *Ring*, whatever happened to *Rasen*?

Rasen, or *Spiral*, had been published in July 1995, a month before the television
première of *Kanzenban*. When the production consortium which subsequently bought
the feature rights to the original novel negotiated the deal, it naturally thought to hedge
its bets and purchase sequel rights in addition. One sequel had already been written, and
so it made financial sense to shoot the two episodes together, with separate crews but
utilising the same cast. To co-feature them in release must surely have seemed like nothing short of genius. If only someone had read *Rasen* before that decision was taken...

Like the novel, the screen version of *Rasen* also begins where *Ring* leaves off. A
mere twelve hours later, in fact. But from that point on, audiences were plunged into
a whole different Ring-world.

> Asakawa thought she had to copy that tape and show it to someone else
> for her son to be able to survive. She went to her parents' house with a
> VCR to copy the tape, and showed the tape to her father. But her son died
> of a heart attack one week later.
> - **Yoshino (Yutaka Matsushige)**, *Rasen* (1998)

The graphic autopsy which opens *Rasen* (as well as Ryuji's cadaver) makes it clear from
the start that this film is going to be about as far from *Ring* in tone as it is possible to
get. Gone is the shadow play of its companion piece, and in its place is the high-key
clarity of techno-horror, in which physical injury is pored over, characters are required
to espouse reams of exposition at a single sitting and everyone acts in such a way as
to imply that they each have a dark side, just waiting to be revealed at the clever whim
of the script. Mitsuo Ando (Koichi Sato) is a suicidal medico, who pines for his
drowned child in the style of Donald Sutherland in Nicolas Roeg's *Don't Look Now*
(1973), and the opening scene in which he fillets his old pal Ryuji is certainly an
attention-grabber. But to have the corpse then sit up on the slab and engage him in
conversation, innards exposed, sends the film into a downward spiral of ghost-train
chills from which it never fully recovers; what might have seemed spooky on paper
merely undercuts what, until that point, has been a gorily-convincing special effect. If
Ring was dark and moody and pensive, *Rasen* breezes in like an out-take from George
Romero's *Day of the Dead* (1985).

The whole of the first reel stays unrewardingly in the blood-red realm of

mortuary horror, where intestines are slopped into waiting trays and fragments of code are prised from subcutaneous tumours extracted from the throat of the unfortunate Ryuji. As the two had played code games with each other at medical school, Ando promptly assumes that the cypher has meaning beyond that of something which Ryuji might inadvertently have eaten but found to be indigestible (and therefore potentially a cause of death), and he sets out to investigate preceding events. To say that the makers of *Ring* had taken a wrong road — at least as far as *Rasen* was concerned — would be an understatement.

'Cardiac infarction caused by a non-malignant tumour in the bloodstream,' is the all-too-prosaic pronouncement of cause in respect of Ryuji's death, and thus the viewer is headed towards a medical rather than supernatural mystery as to what exactly inspired said tumour. The bulk of the action falls to Sato and Nakatani, who supplied little more than a walk-on in *Ring* as Mai Takano; it is Mai's desire to unearth the truth about her erstwhile lover's death which provides the narrative with its forward momentum: "He saw... something," she tells Ando, but this aspect of the story is quickly side-stepped in favour of endless med-school debate on the nature of viruses and much soul-searching from Ando in relation to his deceased son.

Reiko and her son Yoichi also turn up dead, ostensibly as victims of a car accident, though Ando, by then, is more concerned to discover the whereabouts of the suddenly-missing Mai. One or two of Suzuki's shocks transcribe well to the feature, such as the revelation that Yoichi was dead *before* the car crash which supposedly has killed both him and his mother — although prior knowledge of the plot of *Ring* is required to fully appreciate the significance of the fact. Before Ando's analytical abili-

Spiral: *Ryuji Takayama (Hiroyuki Sanada).*

ties are taxed too far, MMB Broadcasting's roving reporter Yoshino turns up holding Reiko's Filofax, in which she has been scrupulous in noting down the events of recent days, thus enabling him to tell Ando the whole story of the cursed videotape in flashback: "Sadako had the power to call down a curse to kill. A curse of hatred," he declares, conveniently, before handing Ando a copy of the video to see for himself. Unlikely, given the circumstances surrounding this gift.

When Ando watches the tape regardless, the viewer is treated to no more than a few fragmentary glimpses of its scenes in close-up, and only those which bear relevance to the new plot. Instead of onscreen warnings, ringing phones, or any of the paraphernalia of the original myth, Ando falls into a reverie during which he witnesses the murder of Sadako at the well; when eventually he comes to, she is writhing around on top of him, as in a dream within a dream. However, a naked Sadako (Hinako Saeki) is no scarier in this film than she was in *Kanzenban*. After it is then established that neither Reiko nor Yoichi died of the same 'curse' that killed Ryuji and the teenagers in the original story, things start to become a mite confusing.

What Suzuki actually did in *Rasen* was to set up another conundrum like that of the four teenagers who all died at the same time in *Ring* — in *Rasen*, the matter of the cryptic note inside a corpse on an autopsy table — then painstakingly work his way towards a *second* solution. But without the iconic references and mystical overtones of the former, *Rasen* seems merely to contrive its conclusions from a series of improbable twists, especially in terms of its interaction with its companion-piece. A guessing-game in which the rules can be changed as its participants progress is no game at all, and the tale turns somersaults to make sense of its increasingly

inexplicable developments. The curse can now be transferred by any means which Suzuki deems to be applicable to his latest plot, from handling the Filofax of one of its victims to sexual intercourse (though presumably not *safe* sexual intercourse, given the outcome). In simple terms, the virus is mutating — but in such a contrived way that all the parameters which were laid out so painstakingly in *Ring* effectively are tossed out of the well along with the rancid water.

Those infected by the virus now dream of Sadako, and their condition is exposed to Ando when they ask of him, "Is Sadako Yamamura's well cracked on the side?" These moments of revelation are intended to impart a *frisson* in the viewer, but coming amidst a veritable onslaught of twists and turns in the narrative towards the climax, they serve only to add yet more. Not that we are allowed to sample the fear of such fever dreams. And with Ando wandering about aimlessly in an increasingly depressive state, even the seven-day deadline under which he labours creates little tension.

By the time that Mai has given birth to a new Sadako who apparently has grown to maturity offscreen and in a matter of days, all credibility is gone and any suspension of disbelief on the part of the viewer in relation to earlier events has followed along with it. The final twist is pure science fiction: Mai and Ryuji are also reborn using Sadako's DNA, as is Ando's son Takanori. The nonsensical manner in which this is meant to be achieved is simply not worth expounding upon; suffice it to say that by its closing reel, *Rasen* has gone completely off the rails. The climax devolves to a ponderous dialectic on the ethics of cloning a loved one from a dubious genetic source. The moral dilemma in this may have fascinated Koji Suzuki — and it works, to a degree, in the novel, if one is able to tolerate the technicalities of a high-concept intellectual argument — but it brings the lower-browed film version to an embarrassing gear-grinding halt.

(One interesting highlight of *Rasen* for die-hard fans is a game of 'Spot the Suzuki', in which the author can be seen to be 'doing a Hitchcock' with his family on board a fairground ride while Ando contemplates suicide in the background.)

Screenwriter-director Joji Iida was partly responsible for the script of *Kanzenban*, which was played as a mystery-thriller, and *Rasen* continues in the same vein. As it was shot concurrently with *Ring*, however, no one involved in its production had the opportunity to see beforehand the revisions which Hiroshi Takahashi and Hideo Nakata were intent on wringing out of the same source material, or be appraised of the fact that they were turning Sadako into a monster on a par with Freddy or Jason or Hannibal Lecter. In the event, the viewing of *Rasen* immediately after *Ring* in the manner that their distributor intended led to a level of disappointment among audiences that would have registered as high on the Richter scale as the Kanto earthquake.

The only points of contact between *Ring* and *Rasen* are the evocation in the latter of familiar riffs from the former and the reappearance of several of the actors involved, most notably Sanada, Miki Nakatani (as Ryuji's girlfriend Mai Takano) and the creepy Yutaka Matsushige as the reporter Yoshino. The films were shot simultaneously, which can be evidenced in a number of cost cutting contrivances, and while Nakata was given the freedom to roam as far afield as Oshima itself, Iida's short-straw sequel was mainly confined to a few sets around Tokyo and its environs.

Shooting the two films together might have seemed like a good idea at the time, but it backfires badly. For a start, all but one of the many flashbacks to events in *Ring* (that of Reiko arriving at the rental cabin) had, through necessity, to be *re-staged* rather than simply be sampled for the 'sequel', so they lack both the mood and the feel of Nakata's dramatisations of the same incidents in *Ring*. Disconcertingly, it is like watching clips from a film which one vaguely remembers having seen but cannot quite place. In some ways, the revisionism of *Rasen* is concomitant with the fact that Suzuki rewrote much of the internal dynamic of his original novel in hindsight, in order to offer a fresh twist on its theme in the follow-up; with a four-year gap in publication between the two, he was able to get away with such sneaky retrospective recastings on the printed page. But the films were released concurrently — they even played as a pair during their opening run — and the detail changes which were necessary for the plot to unfurl soon begin to nag when *Ring* is still redolent in the memory.

Ryuji is a university tutor in mathematics in *Ring*; in *Rasen*, he is transformed into a brilliant medical student. This is consistent with the novels: 'He recalled Ryuji going on to medical school,' Asakawa declares in *Ring*, before telling the reader that he gave up on medicine to lecture in philosophy. Ah, yes — but the Ryuji of the novels

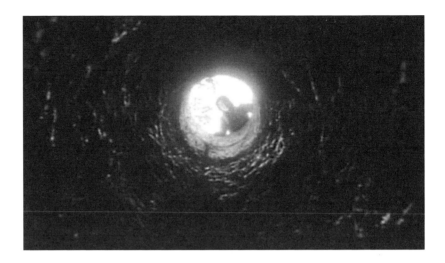

is not the Ryuji of the original film. In his screenplay for *Ring*, Takahashi changed Ryuji's status from existentialist bachelor and self-confessed rapist to that of Reiko's ex-husband, but without reference to *Rasen*, he also changed his profession as well. (*Ring 2* eventually issued a correction of sorts to amend this error.) But more damning is the rewriting of history that was needed to give impact to the new twist in the tale: the shock ending of Nakata's film depended upon the fact that Ryuji thought he had beaten the curse, only to discover that he was to become Sadako's final victim; in *Rasen*, that idea is negated and he is depicted as having been in league with Sadako all along. The jarring disparity between the two is tantamount to treating the audience like fools, and audiences tend to bridle at such blatant attempts at misdirection.

Worst of all is the woeful absence in *Rasen* of the very element which was to bring *Ring* the success that it went on to enjoy in release: the monster, Sadako. And the terror which wrote itself on the faces of her victims is also nowhere in evidence, even when it comes to Ryuji himself. By introducing Sadako as a succubus in a dream sequence, the film misses the best trick of the novel, where Ando is drawn to a mysterious woman in Mai's flat — only to discover that she is Sadako reborn. In *Rasen*, it is Mai herself who seemingly comes back to life.

As Sadako did not appear in *Ring* in any recognisable form, a new actress was cast to play her in *Rasen* — where she not only appears, much as she did in *Kanzenban*, but is also required to make love to Ando in an hallucinatory sequence which results from his having watched the video. Hanako Saeki is nondescript in the role; mysterious as Sadako may occasionally be, she poses little threat in the way that her scenes are handled and in the persona of Mai Takano, where she is played by Nakatani herself, she comes across as just another hokey Hollywood *revenant*, popping up to tell the protagonist about her adventures in the afterlife, like Bruce Willis in *The Sixth Sense* or the family of faithful retainers in *The Others* (2001). What is missing from Joji Iida's *Rasen* is any mood of Terror. The film is simply not scary; not even a little unnerving. In the final analysis, it is an opportunity missed: serving up Suzuki's complicated tale of genetic reincarnation as nothing more than a psychological sci-fi thriller with overtones of medical madness, *Rasen* is prettily shot, precisely constructed and generally well acted, but it has no feel for the genre whatsoever.

Which is not to say that *Rasen* is bad in itself, merely that it suffers by comparison. And that comparison turned out uniquely to be one of the great horror hits of all time. The climax of *Ring* raised a particular expectation in viewers versed in the ways of the horror film as to how any sequel might subsequently unfold, but in adhering to the path which had been set by Suzuki's novel, *Rasen* naturally confounded expectations. While *Ring* went on to be a massive hit, *Rasen* flopped. "*Rasen* had already been made into a film, which played on the same double bill as *Ring* when it was released," Nakata told Jasper Sharp. "Then the president of the publishing company made a very strange offer to us: make *another* sequel to *Ring*. We decided to come up with an original story that would start off almost immediately after the ending of the first one." As 1998 drew to a close, Takahashi and Nakata set about crafting a different continuum to their hit film of earlier in the year. But now they were not the only ones to show an interest in revisiting what was fast becoming a *Ring franchise*.

Ring: The Final Chapter

More *manga* adaptations of the *Ring* saga had now hit Japanese bookstores. That of *Ring* itself was published initially in serial form, subsequently anthologised in two volumes. The story follows Takahashi's screenplay for Nakata's film fairly faithfully, with one or two picaresque addenda to keep things livelier on the page, though the artwork by Misao Inagaki is puerile by Western standards — cartoonish and exaggerated. *Rasen* is a different kettle of well-water altogether. Sakura Mizuki's draughtsmanship is sleek, stylish and mature, and the story went its own way in terms of its source, preferring to ditch much of Iida's film version and return instead to the original for its inspiration. If anything, it improves the pace and structure of Suzuki's novel, though it departs from it towards the close, inserting some graphic horror scenes and turning the reborn Sadako into a cackling harpy reminiscent of Barbara Steele in *El maschera del demonio*. This maverick take only added to the curiosity element which already surrounded *Rasen*.

(Later *manga* adapted *Ring 2*, *Birthday* and *Ring 0: Birthday*, and all featured art-

Spiral: *Sadako*
(Hanako Saeki).

work by Meimu, whose overall style and panel layouts are closer in feel and technique to many of the artists working on graphic novels in Britain and America.)

With the publication of *Loop* in January, Koji Suzuki's 'Ring' trilogy had become what Kadokawa Shoten excitedly christened its 'flagship product' during 1998. "When the film was released, it helped the sales of *Ring*," Nakata explained. "But there were two other volumes called *Rasen* and *Loop*. Inside this trilogy, *Ring* had sold something like 500,000 copies but, after the film, the publisher put on a huge marketing effort and the total reached 1.5 million copies, just of *Ring*. So they helped each other."

The stupendous upswing in sales of Suzuki's novels as a result of Nakata's film encouraged the executives at Fuji Television to try their hands at *another* adaptation of the *Ring* story, only this time in the form of a twelve-part drama serial. *Ring: The Final Chapter* (*Ring: Saishusho*) was an ambitious attempt to produce a definitive version of the theme by combining the plots of *both Ring* and *Rasen*. Two writers, two producers and three directors were assigned to the nine hour project (twelve forty-five-minute episodes), and *Saishusho* began transmission in a 10pm slot on Thursday 7 January 1999, almost a year after the release of the feature.

You must show the video to two other people who haven't seen it. The person who shows the video will then be saved. One person shows it to two people, two to four, four to eight. Gradually, more and more people will have seen the video. But there is a limit to the number of people around. The time will come when the limit is reached. Towards the end, the people who have seen the video won't find anyone else to show it to. They will die. These people will never watch the video. That's because they know that they'll never find anyone else to show it to. So the ones who die will be all these people. Calculate it out and it amounts to one quarter. There's only one way a single videotape can cause the death of one in every four people. Sadako knows that. She knows exactly what she wants us to do...

- **Yoshino (Kotomi Kyono)**, *Ring: The Final Chapter* (1999)

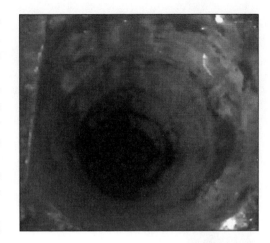

'After thirteen days, the people who videotaped this drama were...'

Saishusho opens on a construction site, over which a screen caption reads 'Three months earlier...' The head of a mechanical digger rears up and roars, like Godzilla on the rampage in Tokyo, then plunges down towards the ground. Its jaws clench tight and it retreats with another mouthful to reveal a narrow opening in the earth. "Hey, go take a look. I hit something," the driver shouts. Beneath the stilled arm of the digger is what looks like the shaft of a well that has been sealed up and buried over. The camera peers down, into the darkness below...

Main title.

This ominous prologue holds more than an echo of *Quatermass and the Pit*, and it sets a similarly apocalyptic tone to that of Nigel Kneale's sci-fi masterpiece for its own epic dramatisation of sentient evil awakened to wreak havoc on the modern world. As Toshiyuki Watanabe's pregnant score ushered in the more familiar *Ring* territory of the mist-shrouded Tokyo home in which a young girl sits alone, the omens were good that this would indeed be the 'final chapter' of the saga.

Above top: Ring: Saishusho *(1999):* prologue.

A simplified plot breakdown for each episode runs as follows:

1. A young girl dies in the bathroom of her home, as in *Kanzenban*: the cause of her death is heart failure. A motorcyclist meets an equally strange fate. Asakawa (Toshiro Yanagiba) and his feisty young female assistant Yoshino (Kotomi Kyono) work for the *Chuo Shinbun* news agency. He is a widower and the father of Yoichi, she harbours an ambition to be the next Mrs Asakawa. Yoshino relates the latest high school rumour to the effect that real-life Sony recording artist Nao Matsuzaki has been cursed — "People die after listening to her songs," she tells him. When his late wife's niece is also found dead, Asakawa's nose for a story starts to twitch: all three died at 8.55pm.

Takayama Ryuji (Tomoya Nagase) is a cultural anthropologist and celebrity

Above middle: Ring: *Japanese manga (1996).*

Above: The Ring: *UK manga (2003).*

Above: Ring:
Saishusho:
prologue.

psychic guru. During a television chat-show debate on supernatural phenomena, he places a three-day curse on the cynical Professor Kaneda to prove his point. Ryuji is the guardian of a disturbed half-sister, Mai Takano (Akiko Yada).

Asakawa traces the niece's recent movements to the Rainbow Resort Club near the Yatsugatake mountain range in central Honshu. He rents the same cabin and sets up a camcorder to record anything untoward. By the now-familiar process of elimination, he sets his sights on a videotape instead; the resort manager has been there before him. "Just as a precaution, I watched it too," the man tells him. Asakawa plays the tape — it is a pop promo of Matsuzaki seated on a sofa, conventional at first sight. He takes the tape back to the office, but the manager is dead, a look of terror on his face...

A countdown caption closes this and future episodes: '13 days left...'

2. Kaneda dies of heart failure at the appointed hour, during a live telecast from his home. The police question Asakawa as to why he left the resort in a hurry. Ryuji is also investigated for causing the death of Kaneda: "There were marks around his neck," he is informed. "You didn't kill Professor Kaneda with a curse. You strangled him!" With all of these coincidences in play, Asakawa goes to see Ryuji himself, who tells him that the curse on the video is the 'real thing' and that if he ignores it, he will die in thirteen days. But Asakawa saw no curse on the tape...

Ryuji shows him a computer analysis of Matsuzaki's pop video. It is overlaid with subliminal images: a baby; a man with a bleeding shoulder; a woman combing her hair in a mirror; a mountain-range... And there is a hidden message: 'A curse has been cast on you. Thirteen days later at this time you will die. There is only one way to be saved and that is...' Static.

'12 Days Left...'

3. Asakawa starts his investigation of the tape. Enter Dr Miyashita (Hitomi Kuroki) from *Rasen*. She runs the pathology department at Musashino Medical College, under the eminent Dr Nagao, and is conducting research into viruses; she was also a friend of Asakawa's wife. Asakawa tries to keep his concerns about the tape to himself, not least for the sake of his son Yoichi, but the devoted Yoshino insists that he should confide in her: 'Everyone will suffer,' she says, in respect of the outcome if something tragic were to befall him — not in relation to the curse. (This line was nevertheless lifted for Samara to utter as a warning in the American remake of *Ring*, but it was edited out of the final cut.) Further examination of the video follows, which uncovers the 'blinking'. "This is *nensha*," Ryuji exclaims. A minor diversion comes when the police think that Kaneda was poisoned. Ryuji is arrested for murder.

4. Ryuji is grilled by the police and his personal history is clarified: he was adopted and Takano is his half-sister, but something murky exists in their communal past. Ryuji asks Asakawa to help in his release from custody by threatening to expose the detective in charge of the case. The body of the resort manager is brought to the medical college for an autopsy.

Operating to some secret agenda of his own, Ryuji encourages Yoshino to watch the tape. Askawa fails to intervene in time and Yoichi, too, is exposed to the video. As a result, Asakawa agrees to blackmail detective Kashiwada and Ryuji is released; when he returns to his apartment, Asakawa knocks him down. In response, Ryuji offers him a new clue: "I'll tell you who's the person with supernatural powers," he says, and points him in the direction of Shizuko Yamamura. Asakawa obtains a can of newsreel footage from his agency's archive and they watch the demonstration in which Shizuko failed in her attempt to project an image onto film using *nensha*. Ryuji

seems increasingly to be troubled by something, and a flashback depicts Takano as a child, screaming 'Brother, stop it!' Asakawa decides to make the trip to Oshima. (This is a more leisurely episode, which gives an impression of time-filling for much of its length.)

Above top: Ring: Saishusho: *Episode 2.*

5. The relationship between Ryuji and his half-sister grows ever stranger: he finds her crawling across the floor of their apartment towards him, chanting "*Unu wa dasen yogora o ageru*" ("You will give birth to a child next year"). The autopsy on the resort manager has turned up a tumour that blocked the main artery to the heart; it is removed for examination, which reveals that the cancerous cells are replicating themselves at an awesome speed. Kashiwada has now resigned from the police force

Above: Ring: Saishusho: *Episode 3.*

Above top: Ring:
Saishusho:

Episode 4.

Above: Ring:
Saishusho:

Episode 5.

as a consequence of the blackmail and is bent on conducting a personal vendetta against Ryuji.

Asakawa and Yoshino arrive at the Oshima island home of Keijiro Yamamura and question him about his cousin Shizuko; he is evasive, telling them that she died on the mainland fifty years before, so they decide to stay the night. They search in the grounds after dark and come upon an old hut. Inside, they find the seventy-four year-old Shizuko. Before they can tackle her about the curse, Keijiro and his son surprise them from behind...

6. Asakawa and Yoshino have been imprisoned in a shed, which Keijiro's son puts to the torch. They manage to free themselves in the nick of time, but when they return to Shizuko, they find her dead. However, she has left them another clue: projected onto the roof of the hut by means of *nensha* is the word 'Tei'. Ryuji has been dogging their footsteps on the island and finding Yoshino alone, he now tells her that he was wrong and that it was not Shizuko who set the curse but someone else. "And we are no match for the killer," he says, doomily. Asakawa and Yoshino realise that 'tei' can be read as 'sada'. They have now established the connection with Mihara, and that the woman in the video was Shizuko, but what of the baby? Looking into the history of Shizuko and her psychic mentor Dr Ikuma, they discover that the pair had a child: Sadako.

7. Inscribed in a notebook in Ikuma's study are the words: 'The devil has been set forth into the world. Soon the world will be destroyed by hatred.' Asakawa now holds all the pieces of the video puzzle, bar one: the man with the wound on his shoulder. He returns to Tokyo and visits the Hisho acting troupe, where Sadako was known to have trained in drama in 1966; her chosen role was that of Salome, in which she is pictured with the head of John the Baptist on a silver platter. Yoshino, meanwhile, has managed to prise an answer out of Ryuji as to how they might all free themselves from the curse, though he still seems unconcerned: "What I'm waiting for is more terrifying

than death itself," he explains, cryptically. (The remainder of this episode is entirely comprised of sub-plots which have little or no bearing on the outcome of the drama.)

8. (The comment on Episode Seven can also be addressed to much of Eight; Sadako's prior history is trawled anew to provide the accumulation of incidents which ostensibly have contributed towards her hatred of mankind.) Asakawa and Yoshino debate the morality of knowingly choosing somebody else to die in place of themselves; opinion is divided on the issue. Ryuji intervenes to intimate that *nensha* weakens with distance... Asakawa reasons that Sadako must therefore be close by and heads off to find the school where the rumour about the curse — and the videotape itself — first surfaced.

9. Under the auspices of Dr Miyashita, Takano undergoes hypnotic regression and more facts emerge about her relationship with Ryuji. She finds out that Ryuji murdered their abusive parents by 'willing' them to death. Asakawa has now sourced the original tape to a school built on the site of an old sanatorium. Yoshino and Kashiwada explore the former home of Takano's parents; Kashiwada is killed and Yoshino finds herself under attack by Ryuji, in a state of possession. She is rescued by Asakawa. Ryuji retreats to the medical facility and threatens Miyashita. Takano escapes. Asakawa catches up with him and demands an explanation. "Soon I will become your enemy," Ryuji says. "I will bring disaster with me. I will turn into the devil..."

10. Events quicken pace. Asakawa establishes that the man who raped Sadako was none other than Dr Nagao, who previously has been involved in all manner of intrigue at the university. Spurred by visions of Sadako, Nagao confesses to her murder and the disposal of her body in a well — then he collapses and dies of heart failure. The culture in the lab has finally mutated into the form of a ring: the Ring virus. Asakawa is puzzled by Sadako's dying remark that she had left 'something precious' behind...

Above top: Ring: Saishusho: *Episode 6.*

Above: Ring: Saishusho: *Episode 7.*

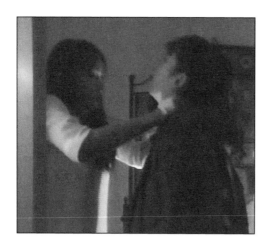

11. Asakawa and Yoshino figure out that the baby in the video was not Sadako herself, but Sadako's child: Ryuji. He has inherited his mother's power, *and* her hatred. There is only one day left for Asakawa, and he now discovers that Dr Ikuma had taken his own precautions against the day when Ryuji would transform and unleash the Ring virus on the world: he had programmed his half-sister Takano to kill him. Ryuji has become the tool of his mother's vengeance. He manages to outwit Takano's attempt to stop him and flees to the focal point of the psychic energy: the well which had been uncovered on the building site by the school. Asakawa confronts him at the rim of the well and appeals to what remains of his humanity to fight the inheritance of Sadako and save his sister. Ryuji experiences a change of heart and throws himself into the well...

Asakawa climbs down after him as the final few seconds tick away. He clutches the dying Ryuji to him as Sadako's ghost appears before them. "Let it go!" he screams, but her hands leap to his throat and she drags him beneath the waters...

12. Asakawa's body is removed from the well, but there is a heartbeat! It transpires that as he was dying, Ryuji transferred the antibodies that were in his own blood to that of Asakawa, thus curing him of the viral curse. A purification

Above top: Ring: Saishusho: *Episode 8.*

Above: Ring: Saishusho: *Episode 9.*

ceremony for the well is disrupted by a wind storm; the curse of Sadako is not over yet. Another schoolgirl has died and the rumours spread anew. A frenzy of tape copying begins, as those who have been exposed to the video try to evade the thirteen-day deadline. Miyashita watches the video for herself and figures out the trigger mechanism: the virus is dormant in human DNA until activated by subconscious stimulus. But Asakawa was saved, and Miyashita thinks that she can create a vaccine from Ryuji's blood; however, Ryuji's body was *not* at the bottom of the well...

Takano has spirited Ryuji's corpse away. Until they can make the vaccine, the only course open to those infected with the Ring virus is to persuade others to watch a copy of the video. Asakawa asks his parents to watch the tape in order to save Yoichi.

They agree, unhesitatingly. He discovers the whereabouts of Ryuji and persuades Takano to give up the body; he has it removed to Miyashita's lab, but time is fast running out for Yoichi and Yoshino...

Asakawa arranges for his parents to watch the tape, but Yoichi refuses to play it for them. Instead, the untried vaccine is tested on he and Yoshino. The seconds tick by and the deadline passes without incident. It has worked: the curse of Sadako is broken.

End titles.

...A television set sits in a darkened room. A tape laces up in the VCR beneath it.

Sudden cut to black.

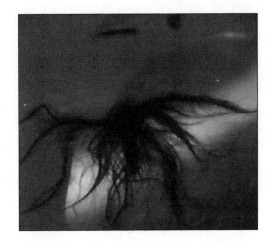

Ring: *The Final Chapter* was shot entirely (and not inappropriately) on video, but aside from its typically muted look it has the attributes of a feature. The scope of the production is a world away from anything similar which might be undertaken, say, on television in Britain. Most of it is filmed in real locations to reduce the cost of sets, but then so was much of *Ring*; it is a feature of modern Asian horrors that gives their chills an authentic flavour which the artificiality of more studio-bound films simply cannot match.

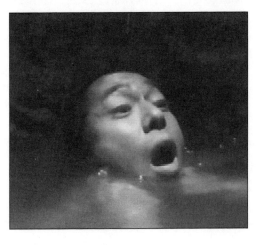

Being a twelve-part serial, it is naturally infested with sub-plots, few of which have been included in the synopsis above. The viewer's first glimpse of Sadako comes in the episode of the Hisho theatre troupe, when she is shown in the guise of Salome. A long digression has theatre director Arima inveigle her into involvement in a bank heist (no less!) which subsequently returns to haunt him, literally. A sidebar to this incident sees Asakawa attacked in a rehearsal room by a young actress (Takamoku Sadahiko) whose body Sadako has assumed for the purpose. The police's investigation into the supposed murder of Kaneda is another lengthy diversion, as is the welter of intrigue which goes on behind closed doors at the medical facility. And there are numerous red herrings, as well, of which Kaneda is one. Entertaining as all these vignettes are, few of them

Above top: Ring: Saishusho: *Episode 10.*

Above: Ring: Saishusho: *Episode 11.*

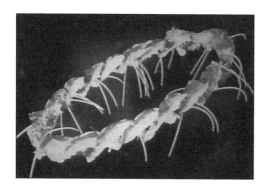

Above: Ring:
Saishusho:
Episode 12.

have a bearing on the real narrative. Following the lead set by *Kanzenban*, Sadako is played in this version by supermodel and sometime soap-star Tae Kimura, but for most of her screen-time in *Saishusho*, she is effectively essayed by the others in the cast (such as Sadahiko) whom her spirit possesses from time to time. She is addressed throughout as Sadako Ikuma, after her adoptive father.

Slowly unveiling the images on the video by computer analysis puts a new spin on the cursed tape and reintroduces the creepiness of the original by another means. More than anything, the style and approach of the show is strongly reminiscent of BBC TV's *Quatermass* serials of the 1950s, or any of the many clones which were later to feature on both British television channels during the early 1960s: each episode is replete with repetitive riffs of over-dramatic incidental music, much meaningful staring off into the middle distance from the principals, and a cliff-hanging ending amplified by the use of screen captions stating that there are 'x' number of days left. It sounds rather trite, but it is actually gripping and engaging stuff, with excellent performances and efficient and unobtrusive direction throughout. *Saishusho* adheres to a format of drama which has been all-but-forgotten in the supposedly sophisticated scheduling of Western networks, with their over-reliance on clichéd formulae of the 'cop-doc-vet' variety.

The reprise of highlights from the previous week's episode, followed by a prologue for what is to come, and all of it featured before the new titles roll is an old-fashioned technique but still highly effective in a melodramatic way. Tension is benefited by the typically Japanese insouciance of male lead Toshiro Yanagiba, who stoically insists on carrying the burden of risk on his own shoulders for much of the way, and only accepts the eager (and often more intuitive) help of female colleagues when he is boxed into a psychological corner by them. Were this to have been shot in the West, the two female protagonists would have commandeered the investigation at an early stage, and half of the twelve episodes would have been redundant in consequence; fortunately, it was not, and the gender rivalries sired by the changing role of women in Japanese society make it a fascinating sociological study to Western eyes, in addition to absorbing drama. "I'm not as brave as you or Yoshino," Asakawa concedes to Miyashita towards the close, in acknowledgement of the end of a thousand years of male supremacy.

As the series nears its climax, the video itself becomes a metaphor for the collapse of post-war capitalist structures in Japan, and the means of its defeat is promoted as the way in which a new age of equanimity might be ushered in. The tone of *Saishusho* is the very antithesis of the nihilism that was expressed in the novel seven years before it; its message is one of hope, in which it urges society to pull together to defeat the threat from within, not to become divided through fear and selfishness. Some two years after the transmission of *Saishusho*, on 26 April 2001, the Japanese electorate voted in to the post of Prime Minister the popular reformer and long-time LDP politico Junichiro Koizumi, and the nation's long transition to a more liberalised Western democracy took another step forward.

Above: Ring: Saishusho*: the 'pop' video featuring Nao Matsuzaki as herself.*

In the demanding role of Asakawa, Yanagiba provides a sympathetic focus for the whirlpool of events in which the characters are mired, and his fraught relationship with the upstart but imperturbable Kyono is by turns formal, funny, patronising or poignant. The idea of transferring the curse to a pop video was an indicator of how (necessarily) adaptable the iconography of *Ring* had now become, and technological development is likely to see the story regenerated on a regular basis, in a variety of different ways.

As a television drama made strictly for domestic consumption, *Saishusho* affords more of an insight into the customs and culture of Japan than the movie version. Some aspects of the production, such as Asakawa and Yoshino's escape from the burning hut, or characters contriving to be at the same location simultaneously, are strictly the stuff of the Saturday-matinee serial. But weaknesses are to be expected across nine hours of broadcasting time. *Ring: The Final Chapter* is thoroughly entertaining; it delivers shocks and chills in equal measure, and it offers up a tear-jerking last episode that must surely tenderise the hardest heart. In terms of a supernatural mystery-thriller with scientific overtones, it knocks the likes of *Sea of Souls* — BBC TV's most recent offering in similar vein — into a deep, dark hole in the ground. It also gave out with something of a mission statement for the *Ring* franchise as a whole: "You examine things too closely and therefore don't see the whole picture. That is the limit of science," Ryuji tells Asakawa. As a pointer to the direction of future entries in the series, it came too late for Suzuki to take on board. But it was not too late for Nakata.

Fuji's sprawling 'Final Chapter' should have been the final word on the *Ring* theme as the millennium neared, but the story of Sadako and her curse proved too

Korean poster for
The Ring Virus
(1999).

powerful a myth to be disposed of that easily. Other sequels were rendered redundant in the wake of its clever combining of both novels and ultimately uplifting resolution; nevertheless, there were still yen to be made from the seemingly insatiable appetite of the Asian film audience for *Ring*...

The Ring Virus

After the striking success of *Ring*, South Korean production company AFDF struck a deal with Asmik Ace to produce a tailored remake. As the Korean *Ring* (or *The Ring Virus* as it would become better known in the West) was to go into production primarily for domestic consumption, it was decided that the setting of the story should be changed to Korea itself, which meant finding an alternative to the volcanic island of Oshima. With more than 3,000 islands at its disposal, it was convenient that Japanese terrors would in large part emanate from them, in the way that an equivalent tale in Britain or America might focus on a haunted house or small backwoods community; *Ring* was no exception. But the Korean film-makers were slightly more strapped for suitable venues when it came to switching the locations of the original to some which were closer to home. For a start, there are no *active* volcanoes in the Koreas, so short of inventing one, screenwriter and director Dong-bin Kim had to come up with an alternative to Suzuki's erupting Mount Mihara to feature in his version of the video. Low-level seismic activity being common in the south-west of the country, Kim opted for a prediction of a tidal wave, or tsunami, instead, and he decided to place the Oshima action of the original on the exotic Cheju Island — Chejudo — which is situated in the Korea Strait, some sixty miles distant from the southernmost tip of the peninsula.

Unlike Oshima, the sub-tropical Cheju is an idyllic and well-developed tourist trap of emerald caves, undulating meadows and ancient stone statues of fertility gods (such as the dwarfish Tolharubang), whose geographical focal point of Mount Hallasan is the highest peak in the Koreas, but its rurality was enough to provide the film with the faint aura of legend which otherwise would have been absent from a shoot based entirely in the Westernised Seoul Studio Complex.

The Korean *Ring* was instigated as part of the country's quota system policy, which requires cinemas to show domestic product for at least 146 days out of every year. *The Ring Virus* was not intended to be a shot-for-shot reprise of Nakata's film. It is more of a hybrid — an alternative take on the source material, utilising elements from the novel which were left out of *Ring* and combining them with sequences from Takahashi's own screenplay (though he received no credit). If anything, it is the remake which preceded that by DreamWorks in 2002, rather than the cloned copy which it is often assumed to be by those who have not seen it. Nevertheless, Nakata was still surprised at how much of his original work came to feature in it when eventually he was able to catch it for himself: "When I first saw that movie I felt really... strange. I wasn't told that they could remake *Ring*. I was told that the Korean version would be based on the novels. I saw *The Ring Virus* in Montreal, Canada, and I didn't know it was a remake because I'd been told that it was a movie based on the same story, not a remake of my movie. But there were so many similar scenes that I was a bit offended. I couldn't smile for an hour or so after I'd watched it."

It is indisputably a fact that *The Ring Virus* borrows from *Ring*, but the impression of lazy duplication throughout really only results from the residue that remains from its climax, which slavishly panders to that of Nakata's version and is nowhere to be found in the novel (see Chapter Seven). It is as much of a fact that *The Ring Virus* is not the same film as Nakata's *Ring* at all.

The opening is quite different. After a teenage girl named Sang-mi is attacked by an unseen assailant in the bathroom of her own home, the viewer is treated to an academic discussion about hermaphroditism at a gallery exhibition attended by reporter Sun-joo Kim (Eun-kyung Shin). "She was in there dead — fist full of her own hair," the mother of Sang-mi tells Sun-joo, who soon uncovers other recent cases of equally inexplicable death 'by fright'. Sun-joo next decides to seek the advice of maverick medico Dr Choi (Jin-yeong Jeong), a world-weary pathologist who has posited 'unrecognisable shock' as the cause of the victims' deaths. In his casual cynicism and arrogant self-possession, Choi is nearer to the Ryuji of Suzuki's novel than was Ryuji himself in Nakata's film; in this and other respects, *The Ring Virus* adheres closer to *Kanzenban* than *Ring*. "It's nothing like you've ever seen," Choi forewarns her, when she determines to investigate further. Unlike *Ring*, this version eschews any mention of the videotape until the action is well underway, but eventually it rears its black plastic head and Sun-joo undertakes the time-honoured trip to the resort at night and during a rainstorm.

The images on the videotape in *The Ring Virus* are more restrained. A blank screen subsides to reveal the disclaimer: 'Watch till the end or else death will swallow you'. A blinking eye is superseded by a sequence of abstracts, like an iris opening and closing. An old woman peers at the screen: 'Playing in water will summon spirits. You'll soon bear a child next year. Listen to your granny,' she intones. A shot of a television set; a shot of a well. A last, fateful caption: 'Whoever watches this will die exactly one week from now. If you want to live...'

Sun-joo careers away from the resort, stopping at a photo booth along the route. A disposable camera in Sang-mi's bedroom had revealed the same warping on the photos of she and her friends that had made its appearance in *Ring*; now Sun-joo wants to test the correlation for herself. She waits for the pictures to process and retrieves them from the tray. Her features are twisted. Mark this one down to Takahashi, even if the images in *The Ring Virus* are marginally more disturbing.

Given that production on *The Ring Virus* was subject to a winter shooting schedule, the following day is the seasonally authentic '1 December'. Sun-joo now turns to Choi for help and he examines the tape in more detail. This version explores the fact that the video revealed originally how to break the curse but that the 'charm' was taped over; a subsequent scene shows an earlier family in the same holiday apartment doing just that. The shots of the rapist are now uncovered as flash-frames, and Choi divides the images on the tape into two types: observational and abstract — a direct reference to Suzuki and the more detailed breakdown which takes place in the novel. As more data is divulged through analysis, Sun-joo's daughter Boram is exposed to the tape. But Choi has got to the bottom of the mystery: "Someone recorded those images through telekinesis," he tells Sun-joo. "A woman with supernatural powers transferred those images from her head to the video." No psychic he; nevertheless, he is affected by what he has seen. "I can feel it," he says. "The damp darkness…"

By 5 December, they are on their way to the island, armed with the knowledge that the woman they seek is Eun-suh. The rest of the story is now revealed: when Eun-suh's mother predicted a 'seismic tidal wave' that would 'swallow the island', the ungrateful villagers condemned her as a witch. At the family home, Sun-joo and Choi experience separate visions of what then occurred: Eun-suh's mother jumped from a cliff and was drowned in the sea (a scene which would feature in the DreamWorks remake of *Ring*), but she left to find work in the city. In a major departure from previous versions of the story, it seems that Eun-suh took a job as a singer in a nightclub. The pair pay a visit to the club and its manager fills them in on the remaining blanks. The flashback sequence that follows is completely different from anything that has gone before, and it gives us our first glimpse of Eun-suh Park (Du-na Bae), the Sadako figure of *The Ring Virus*.

Eun-suh is shown kneeling in front of a television set, which appears to be working despite the fact that the power plug is detached from the wall. She then takes a shower, but she is watched through a spy hole by one of the employees. (A huge close-up of his eye as he ogles her naked body is an obvious nod to the similar scene in *Psycho*, when Norman Bates spies on Marion Crane as she undresses for the shower.) Eun-suh is not entirely oblivious to her secret admirer, though, and when she exits the room, she turns and glares at him. The man screams… "Sunny Park?" the club owner notions in passing. "Singer my ass. She was a gopher for about a year…"

By this time, Sun-joo and Choi have also ascertained the facts about the well and its part in Eun-suh's death. As in *Ring*, a sudden storm strands them on the island, but an opportune flash of lightning illuminates a portrait of Eun-suh on the wall of the

The Ring Virus:
*portrait of Eun-
suh.*

house; when they are finally able to return to the mainland, this chance occurrence leads them to her murderer, for her half-brother was a painter. They confront Chang-jun Sun with the facts as they now understand them, and he confesses all. "I saw male and female in her body," he tells them, in reference to Eun-suh's physical affliction.

The remainder of *The Ring Virus* follows along traditional lines. Eun-suh's corpse is retrieved from the well and the two return to Seoul. An attraction is forming between them, and Choi proposes that he and Sun-joo meet up again soon.

Night, and Choi is at home. As he idly examines some viral diagrams, vague doubts begin to creep into his mind. He crawls across the floor towards the television, to take another look at the tape…

In the subtitled print, there is consistent reference to characters being possessed of 'supernatural' power, though it is clear from the narrative that what is being referred to is psychic ability. Aside from the flashbacks (which tend to imply that Koreans are *all* possessed of such ability), there is little intimation of the supernatural in the film. Even the famous body-in-the-well scene is shot very low-key. And the remark about 'bearing a child' that featured in the video? "You *have* given birth to something," Sun-joo says, when she realises that a copy is needed. In a reversal of the closing shot in *Ring*, storm clouds *follow* her as she drives off into the distance.

In the case of *The Ring Virus*, the charge of 'copy' is, for the most part, unjusti-fied. There are the obvious similarities that one would expect of two films adapted from the same source, but it is really only identical in a handful of scenes, principal among them being the climax. Director Dung-bin Park counters the passivity of Nakata by taking a more hands-on approach in his version. Where Hideo Nakata consciously downplayed the familiar tricks of the horror film — ominous music, rapid cutting, manic first-person camerawork — Kim plays them up. Thus, we have a film that is wholly different in tone: more frenetic, more conventionally 'haunted-house' in approach. But Park's eagerness to please makes for a slick thriller, albeit one that until its final scene exhibits all of the qualities of a B-movie.

The Ring Virus opened in Korea on 12 June 1999.

Rasen — TV

With Ring fever now in full flood across much of Southeast Asia, executives at Fuji Television were desperate to produce a follow-up serial to its own version of Ring, but they had queered the pitch on that score by incorporating the plot of Rasen (Spiral) into the earlier adaptation, which had gone out with the title of 'The Final Chapter'. Having looked at Loop and found it wanting — both in context of the other novels and in terms of the prohibitive effects budget which would have been required to mount it — they were left with no alternative but to adapt Rasen again, this time as a stand-alone serial.

Fuji's version of Rasen begins three months after the events in Ring: The Final Chapter. As high school language teacher Mitsuo Ando (Goro Kishitani) grieves for the loss of his son in a drowning accident, a group of office workers in the Green Tower building in Tokyo are found dead of a mystery ailment which has left their features contorted in terror. Ando's curiosity is stimulated by student interest in a gruesome website, the oddly-named 'Murder's Factory', to which killers themselves ostensibly log-on and discuss their nefarious handiwork; one such is the pseudonymous 'Arita', who claims responsibility for the deaths in the Green Tower. Due to an idiosyncrasy in the typing, Ando realises that Arita has been typing his blog on a keyboard in the same building…

The plot now takes off in a number of different directions, few of which have much to do with Koji Suzuki or his source-novel. Ando is contacted by Natsumi Aihara (Takami Yoshimoto), a former classmate and forensic scientist who suspects her superiors of some kind of conspiracy in relation to a 'digitised' virus which has been stored on computer under the code-name 'Ring'. In the meantime, Ring: The Final Chapter survivor Mai Takano (Akiko Yada) starts to sense that the evil Sadako (also played again by Tae Kimura) is still around. The three form an alliance to investigate the various threads and discover that the Ring virus is a coded message which mutates human DNA to recreate Sadako anew — worse, that the virus has already been 'transmitted' to the surrounding area by a local television station. Mai has herself been impregnated as a result, and she gives birth to a new incarnation of Sadako (played by Yada in this instance, in the manner of the film version of Rasen), who promptly grows to adulthood and sets about strangling all those around her. But there is a flaw in the genetic rebirth, and the Sadako clones are forced to confront an unforeseen by-product of the process: rapid ageing...

Having established its various premises, *Rasen* plugs the gap between problem and solution by devolving into an unending series of supernatural incidents involving black cats, satanic covens, weird dolls, predictions of doom, ghost-girls, psychic phenomena, serial killers and an entire episode (nine) that plays more like a Ring-orientated version of *A Nightmare on Elm Street* (1984) than anything to do with viral curses, complete with smoky dream sequences and Ando dunked into a well of blood. All are tied tangentially to the theme but few add anything of note beyond their purpose of keeping the viewer hooked until the next exciting instalment.

When eventually *Rasen* returns to the matter in hand, the nature of the conspiracy is revealed. Behind it all is the hand of Kyosuke Ota (played by Seiichi Tanabe, who was to feature in *Ring 0: Birthday* a few months later) or *Kyoufu no Daiou*, the 'Great King of Terror', a psychotic lab assistant who had aided lab director Rikuta in secret psychological experiments on children which inadvertently had resulted in irreversible damage to some of those involved and a crop of adult killers in consequence. Ota had sought Sadako's powers of foresight to try to forestall their crimes before they were committed, but he had also become unbalanced in the process and determined to extend his control of events to encompass the entire world. A likely story. This conspiratorial thriller paraphernalia runs parallel to, and entangled with, the spread of the virus on CD, the cloning, and the numerous Sadakos who run around in the background with throttling in mind. It is quite fun to watch in a frivolous kind of way but in terms of storyline, it is a complete overburdened mess.

After much starting and stopping of plot, and more than an Odo Island fisherman's worth of red herrings along the way, Ando manages to take Ota — and himself — out in a gas explosion in his underground lair at the close of Episode Twelve, surviving to tell the tale by Episode Thirteen. But before anyone can utter the words 'Saturday serial', it turns out that Ando did *not* survive either; he, too, has now been cloned. All that remains is the matter of the involuntary ageing. Ando has been given an antidote, but he destroys it, preferring to let nature take its unnatural course. He finally expires on the same beach as did his son, his understanding wife at his side.

Sadako, meanwhile, has unfeasibly repented her evil ways (or her willingness to let them be subverted to the mad schemes of others) and has plunged to her own choice of death from a rooftop.

Given that it was intended to be transmitted at the end of the millennium (from 1 July to 23 September 1999), the thirteen part drama-serial took the opportunity to include the alleged prediction about 'the end of the world' that supposedly is contained in Quatrain X:72 of notorious sixteenth-century French seer Nostradamus' 'The Centuries', popularly (but erroneously) interpreted as any of many variations on the theme of 'The year 1999 and seven months/From the sky will come the great King of Terror/To resuscitate the great king of the Mongols/Before and after Mars reigns by good fortune'.

This mistranslation of Michel de Nostradame's creatively obscure ramblings about the political situation in France at the time was first advanced as ominous prophecy in the 1970s' heyday of obsessions with mystic philosophy by editor Erika Cheetham and others, to insinuate the arrival of a third Antichrist, after Napoleon and Hitler (if one is to assume that either of those were representative of the breed), at millennial midnight. *Rasen* throws it into the mix as the subject of a television chat show about the paranormal like that in *Saishusho*: the enigmatic Toru Kawai (Takeshi Masu) is the evangelical host of '1999: Nostradamus no Daiyogen' ('The Great Nostradamus Prophecy'), a network special that also carries the more worrisome subtitle 'Ima, Jinrui Shuen no Shinjitsu ni Semaru' ('Now — The Truth about Mankind's End is Near'). In the course of the show, he predicts that proof of Nostradamus' warning will come 'from the sky' at 11pm that very evening. Nothing obvious materialises (although the Ring virus is disseminated by the broadcast) and the idea itself is largely dispensed with as the serial progresses, but it plants an embryo of impending catastrophe upon the narrative and good use is made of apocalyptic imagery in early episodes, such as a giant eye that appears in a doorway at the end of a corridor or the looming red moon in the sky, which calls to mind Oscar Wilde's vivid description of mood in *The Picture of Dorian Gray*, after his protagonist has murdered the painter Basil Hallward: 'There had been a madness of murder in the air. Some red star had come too close to the earth.'

Rasen is a sushi of uncooked ingredients tossed onto a platter of popular appeal. As in *Rasen* the movie, the whole is conducted as though none of those involved have ever heard of a cursed video, or any of the associated urban legend which was such common currency in *Ring: The Final Chapter* that its *modus operandi* had reached the pricked ears of every high school student in Japan. Surprisingly, only two writers are credited — Kazuhiko Tanaka and Koujiko Takata — but it seems that neither consulted the other. Acting and staging are far more soap-opera functional than they were in the carefully-crafted *Saishusho*, though the serial nods to its forebear in style. Kishitani has merely to look troubled or terrified by turns as he stumbles upon answers or is stumbled into by the agents of evil; there is a great deal of running around in a state of barely-controlled panic, and all the villains behave in such villainous ways that a blind man with a black bag over his head could have spotted them in a windowless warehouse in the middle of a power cut.

For all its air of urgency and topical dressing of millennial angst, *Rasen* is mostly a matter of sound and fury. The Ring cycle was coming to the end of its natural life in its first incarnation.

The success of *Ring* against the comparative failure of *Rasen* — and in particular the impact of the monstrous Sadako — meant that the film-makers decided to part company with Koji Suzuki in all but a name credit on the billboards when it came to looking for another sequel. If *Rasen* had gone in the wrong direction in terms of how well it might translate into the more rigid narrative straight-jacket of the horror film, then *Loop* was a complete non-starter. So much so, that the call was put out by means of a competition to *any* other writer who thought himself capable of turning in an acceptable screenplay for what now was unofficially categorised as 'Ring 2'. And acceptable in this sense meant one which continued the story of *Sadako*.

"The president of Kadokawa Shoten suggested to producer 'Taka' Ichise and myself that some professional writers could write very interesting stories, so let's ask them to try," Nakata told Javier Lopez. "Kadokawa announced that they would welcome ideas, and four hundred people submitted scripts. Kadokawa, producer Ichise, myself and, I think, Koji Suzuki read them. We discussed the scripts but, unfortunately, we couldn't find the one that could be developed as a movie script. We couldn't use them even as a basis for the story, but there were some interesting ideas, so Kadokawa published them as a paperback." This esoteric addition to the canon was put out under the title of *Ring: Four Scarier Tales* (*Ring: Motto Kowai Yottsu no Hanashi*, 1999), and it featured the stories 'On Air', 'The Well', 'Someone is Watching' and 'Loop of the Ring'.

The difficulty was that Koji Suzuki had come up with too many 'interesting ideas' already. What the film's producers wanted — what the public wanted — was 'The Return of Sadako', 'The Revenge of Sadako', 'Son of Sadako' or something of that ilk, and all because of a sequence in the original film that had created a monster where none such had existed beforehand.

Nowhere in Suzuki's novel does he imply that Sadako is a *revenant*. He is at pains throughout to give her curse a cod-scientific basis in fact; it is the curse, the virus, that survives Sadako's death, not the girl herself in malignant spirit form, and it is this idea which he explores at greater length in the book's sequel, *Rasen* (*Spiral*). When Nakata and Takahashi came to make *their* sequel, however, they realised that no longer could they travel the path which Suzuki had chosen to follow because of the changes that had been wrought to *Ring*. Not only was Sadako depicted as a demonic entity who could be summoned from the very pit of hell by means of an arcane videotape, but she now had power over time and space. With a new and evolving *monster* at their command, the two set about crafting their own variant on *Rasen*, which would soon come to be accepted as the 'real' *Ring 2*.

Ring 2

"The two movies, *Spiral* and *Ring 2*, exist in sort of parallel worlds," Nakata said. "I understand it's a bit confusing! When we made *Ring 2*, we were thinking of John Boorman's *Exorcist II: The Heretic* (1977) — that's a very peculiar horror movie. I shared his desire to make a very strange horror film: scientific, sad, with lots of elegance. His intention is what inspired us." The fact that Nakata and his screenwriter took inspiration from what was widely regarded to be one of the worst sequels to a successful original in the history of the horror film did not bode well for the outcome of their new collaboration.

The experienced Takahashi at least opens the story in the way that the sequel to the screen version of *Ring* should always have played: the body of Sadako Yamamura has been removed from the well and is now the subject of a police investigation. A forensic scientist stands ready to reconstruct her features from the skull and Takashi Yamamura has been summoned from his home on Oshima island to help with the identification of the remains. The white sheet is lifted and he glances at what is left of his niece: "Burn her and do what you like with the ashes," he says. The scene dissolves to a shot of the sea which echoes that of the first film, as Kenji Kawai's *Psycho*-like score reaches a crescendo on the soundtrack. Fade-in titles.

In terms of engendering a tangible sense of anticipation for what is to come, this is a masterful opening, and it buries any memories of the intervening *Rasen* in a matter of minutes. We are once more back at the fade-out of the original, but following the trail of Sadako, not Ryuji. What Takahashi understood and Iida and Suzuki did not (until he penned the short story that was to form the basis of *Ring 0*) is that the core audience for a story like *Ring* expects to see the return of the monster, not one of its victims, nor indeed to be treated to a prolonged debate about its various *modi operandi*. The film then takes more steps in the right direction, returning us to roving reporter Reiko's old stamping ground of MMB Broadcasting, where they are still compiling the feature item about the cursed video that she had instigated before her disappearance — to which has now been added an additional piece of high school tittle-tattle to the effect that the tape has to be copied and passed on in order for the viewer to escape the curse.

At this point, Nakata introduces us to Okazaki, Reiko's replacement on the feature, and his grasp of what is required is further reflected by the casting of Yurei Yanagi in the role; Yanagi had played director Toshio Murai in *Don't Look Up*. Miki Nakatani's Mai Takano also makes a return, still seeking answers about Ryuji's death as she was in *Rasen*, while Okazaki has found himself somebody who not only has a copy of the legendary

*Ring 2: flashback
to the death of
Tomoko at the
hands of Sadako.*

Ring 2: flashback to the death of Tomoko at the hands of Sadako.

tape but has actually *watched* it, in the frightened personage of young Kanae (Kyoko Fukada). Thus *Ring 2* establishes two new narrative threads running in parallel track: Okazaki's ongoing production of a documentary about the video, and Takano's single-minded pursuit of the truth — and behind them both, the brittle bones of Sadako lie in state, and in wait, in a police mortuary.

What the opening reel of *Ring 2* presents is a perfect set up of all the elements that were most effective in the first film, dusted down and made ready to once more weave their macabre magic in a second. Unfortunately for the new 'sequel', Nakata picked the wrong plot to concentrate on. "My films are portraits of women fighting to the extreme to survive," he has said. "Even if, in *Ring*, my main character has to sacrifice her father for her son to live." Flying the flag of emancipation is well and good, but for *Ring 2* to have survived the fate which was accorded to *Rasen*, it might have been better had he sacrificed Takano for the sake of Okazaki. As it is, the twitchy uncertainty of Yurei as he comes into personal contact with the alleged death tape has to play second fiddle to the bland predictability of Nakatani as she embarks on a singularly arbitrary search for some explanation as to what befell her former tutor.

In fact, one of the few concessions that *Ring 2* makes to *Rasen* is in putting right the mistake regarding Ryuji's profession: the script attempts to square the circle by making fleeting reference to the fact that he *had been* a medical student but had given it up to teach mathematics. Not a very likely move. An interesting diversion into media ethics comes when Okazaki persuades Kanae to give him the tape by assuring her that he will watch it (and thus relieve her of the psychological pressure of its seven-day deadline).

She takes him at his word and hands over the tape, but Okazaki reneges on his promise with fatal consequences. When word reaches him that Kanae has died, he locks it away in a drawer. This episode is interestingly developed, providing the film with two of its scariest sequences and the theme itself with another level of development.

When Okazaki subsequently reviews the tape on which Kanae was interviewed for the documentary, he finds that he cannot erase it as he had intended. The interview clip plays in a 'loop' until eventually the image goes haywire and a new scene replaces the old, which shows Kanae head bowed, hair drawn over her face. She raises her eyes and stares straight at Okazaki, who screams in terror... An extension to this scene provides a payoff for the epilogue: Okazaki has been institutionalised as a result of his experience and a nurse enters his cell to take a snapshot of him for his file. As she leaves the room and examines the Polaroid, her face takes on a puzzled expression. Nakata cuts back to Okazaki's face as he senses that someone is behind him. The camera pans to the right to reveal a blurred figure seated at his back. It is Kanae.

However, these are mere interludes in a plot which defers all too slavishly to that of *Exorcist II*. Takano follows the trail of the tape to

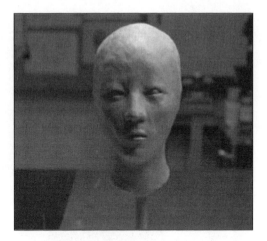

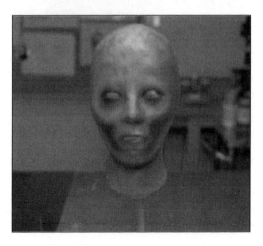

Above: Ring 2: *the forensic model – Sadako by flashlight.*

Masami, the friend of Tomoko's who inadvertently witnessed her death at the hands of Sadako in *Ring*. The girl has been in a catatonic state ever since — a side-effect of which is that she causes television sets in her near vicinity to show images from the video spontaneously — and she is now of interest to Dr Kawajiri (Fumiyo Kohinata). By the mad-lab means of what Nakata has referred to in interview as a 'psych-metre', Kawajiri intends to tap into Masami's subconscious and drain away the negative energy residing there by channelling it into water (a further nod in the direction of *Quatermass and the Pit*). Along the way, Reiko and her son are reintroduced into the narrative; Yoichi is in a similar state of post-traumatic shock after the death of his grandfather, but his presence here serves only to provide Takano with a sympathetic

Ring 2.

'charge' when Reiko is mowed down by an articulated lorry.

Takahashi manages to squeeze into his script another reference to Sadako's mythic origins, when Takashi Yamamura ushers Mai into a cavern at the water's edge, near his island home. "The offering river," he says to her. "Unwanted children were put here so the tide could wash them out to sea." Mai takes the opportunity to ask him the pertinent question: "Who was Sadako's father?" Again, there is no reply. In the context of *Ring 2*, such philosophical quandaries cut no ice, however. This is mad scientist territory.

Nakata's predilection for constructing his films almost entirely out of psycho-kinetic flashbacks reaches fever pitch in *Ring 2*. Takano is now as adept at seeing into the past as was Reiko in *Ring*, even without Ryuji's hand to hold, and the profusion of scenes in which the action is paused for yet another episode of visionary exposition soon starts to clutter up a story that lacked focus to begin with. The increasingly deranged Kawajiri's nutty attempt to combat a supernatural foe with the technological equivalent of crosses and garlic is just so much cod-scientific codswallop. To those familiar with *Exorcist II*, the climax of the film holds no surprises: with Masami seated beside a swimming pool and hot-wired into an array of diagnostic equipment, all hell breaks loose and everyone ends up dead bar those who might be needed by another sequel. "I can see into the next world!" Takano screams while acting as medium for the force that is inside of Masami. "There are no ghosts — no next world, despite what Takayama said," Kawajiri tells her, before going swiftly off his rocker and hurling himself into the pool with a live monitor for ballast.

An earlier scene in which Yoichi sends a couple of cops tumbling simply by star-

Ring 2: *the end of Reiko.*

ing at them harks back to Stephen King's and Brian De Palma's *Carrie* (1976), or even the latter's *The Fury* (1978), and in the melee of kinetic activity which dominates the final half-hour, Nakata quite loses his way as new twists are applied to the original premise with increasing regularity. There are the requisite moments of fright, though too few of them and none that match the heights of terror that the director had scaled in *Ring*. 'Pic notably fails to build on the first movie's wonderfully nasty final scene, and becomes progressively more conventional,' *Variety's* reviewer reported, 'with no special visual style or under-the-skin frissons.'

Ring 2 did well enough at the box-office to float the prospect of a third (or fourth) instalment in the saga but, once it was over, Nakata decided that he had had his fill of Sadako and her video: "Before the release of *Ring 2,* I announced that I'd never make another *Ring* movie. And the scriptwriter didn't regard me as a good horror director at all — actually he hated *Ring 2*, although we're still good friends! Anyway, I was offered to direct it, but I declined. I didn't want to continue making horror films."

Nakata's withdrawal from the series to direct a Hitchcockian psychological thriller called *Chaos* (*Kaosu,* 1999) was not thought by the films' producers to be sufficient reason to look a gift franchise in the mouth. And Takahashi had no such qualms about continuing on with a new script. Fortunately for all concerned with *Ring* '3', Suzuki had followed *Rasen* and *Loop* with the compendium *Birthday*, comprising of three short stories, one of which, 'Lemonheart', went back in time to recount the young Sadako's adventures with the Hisho repertory company in Tokyo, in 1966. On

the face of it, this seemed to be just what Dr Kawajiri ordered.

Ring 2 premièred in Japan on 28 July 1999, but it had been market-tested in Hong Kong for more than a month beforehand, opening in that territory on 10 June. By then, production already was underway on a *prequel* to *Ring*, in the form of the oddly-titled *Ring 0: Birthday* (*Ring 0: Bâsudei*).

Ring 0: Birthday

> Last night, I had this weird dream. There was a well in it. A real old one.
> The edge had crumbled away. Inside, it was pitch black. I couldn't see
> anything. The house looked empty. I went inside. The place was a ruin.
> There was a flight of stairs. I went to go up it, but something told me I
> absolutely shouldn't. I just stood there. I couldn't move...
>
> - **Kiyomi, girl in prologue (Chinami Furuya)**, *Ring 0: Birthday* (2000)

Taking as its starting point the 'Lemonheart' story from *Birthday*, Takahashi's next move was to develop a scenario which depicted the events leading up to the creation of the monster. No film about a psychic adolescent could fail to pay some kind of *homage* to Stephen King's *Carrie*, and Takahashi again intended for *Ring 0: Birthday* to do just that. He telephoned Norio Tsuruta, Nakata's replacement as director of the sequel, and put the idea to him: "For this new *Ring*, I'd like to do a '*Carrie*' about the tragedy of someone with paranormal abilities," he enthused. "How does that sound?" Tsuruta was sold; De Palma's version of *Carrie* was one of his all-time favourite horror films also. "It's not like I was going to remake *Carrie* all over again," Tsuruta noted later. "But it was certainly a major source of inspiration." *Carrie* is a story about a teenage girl with psychokinetic tendencies, who is pushed to the point where the revenge that she eventually exacts on her high school tormentors nevertheless takes place *against her will*. She is not, herself, a monster — any more than the sweet young Sadako of 'Lemonheart' is a monster. To achieve the necessary transition, Takahashi came up with a solution as old as the famous Gothic tale of duality by one Robert Louis Stevenson: *two* Sadakos.

To effect this, Takahashi turned to an influential source of his own — H P Lovecraft, specifically 'The Shuttered Room', in which the protagonist Abner Whateley discovers that he is kin to a monstrous, half-human cousin, who years before had been locked in an upstairs room of the old manse that he has just inherited in Dunwich.

With these two threads in play, *Ring 0: Birthday* was to carve out a whole new path for Sadako to follow.

After a brief prologue set in modern-day Japan in which a teenager relates a strange dream to a friend, the action switches back to thirty years before the events of the two, or more accurately three, previous instalments. Sadako — played by nineteen-going-on-twenty year-old (she was born on 30 October) Okinawa native Yukie Nakama — is a congenitally timid but ethereally beautiful-looking young girl, who aspires to become an actress with a Tokyo repertory company. Her presence within the troupe is a cause of some mistrust among its members, however, who seem to sense instinctively that there is something threatening about her. There are murmurings. They are not wrong. "Are you still seeing strange things?" Sadako's doctor asks her.

On her trail is hard-nosed *Chuo Nippo* journalist Shoko Miyaji (Yoshiko Tanaka), notionally to write an article about her psychic abilities but, in reality, out to avenge the death of her reporter fiancé at Sadako's hands during the psychic demonstration which condemned Shizuko Yamamura as a fraud. (The rationale for Miyaji's actions is never actually made explicit in the film, but it is strongly implied.)

During a rehearsal for director Shigemori's self-penned play 'The Mask', leading actress Aiko is found dead in her chair; moments before, she had watched dumbstruck as a young girl dressed in white had walked across the stage towards her, unnoticed by those around. Shigemori decides that the show must go on, and casts Sadako in the part in Aiko's stead. Former video documentary director Norio Tsuruta, whose first feature this was, clearly gains in confidence as *Ring 0* progresses, but this early fright is badly mishandled: so brief and awkwardly-executed are the early glimpses of the girl that the viewer is hard-pressed to tell what exactly Aiko is fixated on for much of the sequence. It soon becomes clear that Sadako is being shadowed by some kind of

Top: Ring 0:
Birthday *(2000).*

doppelganger, a murderous alter ego that takes the form of a child.

While Miyaji goes about the task of establishing Sadako's guilt with respect to the deaths of all of the reporters who were present at the notorious demonstration, Sadako rehearses the play: "If I can be reborn, even if it violate the will of God itself, I would want to be by your side…" she declaims, as sound-man Toyama (Seiichi Tanabe) starts to fall madly in love with her. When the troupe's director pulls the old "I'll make you a star — I can do that" routine, and persuades Sadako to spend the night with him, a fight ensues between he and her young suitor, and Shigemori is accidentally killed. Toyama hides the body and they make ready for the first night of the new play, regardless. But Miyaji now intends to disrupt the proceedings by swapping the sound-effects tape for a recording that was made on the day of Shizuko's downfall, on which can be heard the voices of the dead reporters.

By this time, costumier Etsuko (Kumiko Aso) has also seen the 'ghost child' while sitting alone in the company dressing room, in a superlatively creepy scene that makes up for the earlier misfire with Aiko. Tsuruta does well in extracting an unsettling mood from the empty corridors and deserted ante-rooms of the theatre out-of-hours, when all breath has been drained from its outfits and where sets which were given the illusion of life with actors present are now

Ring 0:
Birthday:
Sadako
Yamamura
(Yukie Nakama).

nothing but props on a floor. To those unfamiliar with the story on which *Ring 0* was based, the script does a good job of piquing curiosity as to the exact nature of the relationship between Sadako and the little phantom, though it is made tantalisingly clear that there *is* one: "There's someone here with me," she says at length. After the debacle of *Ring 2*, the film makes a conscious attempt to reconnect itself with the mythic undertones which were present in the original; it cannot allude to the images on the latter's cursed videotape directly, for the obvious reason of its period setting (though it heralds them in the strange sounds that are heard on reel-to-reel audio tape whenever Sadako's power is activated), but in the precognitive glimpses to which she and others are subject is one which shows the figure of a man with a towel over his head, pointing out to sea. "Who is my father?" Sadako asks in voice-over.

The play goes ahead, but not for long. At Miyaji's bidding, Etsuko swaps the tapes and the anticipated theatrical effects are replaced by a cacophony of noises from the event of ten years before that the teenage Sadako thought she had forgotten: "Don't let that monster get away!" screams a voice from the past. Her brain reeling from sensory overkill, Sadako — or someone — lashes out psychically, first killing the doctor who has stepped onto the stage to help her and then bringing the fixtures crashing down. As the audience flee the place in panic and Sadako retreats to the wings, the relentless Miyaji notices another presence on the now-deserted stage. "A *second* one," she exclaims.

Sadako finds herself cornered by the others in the cast, their collective blood up at the simultaneous discovery of the body of Shigemori. She cowers before them, but

they beat her to death. "I wanted to do that," Miyaji says, arriving late on the scene.

Reviewers of *Ring 0* have pointed correctly to *Carrie* as the model for its mêlée in the theatre, but the entire theatrical set up is closer in feel to *The Phantom of the Opera* than it is to the tale by Stephen King. The *Carrie* connection is inescapable in any film with a psychic bent, but echoes of *The Phantom* proliferate: the leading actress is killed to make way for Sadako, just as the diva in *The Phantom* invariably is nobbled to let in her understudy, Christine; a lighting rig crashes onto the stage during the performance; after a moment's hesitation, the other cast members bludgeon her to death in the wings, as the pursuing crowd did to Chaney's Phantom; Sadako herself appears on-stage in a half-mask, like Lloyd Webber's musical Phantom.

The half-mask is more pertinent here: "There's another Sadako," Miyaji explains to the assemblage of self-appointed vigilantes. "If we don't kill her, we'll all die under the curse. Dr Ikuma is hiding her alter ego somewhere else." The house by the well which previously had featured in all their dreams is now their next port of call, and they find Ikuma waiting for them. (The role of Ikuma was played by sci-fi soap star Daisuke Ban throughout the series.) "Have you come to kill Sadako?" he asks.

> There was only one at first. But at some point she split into two. One took after her mother; the other one was probably like her *real* father… It drove her mother mad. All I could do was use drugs to stop the other one from growing…
>
> - **Dr Ikuma (Daisuke Ban)**, *Ring 0: Birthday* (2000)

Ring 0: Birthday:
Suzuki meets
Lovecraft in the
shuttered
Yamamura house.

At the climax of *Ring 0*, Takahashi defers once more to his mentor Lovecraft. Still in costume, the theatrical troupe are led into the woods by Miyaji to try to encircle and slay Sadako. Toyama catches up with her first, standing on a cliff edge and staring out to sea. His declaration of love leads to a sudden, offscreen demise — and a high-pitched scream stops the others in their tracks. The woods fall silent. They all stand still, hardly daring to breath, glancing fearfully around. Tsuruta holds the scene for what seems like an age until, at last, the Sadako of *Ring* can be glimpsed through the foliage, slithering by behind the trees. To the crack of a chord on the soundtrack, the first of them falls to the ground, dead; he is followed by another. With these deaths, the rest turn and flee in panic. But one by one, they are struck down until only Miyaji and Etsuko remain. They take temporary refuge in a deserted cabin nearby...

This powerful and compelling sequence borrows unashamedly from Daniel Haller's *The Dunwich Horror* (1970), in which the villagers of Arkham pursue Wilbur Whately up Sentinel Hill, where they also are picked off one by one by his invisible non-human twin. That the Japanese horror film is still as willing as it was in the days of *Godzilla* to embrace and reinvent such influences enhances rather than diminishes its contribution to the field. Screenwriter Takashashi is not merely copying a good idea but reworking it for a new generation of fans like himself. His numerous *homages* display a deep love for the genre, not a lazy, catchpenny approach, and what he has taken from *Dunwich* is not the scene, but a situation that resonates on a level of fear and incomprehension that any soldier who ever fought in a jungle would recognise only too well. Nowadays, the invisible or only partly visible enemy strikes a similar chord in society at large. Sadako is nemesis in *Ring 0* — and not to one, but to the many.

"Who is my real father?" Sadako asks of Ikuma, when the holocaust is at an end.

"I am," he replies, after a beat.

"Of course," she concedes, resigning herself to inevitable fate.

The assault on Sadako is brutal: a long, single take, in which Ikuma features in the foreground while his daughter is seated behind him, reveals that far from having given her a sedative after her ordeal, he has injected her with poison. When the pain hits, she struggles with Ikuma but manages to flee the house, gasping for air. She collapses onto the ground outside and starts to crawl towards the well, her assassin closing behind. As she clambers to her feet beside the well, Ikuma reaches for a wood-axe that lies nearby. She has time only to turn and face him. Two savage blows send her reeling backwards over the edge; Ikuma raises her lower torso into the air to complete her descent into the dark infinity below. "Forgive me, Sadako," he pleads, sobbing. (The violent realism of this scene is only undermined when we later return to Sadako in the well, and no trace of the blows can be evidenced on her forehead.)

If Sadako's earlier recovery in the back of the group's van after having been beaten to death at the theatre recalled that of coachman Gray in Robert Wise's *The Body Snatcher*, the double-twist finale where she awakes after being tumbled into the well to discover that it was all a dream and that she is back in Toyama's apartment — only for her then to wake *again* and find herself alone and bleeding at the bottom of the pit — is straight out of Terry Gilliam's *Brazil* (1985). As with the *Dunwich* sequence, all these referential nods help to weave a tapestry of such textural complexity that it transcends the material from which it is wrought. Shinichiro Ogata's incidental score was similarly complemented by the discreet inclusion in the theatrical sequences of a soulful adagio from Venetian baroque composer Tomaso Albinoni.

Variety's Derek Elley was moderately impressed: 'Taking over helming duties from Hideo Nakata, horror specialist Norio Tsuruta delivers a sustained exercise in dread and expectation throughout *Ring 0: Birthday* that wraps up the whole story without delivering the skin-crawling psycho-horror of the initial, and best, movie. Scripted again by Hiroshi Takahashi, the film necessarily ditches the killer-video paraphernalia of *Ring* and *Ring 2* for a straight-arrow horror mystery. Carefully shot, and drawing a nice sense of menace from the modern theatrical surrounding, pic never delivers any stomach-churning thrills but sustains interest throughout its fairly tight running time.'

Ring 0: Birthday is rich in imagery and imagination, and the best of the four 'Ring' films after the original by a wide margin. In many ways, it is almost a classic in its own right, as is often the case when a horror film seeks consciously to allude to genre greats from the past. *Ring* hinted at an apocalypse to come; *Ring 0* draws back

Above: The cast and crew of Ring 0: Birthday.

the veil on that apocalypse in a way that only someone versed in the modern myths of the cinema of Terror could have achieved, and that *Rasen* failed to do. *Ring* is a great film, with a climactic payoff which will stand for all time as one of the high-water marks of Terror, but for a few seconds in that deserted house on the edge of the woods, *Ring 0* tops even that. *Ring* made you shiver, but *Ring 0* gives you the creeps. Nakata's film was already regarded as a modern classic before *Ring 0: Birthday* was written, but Takahashi's and Tsuruta's *Ring 0* is the undoubted masterpiece of the series.

Ring 0: Birthday went into Japanese release on 22 January 2000, a little under six months after the opening of *Ring 2*. By the time the fourth film in the series hit theatres in the Far East, Hollywood executives had caught wind of the first. The remake rights to *Ring* were optioned by American production company DreamWorks, which discouraged its domestic owners from taking the story any further. It was now up to the Americans to propagate the curse of Sadako in any way they saw fit, and what initially they saw fit to do was to change the name and nationality of its villain.

Reviewing Nakata's original film for *Sight and Sound* in August 2000, critic Kim Newman remarked in closing, 'It's the kind of movie whose reputation spreads like the underground tape-cum-endurance test of its plot, and the malevolent but also pathetic Sadako has a real chance to become a break-out horror character.' With DreamWorks sending a flight to Tokyo with a payload of dollar bills, how right his prediction would turn out to be.

As she had desired so plaintively in her role as the scarred daughter of 'The Mask' in *Ring 0*, Sadako was now about to be reborn for real. ○

Day Five: Exhumation

Everyone will suffer…

- The Ring (2002)

They don't dream, you know. The dead don't dream, and the dead never sleep. They wait… They watch for a way to get back. My baby told me to, just like yours will tell you, and you have to do it — you have to send it back. They stopped me; don't let them stop you. You have to listen to the voices. You know what they did? They let the dead get in. They let the dead get in…

- Evelyn (Sissy Spacek), teaser trailer to *The Ring Two* (2005)

O n the face of it, Steven Spielberg's DreamWorks SKG — the production company that he formed in October 1994 with partners Jeffrey Katzenberg and David Geffen — did not appear to be the ideal home for an American remake of a subtle and scary oriental spook-fest. Better known for animation output (*Antz*, 1998; *Shrek*, 2001) or big-budget spectaculars (*Saving Private Ryan*, 1998; *Gladiator*, 2000), DreamWorks' capabilities in handling horror were as yet unproven. The supernatural shocker *What Lies Beneath* (2000), with Harrison Ford and Michelle Pfeiffer, had delivered the mood and the requisite chills, if a little too histrionically at times, but the previous year's remake of Robert Wise's *The Haunting* was an unmitigated disaster in all departments, as well as an object lesson in how *not* to make a scary movie.

The Haunting had suffered from a surfeit of CGI artists still in thrall to the limitless possibilities of the digital imaging software which had been available to them since the early 1990s, and the opportunity to turn Shirley Jackson's foreboding Hill House into a grotesque cartoon mansion where every ornate carving is imbued with a life of its own proved too much to pass up. *What Lies Beneath* managed to withhold its ghost until the final few minutes of the film, but having exhibited such admirable

restraint, the instinct of director Robert Zemeckis was then to maximise impact and get as much bang for the buck as possible out of his elaborate effect when it did eventually come.

Until the upsurge of new directorial talent during the 1970s, ghosts had never found much favour in Hollywood. The ghost, as the villain of the piece, was too tenuous, too ethereal, too wraith-like for the in-your-face approach of the average Hollywood horror film. Ghosts, by their very insubstantial nature, were fundamentally unable to spring at their victims wielding a meat cleaver, so the potential for a climactic scene of carnage in a supernatural story was always severely limited from the outset. As ever, there were notable exceptions.

Lewis Allen's *The Uninvited* (1944), from the novel of the same name by Dorothy Macardle, was one of the few films out of Hollywood before the 1970s to try to tackle the ghost story head-on. Ray Milland and Ruth Hussey's eventful domicile in a Cornish cliff-top mansion haunted by the malevolent *Rebecca*-like shade of a former tenant was more Gothic romance than Gothic horror, but it did produce a smokily-indistinct spook on the stairs during its closing moments. Discriminating Russian émigré Val Lewton's tenure as a B-movie house-producer at RKO resulted in a clutch of memorably chilling films, but only one of them — *The Curse of the Cat*

People (1944) — involved an actual ghost, and a benign and child-friendly one, at that. Even the appropriately-titled *Ghost Ship* was actually a psychological tale of creeping insanity, where the only ghosts were those in the deeply-disturbed mind of the vessel's demented captain. The word 'ghost', in Hollywood parlance, more often was employed as a euphemism for another return of a commercially-favoured monster, such as in *The Ghost of Frankenstein* (1942) or *The Mummy's Ghost* (1944), although the ghost of a hand made an engaging appearance in Robert Florey's *The Beast With Five Fingers* (1946). But its makers copped out at the end by relegating the film's spectral events to the psychotic imagination of Peter Lorre. (No such negation features in W F Harvey's original short story.)

There was more to this unwillingness to embrace the ghostly than reluctance on the part of pragmatic producers, however. Since the beginnings of cinema, the Church had taken an avid interest in depictions of the spirit world, whereas it was largely unmoved by monsters; censorship intruded upon the more serious-minded representations of the supernatural in film, which were seen to cross the dividing line of spiritual acceptability: *The Uninvited*, for example, had been deprived of its ghost on release in the UK, which led critics to praise its psychological reading of the material!

The conservative Right, which historically had wielded the power in the major studios, had therefore tended to avoid the subject of ghosts, other than to cast them as B-movie bogeymen or comic stooges to the likes of Laurel and Hardy, Bob Hope, Dean Martin and Jerry Lewis or even Bill Murray and his team of *Ghostbusters* (1984).

The scariest supernatural yarn to come out of Hollywood in the post-war years was left to a minor independent producer to direct on the cheap. Herk Harvey's *Carnival of Souls* (1962) was an inventive muse about a girl (Candace Hilligloss) who survives an automobile accident, only to find herself caught in a limbo land between life and death as a consequence. The sudden (and often startling) appearances of a Halloween-faced ghost, played by Harvey himself, obviate their technical crudity by sheer spine-tingling effectiveness, though the ending of the tale can be guessed at by anyone with a passing knowledge of Ambrose Bierce's 'An Occurrence at Owl Creek Bridge'. The other two standout ghost films of the 1960s — Jack Clayton's *The Innocents* and Robert Wise's *The Haunting* — were both made with American money but staged in Britain. American producers, for the most part, preferred to leave 'real' ghosts to the British, the Italians, or, for that matter, the Japanese.

> …Somewhere, between science and superstition, there is another world: a world of darkness…
>
> - **Trailer to** *The Exorcist* (1973)

The first American ghost of note did not arrive until 1979, after AIP purchased the rights to Jay Anson's best-seller *The Amityville Horror*. Here was a genuine haunting, alleged to have been based on a real case, though heavily indebted in truth to the theme and commercial success of *The Exorcist*. There was an *actual* ghost in the film, though it remained unseen by all except protagonist James Brolin, whose eventual possession by said spirit still harked safely back to the clichéd notion that much of what is seen to transpire could merely be 'all in the mind'. Nevertheless, the box-office bonanza which greeted *The Amityville Horror* brought a plague of malevolent spectres to American screens, from the alien-eyed and all-too-visible pirates of John Carpenter's hokey *The Fog* (1980) to the sexually-voracious but frustratingly invisible *The Entity* (1982). The best of the bunch was John Irvin's *Ghost Story* (1981), from the novel of the same name by Peter Straub, but critical antipathy deprived it of the recognition it deserved.

The gradual domination of the industry by 'indie' producers like George Lucas and Steven Spielberg, which started in the 1970s, paralleled the rise of a New Spiritualism in Hollywood, where ghosts began to be seen as something akin to friend-ly aliens, but from the dimension of the dead. The prototype for this revival of inter-est in paranormal phenomena as pseudo-scientific novelty item was Spielberg's pro-duction of *Poltergeist* (1982), directed by Tobe Hooper — a film whose concept of the supernatural would not have seemed out of place among the ectoplasmic contrivances of fairground mediums at the end of the preceding century.

Poltergeist's ghosts were engineered by Lucasfilm's Industrial Light and Magic, of pioneering *Raiders of the Lost Ark* (1981) and *Close Encounters of the Third Kind* (1977) fame; as a result, the same overweening religiosity which had infused the latter was deployed to convey them. The realm of the spirits unfolds on screen in a manner wor-thy of Cecil B De Mille, as a party of psychic investigators peer into a 'haunted' bed-room and a welter of paranormal activity greets their awe-struck gaze: a self-lighting table lamp; a record on a turntable, arm engaged; a book flipping pages — and all of it tripping an airborne fandango, like the surrealistic frenzies of a Tex Avery cartoon. *Poltergeist* did more to snuff out the Gothic flame for the remainder of the 1980s than any other supernaturally-based film; the battering-ram of increasingly persuasive technical effects was all that was needed to convert waverers to its spiritualistic philosophy. Whether it was the depiction of a female figure formed from luminescent ectoplasm or a many-hued mothership full of angelic extraterrestrials (as in *Close Encounters*), the most influential medium in the history of communication had passed into the hands of mystics with a message. *Poltergeist* led directly to the slapstick satire of *Ghostbusters*, which put paid to the idea of fearsome phantoms for the better part of two more decades. (The predictable, if belated, Japanese clone of *Poltergeist* came in 1989 and was called *Sweet Home*.)

This tambourine-banging, New Age approach to all things occult-related lasted well into the 1990s, from the romantic cliché of *Ghost* (1990) to the charismatic delirium of *What Dreams May Come* (1998) and syrupy parapsychological posturing of *The Sixth Sense*. The onset of angst with respect to the impending millennium invoked the harder edge of supernatural horror in films like *The Devil's Advocate* (1997) and *End of Days* (1999), yet the notion of spiritual terror still eluded the power-lunching players of Burbank and Santa Monica Boulevard. After an audit of the numbers from *The Blair Witch Project*, however, they came to realise that a full-blown return to the ghostly was a more effective means of frightening an audience out of its ticket money than the tired antics of cannibal retards and serial killers. Ghosts were suddenly *in*, and in a big way, from the campy, spook-saturated tirades of Dark Castle's William Castle *homages, House on Haunted Hill* (1999) and *Thir13en Ghosts* (2001), to the less visceral menace of *Stir of Echoes* (1999) and *The Others*.

There had been stirrings of a more fundamentalist response to the sham evangelism of *Poltergeist* as far back as 1989, though they were not from America. As Koji Suzuki began to formulate the details of his own tale of Terror, Britain's Channel 4 television mounted an adaptation of a book which, in its theme of a vengeful female ghost, could almost claim to have been Japanese in origin.

> And yet... she had not looked in any way — as I imagined the traditional 'ghost' was supposed to do — transparent or vaporous, she had been real, she had been there, I was certain that I could have gone up to her, addressed her, touched her.
>
> I did not believe in ghosts.
>
> What other explanation was there?
>
> - **Susan Hill**, *The Woman in Black* (1983)

The Woman in
Black *(1989).*

In novel form, Susan Hill's *The Woman in Black* was a return to the great tradition of ghostly fiction inaugurated by M R James, to whom its author alludes at the beginning by advising the reader that hers is *not* a tale for telling at Christmas. The television version was scripted by *Quatermass* creator Nigel Kneale and was faithful to the novel in every particular, save where it sought to highlight events for visual effect. The grimly skeletal 'woman in black' is one Jennet Eliza Humfrye, whose shade comes to haunt solicitor's clerk Arthur Kipps when he is dispatched to the isolated Eel Marsh House to settle the affairs of a Mrs Drablow. As the house is situated along a causeway that floods at high tide, Kipps is forced to spend the night there, alone. Kneale plays this classic situation for all it is worth and, in *The Woman in Black*, it is worth a great deal. But the biggest shock is kept for Kipps' return from his terrifying ordeal: awakened from a fitful sleep, he is made aware of a movement at the bottom of his bed. A doll. As he picks it up, the ghastly figure of the woman appears and lunges towards him — closer… closer, till he is almost smothered in her hideous gaze…

 The Woman in Black had presented its audience with a resoundingly modern ghost, while managing to remain true to the conventions of the genre. The intimidating Jennet Humfrye was no trick of the light — no hazy shadow in a corner. She appeared to be as real as those on whom she preyed. This Jamesian motif of false perception is what fed

The Ring *(2002):*
Samara Morgan
(Daveigh Chase).

into Takahashi's script for *Ring*. But it was the sheer scale of the financial return from *The Blair Witch Project*, with its considerably less substantial 'ghost', that first caused Hollywood accountants to sit up and take notice of a potential new wave in the cinema of Terror. When they did, they plunged into it with a vengeance.

The stalk-and-slash thrillers which had reigned supreme for over two decades were forced to retreat into the backwoods of *Jeepers Creepers* (2001), *Cabin Fever* (2002) and *Wrong Turn* (2003) and, by 2002, the new horror boom was moving at such a pace that demand outstripped the supply of original ideas from traditional sources. Most of Stephen King's oeuvre had been filmed already during the preceding twenty-five years, and the works of Anne Rice had shown themselves to have limited niche market appeal, even when featuring Tom Cruise. No such dearth of imagination afflicted the film-makers of Japan, however, and the decision was taken to test the box-office water with a straight remake of the *other* movie which had started it all — on the other side of the globe.

After seeing Nakata's film during its original Japanese run, Mike Macari, a creative executive with production company New Line Cinema, had spent the best part of two years trying to interest his bosses in the idea of a remake. When that failed, Macari left New Line's 'Fine Line' sub-division armed with his 'Ring' idea and with the intention of becoming an independent producer by shopping it around

Macari showed *Ring* to Roy Lee, co-founder of Vertigo Entertainment, which acts as an intermediary in the sale of remake rights to Asian films. Lee, in turn, showed it to DreamWorks' executive Mark Sourian, who immediately arranged a screening for the company's joint heads, producers Walter F Parkes and spouse Laurie MacDonald. "Mark said, 'I've just seen the scariest movie I've ever seen in my life. You have to see it right away'," Parkes recalled. "Laurie and I cancelled everything and watched the movie on video which, come to think of it, was appropriate for this. We were both frightened and mesmerised by it, and immediately decided we wanted to remake it."

"We felt from the beginning that it was a strong idea, and the Japanese movie gave us a great template, not just in the premise, but tonally," MacDonald added. "Another of the movie's strengths was its wonderfully incongruous marriage of a kind of pop teenage story with a high concept that revealed itself in a very surprising way — more mysterious, more evocative, and with underlying emotional issues that you wouldn't necessarily expect from the genre."

Parkes went on to enthuse: "It was a very vivid and easily-understandable concept about a videotape that caused the death of its viewer within seven days. But the Japanese original transcended that and had interesting characters. It was also about this emotionally-detached mother, so there was the potential evolution for this other story. Finally, that sequence in the original where the woman emerges from the TV set was as frightening as anything I'd ever seen. It was the concept and the potential for exploring characters in more depth, combined with this indelible final image that made it a very appealing project."

By January 2001, *Ring* had caught the interest both of DreamWorks and the Walt Disney Corporation, who entered into a bidding war for the rights. The personal commitment of Parkes and MacDonald carried the day, however, and the deal was done. "This was probably the quickest process from acquisition to release that I have ever been involved in," Parkes said. "We watched the movie from 4pm to 6pm in the afternoon, and by 7pm we had paid $1 million for the remake rights."

In the process, Dreamworks picked up the North American distribution rights to the original film, which it planned to shelve until after the remake had opened; a reciprocal arrangement gave Asmik Ace and Kadokawa Shoten distribution rights to the remake in Japan, as well as a share of the profits. According to Patrick Frater and Jeremy Kay of *Screen International*, the deal was worth $20 million to Kadokawa Shoten alone.

Despite claiming that he had found the concept of the film 'easily understandable', Parkes felt that part of it was 'elusive or downright confusing'. "It embraces ambiguity in a way that American audiences aren't really used to," he told Frater and Kay, before appearing to contradict himself again. "This creates an interesting tension.

We thought it would be prudent not to overly-Americanise the movie."

In his new role as producer of *Ring* (along with Macari), Parkes' next move was to appoint a director and a screenwriter who could straighten out some of the ambiguities which he considered were present in the original. One name that sprang easily to mind for the role of director was that of Tennessee-born Gore Verbinski, who had started out his career by playing guitar with punk bands Little Kings and The Daredevils, the latter of them alongside Brett Gurewitz of Bad Religion. Verbinski had directed *Mouse Hunt* for DreamWorks in 1997, and he had recently completed *The Mexican* (2001) with Brad Pitt; more pertinently, however, he had stepped in to rescue the Parkes-produced *The Time Machine* (2002) when its director Simon Wells was forced to pull out due to exhaustion. "The main reason we chose Gore was that he is a consummate visualist," Parkes qualified. "Having worked with him before, we felt his sensibility was right for this and that he would be intrigued by both the story possibilities and the visual possibilities. He has the expertise and the artistry to create images that in and of themselves can involve you and truly scare you."

Verbinski accepted the assignment and ramped up enthusiasm for the project with a little mythologising of his own: "The first time I watched the original *Ring* was on a VHS tape that was probably seven generations down. It was really poor quality but, actually, that added to the mystique, especially when I realised that this was a movie about a videotape. There's something about that image of a seemingly innocuous videotape… just sitting there, unlabeled. If you're aware of the myth, the object itself becomes both tempting and haunting."

To provide the script, Parkes turned to New York University Film School graduate Ehren Kruger, writer of *Arlington Road* (1999) and *Reindeer Games* (2000). Kruger's previous experience in the horror genre stretched only as far as having stepped in at the last minute to churn out a screenplay for Wes Craven's *Scream 3* (also 2000) but, hey, this is Hollywood. "I'd heard about *Ring* on the underground circuit and had found it at a local video store," Kruger explained to Den Shewman of *Creative Screenwriting*. "It was one of those few movies that stuck with me; I kept thinking about it as I was going to sleep. A month after that, DreamWorks called and said they'd secured the rights and were looking for a writer. I said, 'I'll do it!'"

"I watched the original film about three times, then I put it down and didn't go back to it. I didn't look at the source novel, but I did look at the sequels to the original film to see what light they shed on the back story. Then I went to work on breaking down a structure for it, operating on the assumption that I wouldn't change anything unless there was a consensus that it really needed to be changed."

From the resultant script, it would seem that such consensus was being arrived at on a fairly regular basis. Nevertheless, Kruger continued on with his theories on the

The Ring: *advertising logo.*

Ehren Kruger.

nature of plot construction in relation to oriental mystery-thrillers:

"It was a very interesting process to explore the differences between Japanese and American culture. We have different tolerances for ambiguity; different icons and ideas of spirituality, or ghosts, or the supernatural. If you compare the mainstream American audience to the mainstream Japanese audience, probably a little different tolerance for pacing as well. As far as structural changes between this story and the original, most of the differences come in the middle hour of the movie. This is very much a film that grabs you at the opening, and says that something terrible needs to be averted by the end of the movie. Everybody knows that whatever that mystery is, it's not going to be solved for another hour and a half. It takes work and craft to make the story build tension in a delicious way, such that the audience doesn't go for popcorn. You know where you need to get to, so you break down interesting ways to get there. This story is operating on two levels: one of pure plot (a mystery to solve), and another of character and how this dangerous situation is bringing the characters either closer together or rending them apart. Because it's also a horror film, there have to be some frightening things in the second act. As long as you have some levels in there, you go the usual screenwriting route: what's the obvious thing that would happen next? Then, knowing that, let's try something not quite so obvious..."

The remake was differentiated from *Ring* by the appending of the prefix 'The', and the visual tag of an actual circle of light on promotional items — not that there was any need for differentiation on its home turf, where DVD and video releases of the original were held up by DreamWorks in any event, until after its own version of the film had run its course. Changes to the storyline of *The Ring* were more substantial, however, despite Kruger's insistence about how reverential he had been in his handling of the material. "I came in and said that I'd treat the original with kid gloves; that if it's not broken, don't try to fix it," he had reiterated to Shewman. "That was along the same line of thinking as the executives at DreamWorks. They attached the director, Gore Verbinksi, at about the same time, before I started writing, and that was his feeling as well. We all seemed to be on the same page — which is not to say that it was an *easy* job. Just because you come in and say that you're not going to rework the underlying material, don't let that mislead you into thinking that it's going to be a cakewalk of an adaptation. You fight over everything."

The decision was taken at the outset to set the film in America and merely transpose the plot, but this proved less straightforward than it might originally have seemed. The Japanese elements of *Ring* are integral to the whole and contribute strongly towards the mythic undertones of the story; to remove them was to deprive Sadako of a greater part of her power as a Gothic monster, whose corporeal form lies not dead but sleeping in a dank, underground cavern near a mysterious volcanic isle.

Nevertheless, Kruger set about devising a new back story for Sadako, whose name he changed to a more acceptably Western-sounding (though Arabic in origin) 'Samara', in place of that which Suzuki had researched so scrupulously. (Samara is also the name of a river-region in Russia, formerly known as Kuibyshev.)

"There were a lot of discussions of what precisely the nature of the videotape should be. The central conceit of the film is the videotape that kills you when you watch it, so for the first act of the story there was a lot of suspense about what exactly is *on* that tape. When I first saw the original film — and I didn't know anything about it other than there was a videotape that killed you if you watched it — I said to myself, 'That must be a scary videotape'. For all I knew, you weren't going to see what was on it until the end of the movie. As it turns out, the heroine sees it pretty much at the end of the first act. So for that first act, there's a lot of suspense about what's on there. In the Japanese film, it's very strange imagery, but every image plays an expository role; every image is explained (more or less). I thought it would be nice, and Gore felt the same way, if the videotape was a little less straightforward in our version. If there were a way to make it a little more frightening, in that everything that's on it doesn't necessarily have a correlation in the story. There are some ambiguous, bizarre, obscure things, in an experimental way. That was something that we had to fight for."

It can be read from Kruger's remarks that differences in approach to the

American version of *Ring* had surfaced even before the shooting began. Its producer wanted less obfuscation and more clarity in the narrative, while its writer wanted to obscure aspects which were perfectly clear to begin with. The problem with their respective analyses is that the curse operates to a dream logic — it is the *result* of it that is inexplicable in real terms. Parkes and Kruger had opted to go in the opposite direction to the original film on both these counts, which is to say that they decided to make the imagery on the tape *less* explicable while making the path to its solution more logical. But by disassociating the video from the events of Samara's life, and rendering its images irrelevant, the tape is reduced to the status of mere device whose mechanics theoretically can be unpicked. Nakata's *Ring* had taken the other route: the curse itself essentially is deconstructable, with research and a little legwork; what is less easily fathomable is *why* it does what it does. This is where the supernatural element of the story comes in, and this is what the makers of *The Ring* quite failed to grasp from the off.

Verbinski himself was keen to maintain more of this elliptical element than some of those around him: "The Western desire for linearity and resolution are so destructive to a film like this. It's hard to fight against that and still keep the audience interested. To me, *The Ring* is about the lack of conclusion. This is something that a Western audience is going to have a difficult time swallowing." The debate about how much to elucidate and how much to leave to the imagination of the audience went on into the shooting, by which time DreamWorks had handed a revised third draft of Kruger's screenplay over to script doctor-in-residence Scott Frank (the Academy Award-nominated screenwriter of *Out of Sight*, 1998) to add more depth and humour to the still-thin characterisations of the principals. "The film went into production without a locked script," Verbinski told Javier Lopez. "We worked on it right though production. Ehren Kruger wrote the first three passes and we worked together very well. Scott Frank came on later to do the polish. I admire Scott's writing, but we had very little contact as I was shooting by this time. Much of the visual work was never put on the page because it just wouldn't read as well as it appeared, so I was working from my visual notebook rather than the script for a lot of the film. The story is very similar to the original with a few surprises, and I think we all felt good about where we were going…"

> When I was making *The Ring*, I was like — 'We're doing the shot of the
> doorknob turning! I can't believe it! Couldn't you think of something a
> little more original? I felt embarrassed because it's in a thousand other
> people's movies…
>
> **- Gore Verbinski interviewed in *SFX* (2002)**

The name of the protagonist had also been changed from Reiko Asakawa to Rachel Keller, though this was more understandable. Jennifer Connelly, Gwyneth Paltrow and Kate Beckinsale were all considered, but in line with the fact that the script was being penned by the writer of *Scream 3*, favourite for the role in Parkes' eyes was *Scream* heroine Drew Barrymore, who had since become much better known as Dylan Sanders, one of *Charlie's Angels*. Barrymore was more than bankable, but Macari preferred the idea of a less high-profile leading lady and suggested Naomi Watts instead.

Formerly a native of Kent before moving with her family to Australia at the age of fourteen, the thirty-two year-old Watts was riding the crest of a career wave after ten years of largely inauspicious appearances, including two in previous horrors: *Children of the Corn IV: The Gathering* (1996) and BBC TV's Hammeresque adaptation of Sheridan Le Fanu's *The Wyvern Mystery* (2000). Her overnight elevation to the A-list had come about after her stunning virtuoso performance in cult director David Lynch's dark and discordant *Mulholland Drive* (2001), which had been co-produced by Macari's business partner Neal Edelstein. Verbinski took little convincing. "I saw *Mulholland Drive* and immediately responded to her performance," he said. "I think

Rachel is a tough role, and Naomi is a very gutsy actress."

"What Rachel Keller has to go through has to do with not only her own survival, but also that of her child," Parkes concurred. "As a result, the part demands some very intense, very real, acting moments. Naomi has the ability to be extraordinarily intense, yet she delivers those moments in a way audiences will be able to relate to."

Watts joined in the promotional jamboree. "This is definitely a genre film, but what I think sets it apart is that the story is very clean, very straightforward and moves with a lot of momentum. You watch this video — which is incredibly scary on its own — then the phone rings and you're told you have seven days to live. Right there, that one sentence sets up the kind of suspense that makes your skin crawl and the hair stand up on the back of your neck."

Next, the film-makers expounded on their theories about fear — what evokes it; how best to impart that to an audience...

Kruger kicked off in rhetorical mode: "How do you tell a story that dabbles in the supernatural in a realistic way so that it's going to get under people's skin? It's a tricky knife-edge to walk, but all the really successful horror films — like *Rosemary's*

Baby (1968) or *Don't Look Now* or even *The Shining* (1980) — are able to do that. They're patently fanciful stories and on one level totally ridiculous, but they treat the material with such realism that the audience is sucked in and can experience that delicious fear in the theatre.

"*Ring* plugs into the age-old theme of Pandora's Box and the Garden of Eden and temptation. When someone says 'Don't look at this!' you only want to look at it all the more. In this case, Rachel goes looking for what she hopes she'll find and suddenly has cause to believe that she should never have been looking in the first place. That plugs into something very universal about human nature. In that sense, this movie's a very simple story, but it's operating on this psychotic theme. Hopefully, the audience will find it to be on a personal, intimate scale for something very frightening. It's a tricky film because what makes it effective is, at the end of the day, this sense that evil exists, and evil is not always so easily vanquished. If you take that away — end the story on a note where evil is easily vanquished — you're taking away much of the effectiveness of the movie and, I would posit, most horror movies."

Gore Verbinski picked up Kruger's thread: "I'm a big fan of horror films, but there are the ones that simply shock you and there are those that operate more subversively. These have a particular psychological manipulation going on that the viewer is not completely aware of. When they work, there can be a tremendous residual effect; those films stay with you longer, because they get under your skin. Horror films essentially are derived from a very simple premise, as it is in our film. It's only in the execution that certain films elevate themselves beyond the genre. These are the ones that inspire me because they scare me the most. Ultimately, it's about the craft.

"The tape had to serve two functions," he continued. "It had to contain clues to its origin and to understanding why it was created. As abstract as it might appear at first viewing, those images had to have a reason to be. The video also had to be bizarre, to shock without seeming to have been designed to do so. I started with some of the key images from the Japanese film, because when you remake a movie, you want to keep the great moments from the original. Then I drew on what scared me — my own kind of horrors, and I tried to include them in a way that was compelling but could also make sense from the perspective of the person who made the video..."

This sudden air of expertise on the art of horror among all those involved with *The Ring* was in danger of becoming infectious. "One of the things I first loved about the project was the title," Parkes injected. "Within the context of the movie, it could have a number of different meanings: the ringing of the telephone, the ominous image of an eclipse-like ring of light, or perhaps it's the circular storyline that leads you back to the beginning..."

"Our journey begins with a videotape that comes with a warning. Yet, it is the very warning that makes it all the more interesting to us," Verbinski summarised. "Taboos are always accompanied by temptation; it's an essential quality of human nature — to discover the forbidden. Knowing this about us is what makes the evil essence of *The Ring* all the more horrifying."

After the hype, came the celebrity interviews.

For Alana Lee of the BBC, Watts offered the following: "In *Mulholland Drive*, I played two characters that weren't based on any reality and were very extreme people. I felt that this character, Rachel Keller, was very ordinary, even though she's presented with extraordinary circumstances. She's a normal person who's just a mother and to her, everything is okay. Life is just dandy. Then this horrible thing comes into her life and she's forced to question her sanity. It seems completely implausible, and then the journalist part of her goes out the window and it becomes about survival for her and for her family. It's pretty intense.

"When she discovers her son has watched this videotape, that's when it brings out all sorts of guilt. She's thinking, 'I should have been a better mother. What can I do to protect my child?' And that's it. So, basically, this is more than just a horror film. For me, it's a psychological journey she has to go through.

"I had about a week of rehearsal and that was my preparation. It was a huge movie and things like costume-changes took precedence over any acting preparation. But fear is a pretty simple emotion to play, so imagination was really my key."

For the official press release, Watts' co-star Martin Henderson adopted a suitably sombre tone: "I thought [the screenplay] was extremely scary, and every time I read it, I became more aware of the little subliminal things that you don't notice at first. I think that's the beauty of this movie — you don't know where the evil is coming from. There are images on the tape and, as the movie progresses, you begin to see the connection and understand the origin. Hopefully, the audience will be taken on that ride." He was a little more sanguine when he chatted with the BBC's Neil Davey, however: "Most horror films fail to scare me. I think *The Ring* plays more as a psychological thriller. It's smarter, there's more character development, and some of the themes explored go a little deeper. I realised that, done well, this could be a pretty great film." And the atmosphere on the set? "A lot of the scare factor comes with the editing, the effects, and the music. There were moments when Naomi and I would look at each other and say, 'This is embarrassing; people are going to laugh.' You just hope that somebody makes it scary or you're going to look like an idiot!"

"I thought it was a great yarn — a real page turner," countered Dundee native Brian Cox, the screen's first Hannibal Lecter (*Manhunter*, 1986) and herein cast as the father of Samara. "I was intrigued by where it was going... the twists and turns in the story. That's basically what makes a good script in my opinion." To which the film's

director felt obliged to reciprocate, "From the very start, I had Brian Cox in mind for *Above:* The Ring. the role. I couldn't imagine the part being played by anyone else."

Following on such effusion, all that was left was *The Ring* itself...

The Ring

Seattle, Washington State.

A *Scream*-like start, as the camera closes in on a house where two teenagers, Katie (Amber Tamblyn) and Becca (Rachael Bella), make small-talk in one of the bedrooms: "Have you heard about the videotape that kills you when you watch it?" Becca asks. "You start to play it, and its like somebody's nightmare. Then suddenly, this woman comes on, smiling at you, right? Seeing you... through the screen. And as soon as it's over, your phone rings. Someone knows you've watched it. And what they say is: you'll die in seven days. And exactly seven days later..."

"There really is a tape," Katie replies, revealing that she has seen it, then she makes the confession out to have been a joke. The two friends rib each other for taking such a

preposterous idea so seriously and Katie goes down to the kitchen to fetch a drink. But she *has* seen the video. Seven days earlier.

In an adjacent room, a television set bursts into life. Katie is puzzled, switches it off with the remote, and returns upstairs. But Becca is not responding to her cries. As she reaches the hallway, she notices a pool of water on the floor outside her room. We see, though she cannot, a reflection on the paintwork at the base of the door which indicates that her own set is now switched on. She opens the door... The camera zooms in fast on her face as she opens her mouth to scream... (Unlike the Japanese version, the presence of the supernatural in this sequence is not so much hinted at as laid on with a trowel — a digitally-created 'ripple' pulses across the screen of the television set as Katie jerks the plug from the wall; ominous music wells up on the track; the upstairs hall is swimming in water, up to and including the handle of her bedroom door.)

Reporter Rachel Keller (Watts) has been consoling her son Aidan (David Dorfman) about the sudden death of his cousin Katie, three days earlier. His school-teacher draws Rachel's attention to the fact that he has been making macabre sketches of Katie's dead body. Rachel dismisses her concerns, until his teacher reveals that he drew the pictures more than a week before. (More ominous music.)

Given the fondness of American film-makers for the antics of precocious preteens, the role of Asakawa's son in the original (which even doting dad Koji Suzuki had downplayed in the novel to the level of a narrative ploy) presented screenwriter Kruger with a golden opportunity to craft Rachel's son Aidan into a version of Cole Sear from M Night Shayamalan's *The Sixth Sense* and have him become telepathically 'aware' of Samara's presence. The idea was really imported from Nakata's *Ring 2*, where the boy develops a psychic link with the ghostly girl, but it serves only to point up the obvious in *The Ring*. The script stops just short of having Aidan say, 'I see dead *females*,' but it comes perilously close. Subtle changes of emphasis like this are immediately troubling in Verbinski's version; almost before the plot has got underway, Kruger already looks as though he is beginning to lose it.

Rain and gloom, and the day of the funeral. Katie's mother asks Rachel to come up with an answer to account for the fact that her teenage daughter's heart 'just stopped'. In the middle of the exchange, Verbinski inserts a cutaway to the discovery of Katie's body in the bedroom closet. The features are ghastly; the dead head lolls forward onto the chest. (A subsequent conversation between the two reprised this cutaway in slightly more detail, but it was excised from the film prior to release.) As in *Ring*, Rachel now gleans most of the relevant information regarding the video, the three other deaths, and the stay in the resort cabin from a clutch of Katie's schoolfriends sharing a joint in the garden. Without further ado, she heads off to Shelter Mountain Inn. Almost before she has handed over her Amex card to pay for her stay, she has spotted the video. There is no exchange of dialogue with the manager; she merely drops it into her bag and heads towards the nearest VCR. The rain has temporarily eased, which allows us to focus for a moment on the red leaves of an incongruous Japanese maple on the hillside above the dilapidated cabin. (The cabin number is twelve and not B4 in *The Ring*, in a self-conscious nod to Hitchcock's *Psycho*.) Rachel slams the tape into the machine and instantly, the image of a ring of light appears on the screen. She stares at it, entranced.

The images on the videotape in *The Ring* were created by the Hollywood FX house of Method Studios, which specialises in commercials. Like those in earlier versions of the tale, they divide into two categories — but not the *same* two categories. The images chosen by Verbinski only partially relate to the curse; many of them relate arbitrarily to the narrative in general, as seen through Rachel's own eyes. The logic of this is that the tape would have to alter its content to suit the perceptions of individual viewers. Ergo, there is *no* logic to this. While the images are shown subsequently to parallel incidents which occur during Rachel's quest, the same could not have applied to Katie or any of her friends. As the film also seems curiously intent on referencing Hitchcock, the video in *The Ring* appears to share more in common with the dream sequence in *Spellbound* (1945) than it does with either Suzuki or Nakata.

Above: The Ring: *the 'cursed' video.*

Be that as it may, they break down as follows:

A thick swirl of blood. A wooden chair in an otherwise empty room. The teeth of a comb gliding down long, dark hair in close-up. The familiar shot of the mother-figure, combing her hair in the mirror; she looks at the camera, then to the side. Another figure appears in the mirror; she is younger, enclosed by shadow. A series of more subliminal shots succeeds this last: an upright needle with blood running down it; the outside of a house, with the figure of a man at an upstairs window; a view over a cliff-edge, with a house-fly crawling across the upper right-hand corner of the image; what appears to be a length of intestine telescoping out of an open mouth; a black plastic bag in close-up, a cover sliding into place over a well, as seen from beneath; the maple tree on fire; the tip of a finger being lowered onto the needle…

At this point, there is cut back to Rachel as she grimaces.

We return to the screen. It is filled with maggots, wriggling around. There is a chair by a table, on which is placed a glass of water; an unrealistically-large millipede snakes into view from underneath it. There is a glimpse of a goat in a stable; a close-up of the eye of a horse. The cover slides further across the mouth of the well. A box (rather too obviously produced by 3D modelling) features next, in which lie seven severed fingers. The flaming maple again; the black bag again. The mother looking at camera. The shot of the house, with the upstairs room vacated. The wooden chair spinning like a top, but upside down. A ladder leaning against a wall. A moody shot of dead horses on a beach. The woman again, seen from the rear, falling gracefully from the edge of the cliff. The ladder again, also falling. The cover pushed home, leaving a halo of light… The ladder hitting the ground… Finally, the well itself. Static.

(Several of these images are *never* explained in the extant print, as the references to them were deleted after the first test screenings. Among those left hanging are the goat and the maggots. The first was alluded to along the route of Rachel's investigation, but the maggots made their appearance when Noah turned up at the Shelter Mountain Inn, where he discovered the manager lying dead in a canoe; moving a scrap of paper in the man's office, he finds the table swarming with maggots. [The scene was similar to that in Episode 1 of *Ring: The Final Chapter*.])

As reaction shots of Rachel are intercut with more mood shots of scudding clouds, and the rain returns to pound at the bleak landscape outside the cabin. The

phone rings. For the first and only time in the entire saga, a voice is heard on the other end. "Seven days," it warns. Rachel flees the scene, as rain continues to thunder down…

Above: The Ring: *Noah Clay (Martin Henderson) and Rachel Keller.*

Screen caption: Day 1.

The next shot is a straight *homage* to Nakata, as Aidan meets Noah (Henderson) on his way to school. Rachel has called on her ex-lover (and Aiden's father) for help, and he watches the tape with familiar disdain for all things weird and wacko. She takes it to the audio-visual research room at her office building, to make him a copy and examine it more closely for herself. Her curiosity is piqued by the fly on the shot of the cliff.

Day Two passes relatively uneventfully: Noah establishes that the tape has no 'control track', which militates against it having been produced on a machine. (Nothing further is developed along this line of reasoning.)

By Day Three, Rachel is visiting Becca, who has been institutionalised as a result of the trauma that she experienced when her friend Katie died. A lift from *Ring 2* sees Becca being led along a hospital corridor behind a screen, to prevent her catching sight of the television in the patients' lounge. (There is no pay-off to this scene, and Becca merely intimates to Rachel her own knowledge of the latter's impending fate.) While

printing off some frame-grabs from the tape, Rachel spots a lighthouse in one of the shots. She also becomes increasingly fascinated with the 'fly'. For no sane reason, she reaches out to extract it from the screen; it comes away in her fingers, apparently *through* the glass. She stares at the insect, and her nose begins to bleed…

Day Four, and Rachel is trawling archives of newspaper cuttings. In no time at all, she has the solution to much of what can be discerned on the tape: the woman in the mirror is Anna Morgan (Shannon Cochran), wife of Richard Morgan (Cox), who together had owned a prosperous horse farm on the remote Moesko Island.

The producers of *The Ring* were presented with the same problem as those of South Korea's *The Ring Virus* when it came to Samara's birthplace — no volcano and, in their case, no island either (unless one counts Catalina). Setting the film in Washington State gave them the choice of both, but not together. Mount St Helen's is certainly an active volcano, and the Strait of Juan de Fuca between Seattle and Vancouver Island is filled with more of the same, large and small. In the end, it was decided that the easier route would be to fabricate a fictional island, rather than alter the timeline to suit the eruptive whims of a real volcano. (A little *Blair Witch* veracity was incorporated into the scene by having Rachel check out Moesko in Francis Ross Holland's *America's Lighthouses: An Illustrated History*, which itself is a real volume; the lighthouse that acted as model for the one in the film is the Yaquina Head lighthouse, situated in Newport, Oregon.)

More archives, more research, and the entire story is nailed: the Morgans' live-stock was struck by a mystery illness and had to be destroyed. Anna then committed suicide by throwing herself off a cliff; husband Richard is alive, however, living like a recluse on what remains of his farm.

Day Five. Via the mechanism of the warped photographic image, Noah has now been convinced of the truth of the curse. This is just as well, as there are only two days to go and his son has been encouraged by a voice in his head to watch the video for himself. (Rachel has also experienced her first psychic shock in prelude to this incident, which included a glimpse of Samara and an intimation of psychiatric rehab.)

Day Six. My, how time flies when a Hollywood scriptwriter wants to jettison as much exposition as possible. All her recent research has led Rachel to a startling conclusion: "I think… before you die, you see the ring," she tells Noah, before heading for the ferry and Moesko Island on her own.

At this juncture, *The Ring* is only minutes past its midway point, despite almost six of the allotted seven days of the curse having already expired. Kruger clearly felt that a greater sense of tension would be generated in the audience if all the critical action was crammed into the last day, presumably operating to his previously stated principle that 'everybody knows that whatever that mystery is, it's not going to be

Opposite: The Ring: *Aidan Keller (David Dorfman) and his mother.*

solved for another hour and a half'. He had therefore chosen to split the film into two halves, with the first covering a period of approximately ten days and the second, a mere twenty-four hours, whereas *Ring* had been constructed to a more linear time-frame. Hideo Nakata had been a guest on set and the two had disagreed about this change in the pace of the narrative. "I don't want to say he didn't like it," Kruger remarked, "but it wasn't quite his sense of how he would pace the story."

Another concern on reaching the halfway point in American movies is the matter of audience attention-span, and an action set-piece is often thought to be needed to shake awake any who might have dozed off in the meantime. Observing that rule to the letter, *The Ring* now injects a ludicrous sequence on board the ferry, in which a thoroughbred stallion, sensing something untoward about Rachel, bolts from its box, charges the full length of the car deck, and leaps over the side of the ship to meet a messy end under its propellors. (The swirl of blood in the video.) This might have provided some action for the trailer, but it sure as hell adds nothing at all to the plot.

The salient point of the scene had been delivered moments earlier. Still clutching a handful of press cuttings, Rachel hones in on one in particular. "She had a daughter…" she says to herself, in respect of Anna Morgan. And the rain comes down…

On Rachel's arrival at the Morgan farm, another constructive ploy swings into play: Verbinski intercuts two separate investigations — that of Rachel and her encounter with the mysterious Richard Morgan and Noah's attempts to prise Samara's medical records out of the psychiatric hospital which had treated her mother. Tension in the first comes from the potential unpredictability of the burly Morgan when he discovers that Rachel has the video ("Where did you get that? Is that the only one?" he demands), while in the second, it devolves to whether or not Noah will succeed in his clandestine pursuits. Any notion of suspense at this point in *The Ring* has been reduced to a level of concern for personal welfare — audience anxiety in relation to either party's imminent demise is almost entirely absent.

(Given that Gore Verbinski chooses to include several visual allusions to the films of Alfred Hitchcock in *The Ring*, it is worth noting the difference in approach between the two. The 'Master of Suspense' never lost sight of the concept of *predicament*, and his classic set-pieces of suspense were invariably tied to the central theme of the film in question, usually in terms of delaying or denying a desired outcome. The central theme of *The Ring* is whether or not the protagonists will survive the seven-day deadline of death, and yet there is no 'countdown clock', no sense of time passing, no expression of stress or anxiety as the fateful hour approaches. Instead, the film offers the threat of violence against the person [a runaway horse; the psychotic Morgan], or the threat of discovery while engaged in a crime [Noah's breaking-and-entering], none of which matter a jot in the prevailing circumstances. Were Hitchcock to have directed

The Ring, the end result would have been closer to the Nakata version. Verbinski and Kruger might be schooled in film theory, but Hitchcock and Hideo Nakata both came up the hard way.)

"I don't have a daughter," Morgan tells Rachel eventually and shows her the door, but not before she has established the house as the one which features in the video. She phones Aidan, who has been spending his time obsessively sketching rings; a 'girl' has been invading his thoughts — confiding in him, he reveals. "She doesn't like the barn," he says. "The horses keep her awake at night. She lives in a dark place now..."

Enter the formula staple of the wise shaman. Local doctor, in this instance. Grasnik by name, and played by Jane Alexander (who was hired to provide belated exposition after initial test screenings had left audiences in the dark). Rachel unburdens herself. "I don't know how to say this, but I'm seeing things. In my head. Images. And so's my son... my son; that's why I'm here. And somehow — I don't know how — but it's because of that girl."

Dr Grasnik understands only too well. She promptly relates the tale of the Morgans and their curious child. "One winter they went away and when they came back, it was with Samara. Adopted they said — never did say from where — said the mother died of complications. But they had their baby, they had their horses, everything was fine. Till Anna started coming to see me. Said *she* was suffering visions. Seeing things — horrible things — like they'd been burned inside her. That it only happened around Samara. That the girl put them there..."

Noah, meanwhile, has turned up a series of photographic negatives in the basement of the hospital that appear to have been created by *nensha*, or 'thoughtography', as per those in *The Ring Virus*. But the videotape recording of Samara's time at the hospital is missing, logged out to Morgan.

Back at the Morgan ranch, Rachel has found the missing tape of Samara's sessions with her psychiatrist which Richard Morgan has left conveniently laced up in his VCR: this provides us with our first real glimpse of Samara, played by eleven year-old Daveigh Chase, who previously had put in appearances in Spielberg's *Artificial Intelligence: AI* and Richard Kelly's *Donnie Darko* (both 2001) among others, in addition to providing the voice of Lilo for Disney's *Lilo and Stitch* (2002). *The Ring*'s Samara is therefore a curious miniature of Sadako, with the same white dress and long, black hair — but more of a Damien Thorn for the new age, in truth. The hospital tape reveals the nature of her evil: it is nothing more than that — *evil*. Unreasoning and inexplicable. A signal change from the Sadako of Suzuki's novel or Nakata's film. Victim has become victimiser in the switch of cultural myths. "I don't make them. I *see* them," the film's eight-year-old psychic tells her shrink for the record in respect of the 'thoughtographs'.

Opposite: The Ring.

Rachel squats before the television; she now has most of the answers that she seeks. Verbinski sets up this scene so that the viewer can see Rachel's face as she watches the tape; behind her, the rest of the room is in darkness, illuminated at intervals by a sweep of the lamp of the nearby lighthouse. He cuts away to the image on the screen and then back to a view of Rachel from a slightly different angle. This time, however, the figure of Morgan can be seen standing behind her, in the embrace of the beam. Not only is this shock-cut predictable, it is clumsily staged. And it points up the fundamental difference between the Japanese and American approaches to this kind of material. Had Nakata or any of his peers directed the same scene, there would have been no cutaway back to the television; instead, he would have stayed with the shot of Rachel and the burst of illumination at her back until the viewer was off guard, then the figure of Morgan would have been introduced into the frame almost imperceptibly, so that awareness of his presence was gradual and, ultimately, much more frightening.

Morgan knocks Rachel to the ground and takes himself off to a bathroom clutching an intricate array of electrical equipment, where he commits one of the most elaborate suicides ever put on film in deference to the climax of *Ring 2*. (An electric fan thrown into the water would have done the job just as well, and most of his convulsions ended up on the cutting-room floor, in any event.)

At this precise moment, Noah arrives at the ranch to steady Rachel's frayed nerves. How come? From where? Rachel recalls Aidan's cryptic message on the phone: "She doesn't like the barn…" They head over to a large barn in the grounds, within which they find a ladder to an inner chamber where Samara had been kept a prisoner by her father. "He kept her here alone," Rachel observes. Noah nods to the small television set in the corner of the makeshift room. "Not alone," he replies. (This extrapolation of cause and effect in relation to the cursed *video*, not to mention Samara's fatal fascination with TV sets, is the one significant improvement which *The Ring* makes over previous versions of the story — even though the whole elaborate set-up is culled from *Ring 0*.)

Day Seven is finally reached, and the chance circumstance of finding a *nensha* image of the Japanese maple 'burned' into the wall of Samara's den (as per the circumstance of the painting of Eun-suh in *The Ring Virus*) has led Rachel and Noah back to the cabin at Shelter Mountain Inn. But why? Unlike previous protagonists, they still have no idea of the connection between the cabin and the events on the island. That is because there is *no* connection — no TB clinic — no visits by Sadako/Samara to her ailing father — no subsequent rape and attempted murder. All they know, or now think that they know, is that Samara is dead. But logic would have led them to look for her burial place on the island. Unfortunately, logic has been murdered along with the girl.

Above: The Ring.

The climactic sequence in the cabin is where the structure of *The Ring* departs most radically from the original film. Kruger and Verbinski reconstructed their story so that the well itself became the revelation in the last act. "Before you die, you see the ring," Rachel had said — but what ring? And why has Aidan been sketching concentric circles with a dark core? Why was the viewer shown a glimpse of the well on the screen of the television in Katie's room at the instant of her death? Why did an arm appear momentarily to come out of that same well when Aidan watched the video? More pertinently, why has the shot of the well been the only scene in the cursed video that no one has yet thought to investigate? And still, neither Rachel nor Noah consider the possibility that Samara might be inside a *well*... Time for a little contrivance. Noah knocks a bowl of marbles (yes, marbles) onto the floor of the cabin and they roll towards an indentation under the television stand. Mutual bells ring. The well! The floorboards are prised up, and there it is... The Ring. The promotional icon. Hitchcock's 'McGuffin'.

But these two are not prepared for such a discovery. No ropes, no buckets. A *deus ex machina* then. Psychokinetic rumbles. The television flickers into life. Nails extract themselves from their sockets, as they did in *Close Encounters* on the approach of the saucers. The camera darts to and fro, increasingly agitated. Noah stares into the well — and a swarm of flies bursts forth from the darkness to send him toppling... The television upends, hits Rachel in the back, and sends her hurtling into the abyss... Problem solved.

Only now is the murder of Samara revealed, as a long-dead hand grasps Rachel by the arm and psychic flashbacks are suddenly in vogue...

Samara stands by the well (though how she comes to be on the mainland site of the present Shelter Mountain Inn is not elaborated upon). Anna Morgan is behind her, clad in old-fashioned riding dress like The Woman in Black. She steals towards Samara and quickly envelops her head in a black plastic bag; throws her into the well. (The original version of this scene was extended to include a thump on the head with a rock, but that went along with Richard Morgan's bloodier demise in order for DreamWorks to obtain the requisite PG-13 certificate in America.) The sequence ends with a poignant rejoinder to disappointed parents everywhere: "All I ever wanted was you," Anna eulogises.

The remainder of the well scene is as always. Rachel is 'directed' to Samara's body despite the dark, and she clutches it to her bosom. A CGI-dissolve of the girl's features improves on that in preceding versions. Rescue is immediate.

What? The deadline has passed? Sorry, lost all track of time... Noah muses about how long Samara might have survived down the well. "Seven days," Rachel says. "You can survive for seven days..."

The film now takes a speedy route to conclusion.

Happily ensconced at home, Rachel comforts Aidan, content in the knowledge that the threat posed by Samara's 'curse' is at an end. The following morning, she tells him that they are out of danger, that they have laid Samara to rest. Aidan appears perturbed. "You weren't supposed to help her," he pleads, in defiance of everything that the film has led us to believe. "Don't you understand, Rachel? She never sleeps..." A drop of blood is seen to form at his nostril.

(The notion that Samara 'never sleeps' is touched upon during her therapy sessions at the hospital, and it ties in with her line that 'everyone will suffer', which featured in the trailer but was cut from the final print. As Kruger saw fit to jettison all reference to the viral nature of the curse in his screenplay, these are The Ring's only allusions to the fact that something larger in concept than a single deadly videotape is actually at work. With no parallel theme of contagion present, however, any such idea has necessarily to be left nebulous and vague. The stock-in-trade of all supernatural villains has therefore to plug the gap: 'evil' is what is spreading, apparently. Evil.)

Realisation dawns on Rachel and she jumps in her car; heads for Noah's apartment. It is too late, of course... His television has started to flicker...

Rachel quite unconscionably leaves Noah's current girlfriend to enter the apartment unawares and discover his emaciated corpse. Then she puts two and two together. She has Aidan copy the tape.

It is left to the boy to inject some moral rectitude: "What about the person we show it to?" Aidan asks his mother. "What happens to them?"

Rachel looks away; says nothing.

Several different endings were shot for *The Ring*, the ambiguous (but more faithful) one above being chosen only after the Hollywood practice of endlessly test-screening a film prior to release had produced negative reactions in respect of the alternatives. The original ending had featured actor Chris Cooper as a child killer who, at the beginning of the film, had contacted Rachel and asked her to clear his name. "Because she was a journalist, I was trying to convince her that I had found God and I had straightened my ways and rehabilitated myself," Cooper told website Sc-Fi Wire, the news arm of the Sci-Fi Channel. "I was looking for an out, and she didn't buy it." Rachel is reminded of this incident at the end of the film, and she pays him a visit and drops off a copy of the tape. "It was what they call a bookend," Cooper said. "I opened the movie and I closed the movie. It was two scenes, and I was a serial rapist or a murderer. In the tail end, she pays me a visit and gives me the tape. What I hear is that when they ran the screenings, it was more a disruption than anything. So they cut it all."

A second ending was included in the deleted scenes chapter of the subsequent DVD release. Another early interlude — also cut — had shown Rachel hiring a video-tape from a rental store and being admonished by the shop assistant over her choice of movie; the last scene of the film was then to have been a long, slow tracking shot through the same store until the camera stops at a shelf labelled 'Employee Picks', on which the video is seen to be lying. To those in preview audiences, it must have been obvious that such a ruse would not have guaranteed the video being viewed within the required seven-day period. With neither an ironic nor a darkly humourous ending hitting the relevant spot, DreamWorks settled for the open-ended one that the film's director had wanted in the first place.

Kruger and Verbinski's desire to cover all the angles had inspired them to go much further than *Ring* when it came to acknowledging sources. All of the original four films had been plundered for material, including the Korean remake, and nods were present both to *Ring: The Final Chapter* and Nakata's *Dark Water* (see Chapter 6) in addition. In the case of the latter, they come in the form of the pools of water which presage Samara's incursions onto the material plane, though inconsistency is introduced along with them: Katie's mother makes no mention of having slipped on a wet patch before discovering her body, while the very idea of water running down and around a live television set is enough to inspire a different kind of terror in the aver-

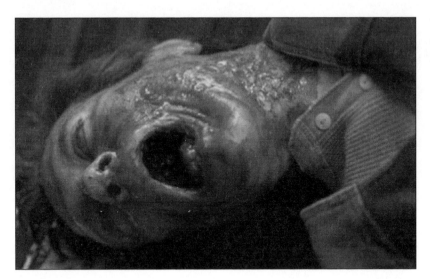

The Ring: *victim on the cutting-room floor.*

age electrical engineer, and it was something that the Japanese film wisely avoided.

Working to the principle that no scene could be allowed to go by without some sign or portent of impending disaster, *The Ring* also invests the myth with an abundance of new motifs: characters are suddenly subject to nose-bleeds for no apparent reason, and they seem strangely prone to scratching off the faces in photographs with a graffito that emulates long dark hair. If all that were not enough, there are the in-jokes: a newspaper advertisement which states 'The End Is Near! — Going Out Of Business Sale' is given prominent display. One especially risible incident sees Rachel wretch up a long strand of dark hair, on the end of which is an electrode! (The inclusion of this episode as part of a 'dream' that Rachel experiences while Aiden watches the tape is even less palatable in context when one realises that its purpose is merely to ape the 'intestine' scene in the video.).

In addition to cluttering up the story, Verbinski and his art department added some unnecessary visual clutter to their film as well, such as injecting 'ring' *motifs* wherever practicable and incorporating shots of a 'flaming' Japanese maple, which looks like it might better have belonged in *The Ten Commandments*. "The tree is a focal point of the movie," production designer Tom Duffield sought to explain. "It kind of unifies the different elements — everything always seems to come back to that tree. Every time we put it up, the wind would come up and blow it over. In Washington, we put it up three separate times, only to have it knocked over by nearly 100-mile-an-hour wind gusts. We tried it again in Los Angeles when it wasn't windy at all, and that night we had sixty-mile-an-hour winds that blew it down all over again. It was very strange," he added, in echo of similarly portentous statements made by the crew of *The Exorcist* when that film was in production.

This tree, perched on an isolated hilltop, typifies Verbinski's predilection for trying to conjure mood out of evocative shots of landscape. Much use is made of cutaways to ominous green skies, reminiscent of those that Roger Corman used to inject at intervals into his Poe films. But Corman's plots invariably were pregnant with foreboding which such inserts helped to underscore; the Andrew Wyeth-inspired rural abstracts with which Verbinski punctuates *The Ring* are *intended* to be prescient of some advancing horror, but what precisely is never clear. Thus they seem often to be empty exercises in Gothic style, and most of them ended up on the cutting-room floor in the event.

This being a Hollywood film, more scenes than those shot for Sadako's video were quietly being earmarked for complex digital treatment. The American film crew did not have the luxury of 3,000 islands to choose from when it came to picking a suitable location for Sadako's birthplace so, instead, they simply painted one in. A key establishing shot was meant to soar over the digitally-created Moesko Island and show Rachel Keller travelling by road to the Morgans' coastal horse ranch, but there was *no* coastal horse ranch. The call went out to an effects house named Matte World Digital: "Gore Verbinski wanted the scene to start with a helicopter shot flying over the ocean, then over a lighthouse and down onto a road," visual effects supervisor Craig Barron explained in *Cinefex*. "A ranch location was chosen, but it was nowhere near the water. So Charles Gibson (who was effects supervisor on Verbinski's *Mouse Hunt*) and I shot a scene from a helicopter, looking down on the road as the pickup arrived at this ranch. Then we shot a piece of film of the ocean flying by the lens and pitching up to reveal the coastline, which was shot off the Oregon coast. We had the water and we had the horse ranch location, but we had to create everything in between: flying up to the lighthouse to view the island before the camera dives down towards the truck arriving at the ranch. It was all done without flying in or out of clouds — no wipes, no tricks," Barron declared. "No one could have done a shot like that ten years ago, using traditional techniques." Maybe not, but all this was for a scene which the Japanese had acquired simply by hopping a ferry.

The Ring is two different films joined at the hip: a schlocky remake of a successful Asian horror with American actors mimicking the motions, and an experimental short filled with disturbing and sometimes distressing subliminal images, designed to exert a malign influence on the beholder. The first was pulled together from predictable studio brainstorming techniques, while the second could as easily have been purloined from a defence department study into methods of psychological warfare. The effect is like watching Disney's *The Haunted Mansion* (2003), then suddenly find-

ing oneself overcome by the desire to kill on leaving the theatre. It is *The Manchurian Candidate* for real. What *The Ring* does, in essence, is induce not pleasurable 'fear', life-affirming and cathartic, but rather depression and psychosis, unhealthy and downright dangerous.

Above: The Ring: *the Psycho shot.*

'The shots of the victims' horrified faces will make your skin crawl,' wrote Shirley Hsu, of the Asia Pacific Arts review. Baker made light of his achievement — as well he might, working with this kind of material for a living: "We just wanted to make them look scary. I did some Photoshop designs, just playing with what I thought might look kind of good. I originally had wanted to do this weird blurred image, you know? And it ended up just being slightly twisted and tweaked and distorted. And scary!"

The sight of Noah's emaciated corpse seated *Psycho*-like in a swivel-chair is little more than a flash-frame in the finished film, but actress Amber Tamblyn's death mask as the unfortunate Katie is featured more substantially, as Verbinski chose to cut away to the discovery of her body in the closet at an unpredictable moment in the narrative. (The more predictable moment, when Katie's mother tells Rachel of the discovery, was cut prior to release.) This shot is the most shocking in the film. "That was a complete dummy of her," Baker said. "I thought it would be easier to have the neck move than to have it fixed in one position, in case the camera angles weren't good. We made it so that the neck was like a mechanical neck, and the head and neck could turn and move. I thought it would be interesting and I did a little movie and showed it to Gore. We did a number of takes — some still, some moving — and that's just the one that he decided to use. So obviously, he felt it worked the best!"

Where the remake triumphs is where American films of this sort always triumph, in sheer, gut-wrenching, visceral horror. *The Ring* is less concerned with the terror that is inspired by the curse of Samara than it is with what she leaves in her wake: the corpses of those who have come face to face with her awesome power. Having tried every trick in the book to create an atmosphere of fear, from moody skyscapes to spooky surrealist imagery, *The Ring* defaults in the end to the gruesome depiction of death. Its horror is that of physical dissolution, not spiritual conundrum. For all its self-professed Christian certainties, it is Death, rather than imaginary phantoms, which still petrifies the West.

The concision which Nakata had applied to his version of the story was sidelined in favour of 115 minutes of often plodding exposition. Nothing is left to the imagination of the viewer which might otherwise be spelled out in graphic visual detail, even to the extent of telegraphing the famous climax, where a fly which at first appears to be a part of the image as Rachel examines the video on an editing console mysteriously transfers itself to the *surface* of the screen. This inane sequence would have called into question the very laws of physics themselves were it to have occurred in any other context, and an investigative reporter as alert as Keller is purported to be would have had the place swarming with theoretical physicists in short order as she realises that she has stumbled upon the scoop of the century. But no — she takes the fly in her fingers, examines it for signs of damage and moves on. Faced with a scientific breakthrough equivalent to the splitting of the atom, she acts as though something of mere passing curiosity has taken place. This matter-of-fact acceptance of the outrageously incredible deprives *The Ring* of any real power to frighten as assuredly as if it were an episode of *Scooby-Doo*.

After the liberal Clinton nineties, political undertones in the Hollywood horror film have once more hardened into ideological extreme, and the supernatural nuances which Nakata incorporated into his version of the tale are eschewed by *The Ring* in favour of a complete *Exorcist*-style makeover in which Sadako is transformed into a tenement of fundamentalist demonic evil. The Kruger-Frank rewrite postulates a reading which is a far remove from what was intended by Koji Suzuki. In Verbinski's film, the concept of Terror takes on a quite different ring.

Samara is isolated, alienated and humiliated; probed, persecuted and pointed at,

The Ring: *deleted scene at the well.*

till she herself becomes a breeding-ground for urban Terror. All it needs is the final act of vilification to complete the vicious circle of hate which has been hers since birth. Right on cue, she is brutally murdered by a mad capitalist in whose eyes she is to blame for the fact that his thriving business has gone down the toilet. *Voila* — Samara is reborn as Death Incarnate, undercutting the security of the innocent through their window on the world: television. She is not an image on a video, nor even a virus; she is real, and she intrudes into the living-room in the climax of the film in the way that grief has intruded into the lives of so many who initially assumed that they had been watching mere telecasts of events which had little or nothing to do with them. *The Ring* went into production on 2 December 2001, just under three months after the terrorist attacks of the World Trade Center in New York; production wrapped four months later, on 21 March 2002.

The Ring is really not a scary film. The viewer does not believe in the cursed video, the history of the tape, or Samara's plight — let alone her power — for a second. But it is a deeply unsettling one. Not because of its theme or its intensity as a work of genre, but because of the lengths to which its director has gone to play mind-games on its largely unsuspecting audience. The use of subliminal and/or semi-subliminal images is a deceit that Verbinski had borrowed from William Friedkin, whose *The Exorcist* made discreet use of demonic subliminals to complement the palette of scares already on offer. When Katie dies of fright within the film's opening minutes and her mouth elongates into one of Rick Baker's rictus death masks, the image is digitally enhanced, frame by frame, in those final fractions of a second, to implant a sensation into the mind of the viewer that is more unsettling than might otherwise be expected from Baker's make-up alone. What frightens in *The Ring* are its visions of death, not the power supposedly wielded by its psychic protagonist; the root of its terror is charnel, not spiritual. Verbinski's *The Ring* does not understand the nature of fear, but it *does* understand the nature of horror. The film itself is a cursed video; it employs the same tachistoscopic techniques to threaten the mental well-being of those who view it as Suzuki's fictional tape is supposed to do in the novel.

Whereas *Ring* imparted a pleasurable *frisson*, *The Ring* merely disturbs. This is no doubt due in part to Verbinski's disconcerting use of the aforementioned subliminals. The film has an unhealthy aura, entirely at odds with its Japanese counterpart. *Ring* sent its audience away from the theatre still tingling with the thrill of fear; *The Ring* sends its patrons out into the cold night depressed about the condition of man, and concerned for the minds of those who could serve up such a nihilistic vision in the name of entertainment. *Ring*, when all's said and done, is a Gothic fairy tale in the esteemed tradition of the *Konjaku monogatari*. *The Ring* is merely another moribund example of the moral vacuity of the Hollywood movie machine; it is a film which reeks of fear, but the desperate anxieties that the story expresses are a far remove from the mythic allegory which was embodied in Suzuki's original. *The Ring* is a scream in the night, wrenched from a society that is *living* in fear: fear of its children, of death and decay, of failure and self-doubt. Above all, fear of itself. What it does *not* reek of is the fun of the ghost train that always was there in Nakata's version. Verbinski's ghost train travels along a track littered with real corpses, and with no obvious way out. Instead of a Gothic plane inhabited by monsters and mortals striving to comprehend the complexities of an unknown universe, it offers the bleak vista of dysfunctional families and the price that will have to be paid for their myriad neuroses. By placing the Morgans to the fore, the emphasis of the tale is subtly altered. *The Ring* is *their* story, not that of Samara (or Sadako), and the film becomes a typical parable about the sins of the parents being visited upon the child. It stares into a world on the verge of collapse and suggests self-interest as the route to survival. It is a frightening film, but for all the wrong reasons. And what the hell are the horses about? Even the animals are in there only to be slaughtered, or to go mad.

Presumably the makers thought that raising the prospect of a dead sorceress would undermine the essential veracity of all they were trying to do. But what could be more idiotic than the idea of a videotape that kills the viewer in seven days? (Unless it happens to be filled with recordings of *The Richard and Judy Show*.) Either one buys into the concept of wholesale suspension of disbelief, or not. DreamWorks, apparently, could not. What *The Ring* really needed was legend-haunted Arkham to give its tale of occult voices from the past some mythic credibility. What it offers is a horse farm.

The Ring: *alternative ending and fade-out.*

The almost unanimous praise which had greeted Nakata's original was not lavished on the DreamWorks remake. 'The Ring is a stylish Hollywood remake of the Japanese horror sensation that unfortunately has little personality of its own,' *Variety* reviewer Todd McCarthy wrote when the film was released in the States on 18 October 2002. 'Insinuating creepiness of this tale of a bizarre videotape that brings death to those who watch it comes across in muted fashion, with uninvolving characters and lack of genuine excitement or fright, creating a second-rate, second-hand feel… The leads that enable Rachel to pursue the case are often implausibly discovered and connected, timelines and logistics don't convince, and the principal characters reveal themselves as conventional, one-dimensional types of no distinction, quirks or special interest.' It was a view with which Claudia Puig of *USA Today* concurred: 'The Ring starts with a winningly chilling premise and provides some eerie jolts, but ultimately it stops short of being truly effective. Aspiring in the psychological-thriller vein of *The Exorcist* and *The Omen*, it creates a gloomy and disturbing mood, set in the grey Pacific Northwest. But as *The Ring* weaves to an end, too many threads are left dangling and the movie ultimately proves too implausible to put alongside those horror classics.'

When the film opened in Britain four months later, on 21 February 2003, opinion was similarly muted. *The Guardian's* Peter Bradshaw was typical of many: 'As for this remake of the cult Japanese horror film *Ring*, well, it's disappointing, losing most of the original's flavour, while retaining and amplifying what was muddled and unsatisfying about it in the first place. It is a brilliant premise, stretching back to M R James' 'Casting the Runes'… but at least part of the tension and the sheer hold this storyline exerts consists in wondering — how exactly did this terrifying video come to be made? And on this point, here as in the original Japanese movie, there is ultimately nothing but bafflement and exasperation.' *The Independent's* Anthony Quinn was little kinder: 'The film stumbles in the final reel when writer Ehren Kruger tries to elaborate upon the original, dragging wild horses and Brian Cox into a plot that has no need of either.' It was left to Tim Robey in the *Daily Telegraph* to deliver the consensus: 'The original's low-fi inscrutability was so much eerier.'

Guerilla or 'viral' marketing (as the technique coincidentally is known) of the kind that was utilised by *The Blair Witch Project* featured heavily in the selling of *The Ring*. Numerous 'dummy' sites were uploaded to the Internet to attract search engine spiders, including ones which directed users to the fictitious Moesko Island or even the Morgan ranch, and sympathetic pre-existent fan sites like www.theringworld.com were also roped into the promotional loop. The invaluable chat-room word of mouth that resulted from such tactics helped the film to an opening weekend of $15 million in America, lukewarm reviews notwithstanding. A domestic box-office take of $128 million (against a budget of $45 million) in the six months before the release of the DVD ensured the American remake its own sequel, even before its world-wide gross of $230 million (to date) was reached, and those who survived in the original were sought out to pit their wits against Samara once again.

Screenwriter Ehren Kruger was game. Gore Verbinski, however, had since moved on to spend the remainder of 2002, and much of 2003, with the bigger boys of Johnny Depp and the *Pirates of the Caribbean* (2003) and professed little interest in helming a sequel to *The Ring*. "It's no fun making a horror film," he had declared at the time of the first film's opening in October 2002. "You get into some darker areas of the brain and, after a while, everything becomes a bit depressing. I'm pleased with the result, but it's not something I'm ready to jump back into right away." With the passage of another year, his opinion had not changed radically. "It would depend. I'd only want to direct it if it was a really good story. I've not seen the prequel or sequel. Ehren Kruger's the expert on *Ring*, so he knows that stuff. I think what he'd do is grab from between the prequel and sequel and try to create something there."

Star Naomi Watts was less reluctant. "We did a lot of script changes while we were shooting and we shot a few different endings and we didn't know what we were going to use, but the way they played it out was really smart and I love the way it ends," she said. "So I feel inspired and encouraged by that and hopefully Gore will be able to do the sequel too." A reported $15 million pay cheque secured the services of Watts, but Verbinski was not so easily persuaded. In his place, Parkes hired commercials director Noam Murro for his first feature, and filming of *The Ring Two* (spelt to differentiate it from its Japanese forebear) was pencilled in to start in January 2004.

In the three years between the production of the last *Ring* sequel (*Ring 0: Birthday*) in Japan and the first of the Hollywood spin-offs, however, the influence of the original film had impacted on horror product from across the whole of Southeast Asia.

While American producers operated in a time warp that saw them trapped in 1998, the Asian industry had absorbed and abstracted *Ring's* iconography of the dark-haired ghost, the death curse, supernatural rebirth and the paraphernalia of techno-terror in a multiplicity of ways which had sought to move the genre on beyond the boundaries set by Nakata's seminal work.

Before the executives at DreamWorks had even viewed their copy of the video, the Ring virus had already spread. O

Day Six: The Ring Virus

He bent above her — and looked — and shrieked — for the sleeper had no face! Before him, wrapped in its grave-sheet only, lay the corpse of a woman — a corpse so wasted that little remained save the bones, and the long black tangled hair.

- **Lafcadio Hearn**, 'The Reconciliation' *Shadowings* (1900)

So seismic was the impact of *Ring* that in no time at all, the whole Southeast Asian film industry wanted in on the act, and enterprising producers from Hong Kong to Bangkok and all points between looked to *Ring*-style supernatural thrillers to turn them a profit. Asian horrors in the wake of *Ring* started with an advantage that is rarely gifted to their Western counterparts: audiences came to them expecting a fright. This allowed them to concentrate on building mood and atmosphere, both of which are essential to the good ghost story. With the audience suitably primed in the immediate post-*Ring* years, Asian cinema turned out some very good ghost stories indeed.

Before the iconography of *Ring* could fully be absorbed into the body politic of the genre, a number of directors picked up on elements of it that seemed to have captured the public's imagination, the two most obvious of which were mystic landscape and the Japanese staple of the *revenant*, or 'one who returns'. The straight Sadako clone took a while to make its appearance in other horrors, as did the hi-tech apparatus of her curse, but her influence in the shadowy corners of even the most conventional of thrillers was such that all underwent a subtle change from which there was now no going back.

The Thursday evening transmissions of Fuji Television's drama serial *Rasen* during the summer of 1999 had been coincident with the 28 July opening of Nakata's *Ring 2*, which was paired in release with a more typical supernatural yarn, in the manner of the horror double bills that were once the norm in the West. Despite its shortcomings as a support feature and awkward air of entrapment between ancient and modern,

Ring 2's stable-mate was an inaugural entry in what was soon to be a new and vibrant chapter in the history of the Japanese horror film, sired by a public demand for ghostly tales that showed little sign of abating.

> *Fumiya:* The Underworld?
> *Oda:* Yes, the land of the dead. But a land in which the dead still have bodies. In the myths, the gateway is always a cave like this…
> - **Michitaka Tsutui and Taro Suwa**, *Shikoku* (1999)

Media conglomerate Kadokawa Shoten had been among the first to try to cash in on the craze by backing *Ring* executive producer Masato Hara to personally produce a ghost story called *Shikoku* (1999), from a screenplay that was co-written by Takenori Sento, who himself had been a line producer on both *Don't Look Up* and *Ring*. But the result was a ham-fisted mishmash of supernatural themes old and new, few of which gelled in any coherent form, and all of which seemed to have been knitted together to take advantage of the fact that a minor change in the *kanji* transcription for the island of Shikoku alters its meaning from 'the four provinces' to 'the land of the dead'.

Hinako (Yui Natsukawa) returns to the village of her birth to see old schoolfriends Fumiya (Michitaka Tsutui) and Sayori (Chiaki Kuriyama), only to discover that Sayori has long since drowned. Her shade appears nevertheless to be haunting the locale, and the two remaining friends arrive at the conclusion that Sayori's grief-stricken mother is engaged in an occult ritual designed to raise her daughter from the dead. She succeeds in her quest at a mystical site that is held to be a gateway to *Yomi* (the underworld), but the timely intervention of a Buddhist holy man sends the reincarnated Sayori back into the darkness from whence she came.

In both mood and its adherence to traditional beliefs, *Shikoku* is more distinctively Japanese than many of its immediate ghostly predecessors, but dig beneath the mystical surface and Western genre influences are there in abundance. The arcane ritual in which Sayori's mother indulges in order to 'open the gate' is pure H P Lovecraft, as is the premise of an island sanctified against the intrusion of spirits by a ring of strategically-placed temples, while the theme of a revivified offspring harks back to 'The Monkey's Paw'. Sayori's defeat by the Japanese equivalent of Van Helsing represents a different source altogether. Either of these stories would have been sufficient in themselves, but scripter Sento opts to deploy them in tandem, so that each of them impedes unwelcomely upon the other: his magic spell has the power to raise the dead in general, and sundry minor *revenants* are glimpsed along the way to the climax, yet only Sayori manages to make it through in the end; similarly, the emphasis on her own return is cluttered by constant references to a veritable epidemic of grave openings should her mother succeed in her task. *Shikoku's* ambitions far outstrip its abilities in either regard, and the impression is of a semi-professional effort struggling valiantly with a storyline which really required the vision and facilities of a much larger production.

None of this is helped by the annoyingly wilful hand-held style of director Shunichi Nagasaki. After a literally shaky start in which the action is not so much directed as has a camera pointed towards it, and none too precisely at that, the film settles down into a rhythm which better befits the languid pace of its narrative. But the nervy camerawork remains a distraction, despite the film's preference for location shooting and effective use of natural light. By the time of its set-piece climax (staged at a studio mock-up of a pagan temple), Nagasaki is left with little choice but to defer to convention and go for more formalised framing, even though the sequence is photographed with a camera still strapped manfully to his cinematographer's back. 'Asian horror buffs will get the most out of *Shikoku*,' was *Variety's* take. 'A bold attempt to inject psychodrama into a ghost movie that taps into some of the same creepiness as recent Japanese hit *Ring*.'

Twenty-four year-old Chiaki Kuriyama, who is petulant but hardly petrifying as the resident wraith of *Shikoku*, went from this film into the supernatural V-cinema drama *Ju-on*, alongside *Don't Look Up* and *Ring 2's* Yurei Yanagi, but she was even better served three years later when she was cast by Quentin Tarantino to play Gogo Yubari in *Kill Bill* (2003).

Producer Masato Hara's seeming predilection for experimental ideas was to surface again in *St John's Wort* (*Otogiriso*, 2001), though any connection to *Ring* was merely a result of the film's fixation with high-technology. Instead, this was a deliriously campy hymn to the Poe-scapes of Roger Corman, a veritable *House of Usher* (1960) on acid. Utilising the structure and techniques of the video game, two friends explore an inherited Gothic mansion while their compatriots tune in to their every move via camcorder, cell-phone and laptop connections. The very un-Japanese house is filled to the rafters with creepy dolls, weird paintings, mummified corpses, psychotic caretakers and the Sadako figure of a lost twin sister/brother hiding in the attic, and it turns out that it was the studio of a mad artist who got his aesthetic kicks by painting tortured children. In keeping with its PC game concept, two endings are offered, the most appropriate of which is a typically Cormanesque conflagration.

St John's Wort is an interesting diversion, though less substantial than its technical prowess might lead one to believe. Hara gave up on the horrors after this, his patience exhausted by all the psychedelic posturing in pursuit of a good scare. (Strange how the batteries in electronic gadgets seem to last much longer in films like this than they ever do in life, whereas the legendary reliability of Japanese cars turns

Another Heaven
(2000): Detective
Tobitaka (Yoshio
Harada).

belly-up — that of the protagonists failing to start when required, with the result that a tree crashes onto it and strands them at the house overnight.)

> How terrible for the earth and the sea! The Devil has come down to you,
> and he is filled with rage, as he knows that he has such little time left.
> (Chapter 12, The Revelation to John.)
> **- Screen caption**, *Another Heaven* (2000)

In 2000, writer-director Joji Iida went from *Rasen* into the *Se7en*-style, multi-genre supernatural thriller *Another Heaven* (*Anazahevun*), one of whose male leads was also Yoshio Harada: Ryuji in *Ring: Kanzenban*. In its formulaic 'buddy movie' tale of two Tokyo detectives (one old and world-weary, one young and idealistic) pitted against a serial-killing, body-hopping entity from another dimension, *Another Heaven* is a cross between Fincher's 1995 film *Fallen* (1998) and the Keystone Kops, with a liberal splash of *Rasen* for good measure.

Iida's film begins on a promising note: a team of policemen are called to the scene of a gruesome murder, where the victim's body lies sprawled on the floor while a large cooking-pot bubbles merrily away on a stove behind them. "Smells nice," one remarks. "Chicken stew?" A clumsy SOCO (Scenes of Crime Officer) stumbles against the dead man's head and the top of the skull swings back to expose an empty cranium. All eyes turn towards the stew-pot. Manabu (Yosuke Eguchi) lifts the lid and spoons out the contents: the main ingredient is the victim's brain. So far, so gross —

Top: Pulse *(2001).*

Bottom: Pulse:
the human 'stain'.

but the next shot sees the door to the apartment burst open as those present rush outside to wretch noisily at the discovery. Not only the real policemen who entered the
North London flat of killer Dennis Nilsen were entitled to think this reaction a little
over-egged.

Along the way, Iida indulges in some hypocritical sideswipes at the corrosive
effect of violence in the media, but as the body count mounts faster than police can
record it, suspicion falls initially on a young female student named Chizuru (Yukiko
Okamoto). Correctly, it turns out, as the film switches point-of-view to show her

picking up three likely victims in a bar, despite the curious tear of blood which runs down her cheek as she gives them the come-on. Thinking little of it, they take her back to their apartment where she rapes one before breaking his neck. A second flees and summons the police, who arrive to find Chizuru dead and the remaining victim traumatised. Not for long; soon, third man Kimura (Takashi Kashiwabara) assumes the mantle of superhuman killer, and what began as a murder mystery takes a leap in the dark (as does he, from one building to another during a chase) to become a paranormal sci-fi thriller that echoes uncannily of *Scream and Scream Again* (1969).

The killer is revealed to be a demonic spirit that delights in adopting human form to engage in acts of ultra-violence, but the film's mood-swings from moments of slapstick comedy to bouts of savage brutality and sober reflection are as indicative of Iida's lack of focus as was his cursory approach to the body-hopping antics of Sadako at the finale of *Rasen*. There is a potent theme in play beneath the surface of *Another Heaven*, but it is accorded a treatment that borders on the surreal.

Another Heaven is similar in feel to the many inventive low-budget horror-thrillers that American writer-director Larry Cohen cranked out at irregular intervals during the 1970s and 1980s, especially *God Told Me To* (1976). It is stupendously silly, but it has a heart, it makes a strong moral point, and it throws everything but the kitchen sink into the mix on the basis that if one scene fails to work, then the next one just might. Iida's scattergun approach to the material is never less than interesting, although his directing is better than his writing (if the curiously-subtitled English print is anything to go by!), but he has a way to go yet if he is to attain the dizzy heights of Cohen's *Q: The Winged Serpent* (1982). The film was released simultaneously with an eleven-part continuation of the same story on television, in the manner of *Ring: The Final Chapter* and *Rasen*. The serial was transmitted between 20 April and 21 June, but according to *Dorama Encyclopedia* author Jonathan Clements, its 'extremely complicated plot turned a number of viewers off'. Condensing more than eight hours of television into a 132-minute feature may have had a bearing on the equally hybrid nature of the screen version.

Japanese teen pin-up and occasional pop star Takashi Kashiwabara turned up again in the Toho-distributed *Tales of the Unusual* (*Yo nimo kimyo na monogatari-Eiga no tokubetsuhen*, 2000), where he played a prospective groom who has pause for thought about his impending nuptials after he and his intended experience their future together in 'The Marriage Simulator', the last of a compendium of four stories in *Twilight Zone* mould. Kashiwabara's contribution to the quadruple-authored and directed *Tales of the Unusual* is a bitter-sweet slice of romantic sci-fi that ends the film on a feel-good note, while preceding it are 'One Snowy Night', 'Samurai Cellular' and 'Chess'. The middle two tales are essentially whimsical in nature, though Mamoru Hoshi's brilliant direction

Above: Danny Pang.

of 'Chess' is reminiscent of the lyrical expressionism of British cinema in the days of Michael Powell and *The Red Shoes* (1948). Only 'One Snowy Night' takes a stab at the Terror film, with a vengeful ghost that plagues a quartet of survivors from a plane crash who have sought refuge in an isolated cabin; madness ensues, and one of the party becomes the murderer of the others — but is there more to it all than warped psychology? A final, chilling shot of a headless ghost wandering in the snowy wastes is enough to freeze the marrow. All four segments are splendidly realised but a close examination reveals little evidence of the Ring virus. By the time 'Chess' player Shinji Takeda showed up on the set of *Cure* director Kyoshi Kurosawa's *Pulse* (*Kaīro*, 2001), however, he exhibited every sign of having been Ring-positive all along.

> It all began one day without warning, like this...
>
> **- Screen caption**, *Pulse* (2001)

Pulse starts well enough, when Michi (Kumiko Aso) decides to call on a co-worker from the Sunny Plants emporium who has been logging on to a strange website, only to have him commit suicide in her presence. As she and her fellows investigate the death, another young computer nerd named Kawashima (Haruhiko Kato) also connects to the Internet, and amid an unnerving series of images of indistinct figures, a voice asks him: 'Would you like to meet a ghost?'

At this point, logic and plot fly out of the window and the story descends at a dead pace into a surreal muse on solitude and the disintegration of traditional societal ties in a world where the Web itself is merely a symptom of increasing isolationism in human contact. Kurosawa's turgid and consciously avant-garde variation on the theme of *Ring* devolves into a cross between Don Siegel's *Invasion of the Body Snatchers* (1956) and George Romero's *Dawn of the Dead* (1978), whose advertising slogan — 'When there's no more room in Hell, the dead will walk the Earth' — could have served *Pulse* equally well: the fields of Elysium have become far too full of ghosts, and they are spilling out into our earthly domain to make more ghosts of all who encounter them. This opens the way for a series of barely-connected vignettes in which the characters in the film come upon various examples of the breed, whose commonality appears to be that they move with a steady (and sometimes stumbling) gait and leave a visible 'stain' in passing. Of course, the ghosts in *Pulse* are not 'real' ghosts at all but a metaphor for the illusion of life and the transience of the human condition. And there were you thinking that *Pulse* was a horror film. Takeda's role is a sympathetic one of a computer software designer, but he soon disappears into the decor with all the rest.

Above: Oxide Pang.

The frights that Kurosawa is able to conjure out of so overblown a concept are few in number, and they diminish in ratio with his film's inexorable retreat from reality. As the viewer begins to realise that nothing much makes sense and that all action is bound to a philosophical conceit, *Pulse* loses its power to feed the imagination and descends instead to the level of mere curiosity. Kurosawa's staging is often effective, but his way with engendering fear is to ratchet down the action to a snail's pace, and his directorial mannerisms soon become wearing: the camera habitually switches point-of-view ahead of the actors, as though their every move is pre-ordained. This might have been deemed to suit the theme but it gives a distinct impression of affectation. Some resonance is to be had from the 'stains' which are left in the wake of the ghosts, however, reminding as they do of the mortal shadows which were to be found on walls after the atom-bombing of Hiroshima.

The cleverest touch in *Pulse* is the subtle way in which Kurosawa removes from the drama all human presence except that of his protagonists; only when the story is some way in do we realise that everybody else seems suddenly to have vanished. Kumiko Aso came to *Pulse* from *Ring 0: Birthday*, in which she played the role of Etsuko. She does what she can with a thankless part which asks little more of her than to look perturbed when her companions disappear before her very eyes, leaving only glutinous puddles behind, and Tsuruta's film proved in retrospect to have been a better stretch of her talents.

'Cross the Ring series with *Invasion of the Body Snatchers* and the result wouldn't be far from *Pulse*,' *Variety* noted. 'Result is always watchable, occasionally creepy and teasingly pitched halfway between a genre riff and a genuine scare-fest.' Ian Berriman, writing in *SFX*, was somewhat more enthusiastic: 'Bleak, cold and nihilistic, with some haunting imagery and an oppressive sense of impending doom, *Kairo* is a film about urban isolation and loneliness, which explores the effect that communications technology — the Internet, mobile phones — is having on modern society.'

Thailand's contribution to the Ring cycle of vengeful female ghosts was the first and last segment in Oxide Pang Chun's variable compendium of spooky tales, *Bangkok Haunted* (2001). The first story is the traditional Asian one of a young woman scorned and brutalised, whose unquiet spirit, along with her severed arm, becomes trapped as a result inside a tribal long-drum; the second devolves to another distant cousin of W W Jacobs' short story 'The Monkey's Paw', in which a lovesick office worker is coerced into employing a love potion on a prospective mate which, unbeknown to her, has been distilled from the blood of fresh corpses; the third and last is an intricately-plotted tale of revenge, once more enacted by the ghost of a young girl alleged to have committed suicide. The three episodes of *Bangkok Haunted* are each unfolded at a leisurely pace and interwoven by a convoluted twist-in-the-tail, which tends to obfuscate even further an already obscure narrative. Oxide Pang's edgy and violent gangster thriller *Bangkok Dangerous* (1999), which he co-wrote, directed and edited with his brother Danny, was a much more exciting and satisfactory affair to Western eyes.

With VCRs predicted to be on the wane as 'old' technology even before the release of *Ring* (though not when Suzuki wrote his novel), it was only to be expected that *Ring* clones in the new millennium would choose to align their terrors with the technological times. The weird website of *Pulse* now seemed a more suitable domain for the hosting of supernatural phenomena than an anachronistic videocassette, and while DreamWorks and Disney fought over which of them was to reinvent the original, a American-British-German consortium embarked on a variation of its theme which cross-pollinated Nakata's film with the gory extravaganza of Dark Castle's *House on Haunted Hill*.

FearDotCom (2002) was directed by William Malone (of *House on Haunted Hill*), and he wastes no time in confirming Nakata's film as the source of his inspiration: a computer programme springs to life of its own accord, as per Sadako's self-activating videotape; forty-eight hours after logging onto the 'FearDotCom' website, the unwitting surfer dies of his or her greatest fear; the 'ghost' calls its victims on the telephone; the human remains of the vengeful spirit are discovered underwater at an abandoned steelworks. And so on and so forth. The frenetic visual style and virtual impenetrability of much of the action blurs exposition to such a degree that despite all the riffs from *Ring*, nothing about the film makes much sense until the climax, when the reason for the ghostly revenge is revealed; the phantom femme was but one victim of a Hannibal Lecter-like serial killer named Alistair Pratt (a somnambulantly-slumming Stephen Rea), whose *modus operandi* involves torturing them on his very own live-cam 'death' site. This mar-

riage of slasher flick and ghost story enables Malone to indulge his predilection for gratuitous scenes of sadism, but it adds little of merit to the film as a whole.

Above:
FearDotCom
(2002).

(Similar web-cam ground was trodden by Working Title's *My Little Eye* in 2002,
in which a group of teens are ensconced in a 'Big Brother' house, ostensibly in service
of a pay-to-view website — until they all start to meet typically gory ends.)

FearDotCom is the usual visceral assault on the senses, completely devoid of
mood or menace, and it bears witness to the fact that Western directors still have a lot
to learn from their Asian peers when it comes to making scary movies. What Malone
quite fails to realise is that watching people die diabolical deaths without any kind of
rationale to them is just not frightening. Passing references to Dr Gogol (the name of
Peter Lorre's mad surgeon in *Mad Love*, 1935), and Polidori (Lord Byron's personal
physician, who wrote 'The Vampyre' in 1819) attempt to curry favour with the
cognoscenti, and Brian Yuzna regular Jeffrey Combs, of *Re-Animator* (1985) fame, is
imported into the proceedings to inject some cult credibility, but he goes largely unnoticed in the resulting cyberpunk melee and lacks conviction even when nailed to a
makeshift cross at the finale. The always creepy Udo Kier turns in the only performance worth speaking about, but he is taken out by a subway train within minutes of
the film's opening. *FearDotCom* was shot in Luxemburg and Montreal, but its notional

setting of New York might account for the perpetual gloom in which everything is required to be bathed throughout.

No sooner had *FearDotCom* hit American theatres in August 2002, seven weeks ahead of DreamWorks' *The Ring*, than another foray into the same murky territory surfaced on screens in Korea in November. *Unborn But Forgotten* (*Hayanbang*) was the distinctly unmemorable title translation for a rather sordid story in which a number of women are found dead after logging on to a weird website called 'The White Room' and suffering phantom pregnancies as a result. Cybercop Lee-seok Choi (Jun-ho Jeong) is allocated the task of tracing the culprits, to which end, he is aided by a television documentarist named Soo-jin (Eun-ju Lee), who is shadowing him for a feature but who also happens to have logged on to the site and is herself now subject to its doomy fifteen-day deadline.

After much needless complicating of a none-too-sophisticated storyline by director Chang-jae Lim, the villains of the piece are revealed to be the deceased girlfriend and stillborn baby of a high-flying television anchorman. How this unlikely pair of ghosts managed to create a website — or why — is not explained, any more than is reason given for their ire being directed against innocent young women, rather than the self-serving seducer who left them to their fate in the first place. A moderately scary night is passed by Soo-jin in the apartment that serves as a focus for the ghostly disturbances, but any film whose plot twist depends upon the trick of perspective that was employed by Hans Holbein in his 1533 painting 'The Ambassadors' has to be strapped for ideas. *Hayanbang* is actually subtitled 'Unborn but *Un*forgotten' on the print itself, which not only makes for better grammar but is more logical in the context of the story.

September 2001 brought the release of *Kakashi* (*Scarecrow*), which turned out to be a complete misfire from Norio Tsuruta, director of *Ring 0: Birthday*. Something of a cross between *The Wicker Man* (1973) and *Children of the Corn* (1984), but without the logic or suspense of either, *Kakashi* was nothing more than an overripe example of the isolated-community-where-all-the-locals-act-strangely scenario. Kaoru Yoshikawa (Maho Nonami) journeys to the remote mountain village of Kozukata in search of her missing brother, only to find the place inhabited by sullen farmers seemingly obsessed with the construction of scarecrows for a local 'kakashi' festival. Instead of doing the sensible thing and getting the hell out of there at the earliest opportunity (in spite of the fact that her brand new supermini has inexplicably broken down on the way in), Kaoru wanders around oblivious to the general air of hostility, vainly attempting to prise some snippet of information from the uncommunicative villagers. Even when she is attacked by a living scarecrow in a civic building (in daylight), she appears to think little of it and simply continues on with her quest. The secret behind this arrant

Dark Water
(2001).

silliness has been obvious to all but the girl from the start: the scarecrows are a gate-way between life and death — the means by which the dead are returned to life dur-ing the festival. A Sadako figure named Izumi (Kou Shibasaki, who is best-known in Japan for advertising Pond's face cream) is central to the shenanigans, but her presence in *Kakashi* is merely another tired nod in the direction of *Ring*. Utterly devoid of mood and not in the least bit scary, *Kakashi* was a contrived cash-in affixing the now-familiar elements of J-horror, such as the mysterious long-haired devil-girl, to a formulaic Hollywood-horror backwoods plot involving the pagan rites of retards. When a gath-ering of scarecrows comes to life in the film's set-piece climax, it is plain to see that the straw figures in the preceding shots have been replaced by actors in rags, and in *readi-ness*, before one of them so much as moves a muscle.

In 2001, Hideo Nakata had re-teamed with *Ring* series producer Taka Ichise and author Koji Suzuki for a low-key return to the more familiar territory of the tra-ditional ghost story. *Dark Water (Honogurai mizu no soko kara)* was adapted by screenwriters Yoshihiro Nakamura and Kenichi Suzuki from the short story 'Floating Water', one of seven H_2O-based psychological horror tales in a Suzuki collection entitled *Dark Water*, which had been published by Kadokawa as a horror *bunko* in 1997. 'The collection as a whole bears more of a resemblance to *Ghost Stories of an Antiquary* by M R James than it does to Clive Barker's *Books of Blood*,' opined The Agony Column's book reviewer Rick Kleffel. 'There's no blood in this book. But there is a sense of fear and unease in its unsparing portrait of our willingness to brutalise and be brutalised emotionally. This is not to say that these are simply portraits of urban angst. By bringing in the supernatural feel — if not the supernatural —

Suzuki allows the reader to absorb his unpleasant message in the context of a predictable ghost story.'

Suzuki's story is more of a character study than an exercise in Terror, and the
film had to expand considerably on 'Floating Water' to produce a 101-minute feature. As a result, Nakata's *Dark Water* is a slight but engaging tale whose origins in
a short story with a simple, if effective, premise are never far from the surface,
despite the care that its director lavishes on the thin material. (In a wry aside, Suzuki
takes a pot-shot at the kind of writing that he disdains by having a heroine whose
mental breakdown has been brought about by proof-reading too many 'graphic and
sadistic' horror novels!)

Fastidious and highly-strung divorcée Yoshimi Matsubara (Hitomi Kuroki) and
her six year-old daughter Ikuko (Rio Kanno) move into the sixth floor of a run-down
Tokyo apartment block while she searches for a job and engages in a bitter custody
battle with a vindictive ex-husband. Water motifs abound from the off, from the pour-
ing rain that accompanies their trip to view their new home, through the spillage in
the elevator and condensation in the building itself, to the nasty, spreading stain that
is a main feature of the bedroom ceiling. The incessant drip-drip from the damp spot
becomes a metaphor for the strains of hand-to-mouth existence as the increasingly
neurotic Yoshimi has first to fend off the legal challenge to her rights as a mother, and
then deal with what seems to be the ghostly presence of another six year-old who disappeared from the apartment above them two years before. A red child's handbag
becomes annoyingly recurrent, as do glimpses of a girl dressed in a yellow raincoat.
The stain in the ceiling grows larger by the day, as though mocking Yoshimi's power-

lessness in the face of fickle fate, while the ghost begins to draw Ikuko into its icy game-plan.

A history of neglected children litters the downbeat narrative, from Yoshimi herself to the revelation that the ghost on the seventh floor is little Mitsuko Kawai, who, left to her own devices by an absent parent, tumbled into the building's ancient roof-mounted water tank and drowned. But in a chilling finale in the elevator outside the Matsubaras' waterlogged apartment, it turns out that the phantom Mitsuko is not after a childhood friend at all, but a proxy *mother*. The resolution to the story is an unhappy one, and an extension of the well scene in *Ring* where the long-dead corpse of Sadako is redemptively clutched to the bosom of its erstwhile rescuer.

The *Variety* staff reviewer said it all: 'Rarely has H$_2$O seemed so demonically scary as in *Dark Water*, the latest psycho-thriller from Japanese maestro Hideo Nakata which spreads a clammy hand of slow-burning fear across 100 minutes and delivers several real shocks along the way.'

With *Dark Water*, Nakata once again showed himself to be a master of atmosphere and graduated shock tactics, though the film can also be read as an allegory of a mind in inexorable collapse, and with the inevitable result, especially in its elegiac epilogue. If nothing else, it showed that the Japanese ghost story remained alive and well, despite the all-pervading effect of *Ring* on the form as a whole. The Kadokawa production was released domestically during January 2002, and has since been remade by Miramax subsidiary Dimension Films. Expect the allegory to vanish with Yoshimi in the transition.

In November 2002, the Kadokawa Group purchased the assets of the former Daiei Company to create Kadokawa-Daiei Pictures; the deal included a library of 1,600 titles available for recirculation and an 11,000 square-metre film studio. Kadokawa's annual report for 2002 showed that its own distribution of DreamWorks' *The Ring* had pulled in two billion yen at the Japanese box-office (approximately US $14 million). To end the year on a higher note still, Kadokawa Holdings celebrated the achievements of its *Ring* franchise by acquiring a 2.83% stake in DreamWorks SKG itself.

Ring-tones

While those already infected with the virus spread the effect of it further afield, the shadow of contagion also fell across a range of genre films which might otherwise have appeared in more conventional form. Byeong-ki Ahn's *Phone* (2001) is a case in point. Picked up for distribution by Disney's Buena Vista subsidiary (presumably to make up for the fact that the company lost out to DreamWorks in the *Ring* remake race), *Phone* is an intricate supernatural thriller which owes a great deal more than it should to

Phone *(2001)*.

What Lies Beneath, in that the mystery at the heart of its tale of a haunted cell-phone relates to a married man's affair with a young girl who has since disappeared, presumed dead. The ghost of the scorned lover soon makes its presence felt by calling the number that once belonged to her own phone but is now allocated to that of reporter Ji-won (Ji-won Ha); unfortunately, the call is answered by six year-old Yeong-ju (Seo-woo Eun), who transforms into a vengeful sprite with a father-fixation as a result.

Stripped of its diversions into *Ring* territory, *Phone* is really a murder mystery with supernatural overtones, but it was unable to resist the appending of elements that might better have suited an all-out occult assault of the *Pulse* variety. Its Sadako-like spirit is the precocious Jin-hee (Ji-yeon Choi), whose malevolent presence pops up in a number of ways and a variety of guises, including the predictable long-haired one. The twists in the tale are satisfyingly surprising, but ellipses in the narrative often make it difficult to differentiate between dream and reality. The film's two most striking scenes are also its most understated. The first sees Ji-won pick up a hitchhiker at night, who sits strangely silent like the ghost in many an anecdotal tale; the second takes place in daylight, on a deserted stretch of coast: Ji-won quizzes a former classmate of Jin-hee's. The woman, now blind, becomes aware of another presence: "You didn't come alone, did you?" she asks. "Jin-hee came with you, didn't she?" As the nape of Ji-won's neck turns literally to goose-flesh, the icy chill of fear descends upon the scene.

Phone is thoroughly derivative, but no less involving for that. Much use is made of Beethoven's 'Moonlight' Sonata, to add an air of Gothic romance to a film that director Ahn's self-confessed admiration for *Ring* ultimately turns into a patchwork of spooks, stalkers, surrogacy and sexual intrigue. Its climax even nods to Poe's 'The Black Cat', though it is a *phone*, rather than a cat, that is walled up with the corpse. But while most of its frights may be formulaic, little Seo-woo Eun still makes the possessed Yeong-ju one of the scariest tots in the history of the horror film.

Variety's enthusiasm was muted: '*Ring* meets South Korea's cell-obsessed culture in *Phone*, a neat psycho-thriller that will resonate equally with those who love and hate the warbling little handsets. Ahn piles on the shocks and false leads in the first few reels, to the point where the viewer wonders whether the plot is going to amount to anything more substantial than a pure teaser. Then, at the fifty minute mark, a key fact is revealed and with sizeable flashbacks (incorporated without any warning), the yarn swings into a higher gear.'

While Korea incorporated *Ring* motifs into its home-grown horrors in an altogether arbitrary way, Thailand's two-man film industry, the Pang Brothers, took another — and far superior — stab at a supernatural thriller with *Ring* overtones in *The Eye* (*Khon hen phi*: literally, 'Seeing Ghosts', 2002).

Mun Kar Wong (Sin-je [aka Angelica] Lee) has been blind since the age of two but receives a cornea transplant from an anonymous donor. As her mind begins to adjust to the sensation of sight, she experiences certain anomalies: her room takes on a different aspect at times, and she is assailed by mysterious figures who seem not to be part of the same plane of existence as she. Mun comes to the awareness that she literally is 'seeing ghosts' and asks psycho-surgeon Dr Wah Lo (Laurence Chou) for help. Between them, they trace the cornea donation to a suicide named Chiu-wai Ling, a Thai-born Chinese girl who took her life after being condemned as a witch by her peers for possessing the Sadako-like gift of second sight (apposite in the circumstances). "The

The Eye *(2002):*
Wong Kar Mun
(Sin-je Lee).

children treated her like a monster," local physician Dr Eak (Pierre Png) explains. "She foresaw death." Ling's precognitive abilities have not ceased with her own death, however, and despite the subsequent calming of her restive spirit, she still appears to have something else in mind for Mun…

The plot of *The Eye* is a literalisation of Cole Sear's oft-quoted line from *The Sixth Sense*: "I see dead people" — except that most of the people whom Mun sees are *about* to be dead. The film realises its theme splendidly, and one of the reasons that it works so well is that it cross-hatches the shadow-realm of the ghostly with the twilight world of the partially-sighted, as Mun struggles to comprehend what she can only perceive as distorted imagery, some real, some determinedly spectral. "The shadows… they come to bring the dead," she says eventually, as the spooky encounters accumulate to convince her that she is actually staring into another realm. The first half of *The Eye* harks back to *Carnival of Souls*, with dark-eyed visitants wandering in a limbo between this world and the next, and the scare factor is maintained by some nicely managed optical effects which keep Mun in sharp focus while all around her is blurred and indistinct — a simple ploy that adds weight to the almost palpable sense of tension which the Pangs manage to induce whenever scary interludes are in the offing.

The film features several superbly-executed shock scenes, from the unheralded leap of a spook at a calligraphy class ("Why are you sitting in my chair?") to the ghastly but all-too-real visage of a 'floating' ghost in an elevator that recalls some of the nightmare imaginings of Italian *giallo*-maestro Dario Argento. But the creepiest moment comes in a subway train in daylight, when Lo shows Mun a photo of herself and she asks who it is. "It's you," he replies. "Don't you recognise yourself yet?" Mun stares at the image that is peering back at her from the window opposite her seat, and the viewer realises at the same time she does that since the day of her operation, she has been looking into the face of *someone else* in the mirror. This delightful *frisson* is made doubly effective by the Pangs' clever staging of the scene: Mun and Lo are in frame, and no cutaway to the face in the window is provided, even when Mun leans forward to camera to stare at it. The reason for this apparent omission is that the viewer has been given a glimpse of the ghost-face already, though quite without realising it; it had earlier been reflected in a pane of glass above Mun's head. (This is another Argento trick, though of perception this time, such as was used in *Deep Red* [*Profondo rosso*, 1975], and less alert fans of *The Eye* might want to watch the sequence in light of the above.)

The Eye falters on the way to a climax by taking a long detour into Ling's personal history and the events leading to her suicide, much of which is simply copied from the story of Shizuko Yamamura in *Ring*, but it picks up speed again for a spectacular finale in which Mun tries to warn dozens of motorists caught in a traffic jam of the imminent explosion of an overturned gas tanker. The handling of this large-scale action set-piece is a textbook example of montage, with fleeing ghosts, flashbacks, and the minutiae of the chain reaction leading to the explosion all combined in the editing to mask the fact that it is largely created by CGI and a series of individually-staged vignettes. Nevertheless, the Pangs end their film with a bang and add another mini-classic to the fast-expanding *Ring* sub-genre.

'While *The Eye* starts out like a *Sixth Sense* clone with some *Blind Terror* thrown in, this psychological horror thriller gradually takes its share of more original turns,' David Rooney offered in *Variety*. 'A departure for directors Danny and Oxide Pang from the Thai gangster turf of their previous joint outing *Bangkok Dangerous*, the slick Hong Kong production could have used cleaner narrative lines and fine-tuning of love interest elements. But its sharp visuals and genuinely creepy atmosphere combine with enough chills to secure scattered sales and suggest significant remake potential...'

The Eye also broke local box-office records when it opened in Hong Kong in May 2002 and, two years later, the brothers tried to repeat the performance with *The Eye 2*. By then, however, much of the original chill had gone.

Even before the Kadokawa Group's moves to become a player on the international stage, the Ring virus seemed to some to be running its course. "Nowadays, the fashion for ghost stories is fading in Asia," Hideo Nakata stated at the time. "I'm in talks to do another kind of film which I'll direct in America. I'm lucky in that my intermediaries there had seen not only *Ring* and *Dark Water*, but *Chaos* and other films of mine which aren't horror films." While Nakata explored the avenues that he now felt

were opened up to him in Hollywood, however, January of 2003 saw the release in Japan of the first cinematic ghost story since 1998 to give *Ring* a run for its money.

> Ju-on: the curse of one who dies in the grip of powerful rage. It gathers and takes effect in the places that person was alive. Those who encounter it die, and a new curse is born.
>
> **- Screen caption,** *Ju-on* (2003)

Takashi Shimizu's *Ju-on* (*The Grudge*) is quite simply the best and most inventive 'haunted house' thriller since William Castle's original *House on Haunted Hill* (1959), even if its passage to the screen was almost as convoluted as its intricately interwoven storyline about a curse — and a ghost (or ghosts) — that attaches to anyone who sets foot inside a singularly inauspicious house in the Tokyo suburbs.

Ju-on's fragmentary narrative takes the form of numerous self-contained vignettes, whose common link is that the participants in each have come in contact either with the house itself or each other in preceding episodes; this is a clever strategy which calls to mind the portmanteau productions of Amicus Films, such as *The House That Dripped Blood* (1970) or *Asylum* (1972), except that the individual segments in *Ju-on* are better integrated into the film as a whole. The back story that provides the rationale for all the ghostly infestations is the archetypal *Amityville Horror* one of the gruesome murder of Kayako Saeki and her son Toshio by husband Takeo, the three of whom were previous tenants of the house in question.

Above: Ju-on: The Grudge *(2003):* Kayako *(Takako Fuji).*

Building on this premise, the film unfolds as a series of overlapping tales, each one focussing on a particular individual and all ending with a supernatural payoff. The first and last are centred on Rika (Megumi Okina), a trainee social worker, whose casework introduces the viewer to the house and its occupants, past and present. In

Ju·on: The Grudge: *the 'grudge' house.*

between, the ghostly duo of Kayako and Toshio plagues Hirohashi (Chikara Ishikara), Rika's boss, a brother and sister named Katsuya (Kanji Tsuda) and Hitomi (Misaki Ito), three friends in high school, and an ex-police detective named Toyama (Yoji Tanaka), who tries and fails to burn the house to the ground; a late investigation by Rika reveals the identity of the ghosts, but resolution of the affair comes at a price…

For all its novelty and determination to wring something more substantial from the ghost story amid the obvious rip-offs of *Ring*, the screen version of *Ju-on* was actually the *third* time that this particular idea had been committed to film. Three years before, the twenty-seven year-old Shimizu had attended night classes at the Tokyo Film School where he had come to the notice of *Pulse* director Kiyoshi Kurasawa, who was teaching there at the time. "Kurosawa introduced me to a producer at Kansai-TV who was producing a ninety-minute feature for television," Shimizu explained to Patrick Macias. "It was going to be a horror anthology and I was assigned to write and direct, but because I had no previous professional directorial experience, the producer had no confidence in me. He asked me to direct two segments and to cut them down to three minutes apiece. Those two short segments that I made are actually the foundations of *Ju-on*. They lay out the basic premise of the curse and are almost the true prequel to the story."

Shimizu's three-minute shorts were seen by Taka Ichise, producer of *Ring*, to whom he pitched his idea for a film about a haunted house. Ichise was impressed, and he brought in screenwriter Hiroshi Takahashi to help develop the story (Takahashi was credited as a creative consultant). The result was a 106-minute feature designed for the V-cinema (straight-to-video) market. However, Ichise felt that the finished film might play better in two parts, so *Ju-on* originally was released in February 2000 in a seventy-minute version, while *Ju-on 2* followed a month later and clocked in at seventy-six (forty of which were merely a reprise of footage from Part One). The *Ju-on* videos quickly attained cult-status in the fan-fraternity and Ichise encouraged Shimizu to turn his story into a full-length feature. In 2002, he did just that, and a feature version of *Ju-on 2* was also put into production after the huge success of the first big screen version.

"I didn't expect the video version of *Ju-on* to be such a huge hit," Shimizu went on. "When it was, the producer asked me if I was interested in doing a movie. Since I still had a lot of ideas that I wasn't able to explore in the video, I agreed. But the main difference between the video and the film is that the video *Ju-on* didn't really have a main character. You could say that the main character was the cursed house itself. For the movie, it was agreed that we'd need someone to be the protagonist, either a hero or a heroine. It took a long time to come up with a *Ju-on* story that would work with just one main character. There were many scripts and all of them were radically different from each other; some were simply about the origin of Kayako, the first victim and the ghost in the video. But I decided that I didn't want to make the film a prequel. I wanted it to have a male protagonist, a working-class middle-aged guy, but the producer said, 'Who wants to see some old guy?' So that's how we ended up with such an attractive female cast!"

Unlike *Ring*, where all the films, no matter how diverse, were drawn from the same source-novel, the V-cinema release of *Ju-on* was *itself* the source for subsequent films, and any appreciation of *Ju-on: The Grudge* has first to take it into account. In place of Rika, *Ju-on* (*The Curse*, as it has since become known) pivots its narrative on primary schoolteacher Shunsuke Kobayashi (played by *Ring 2*'s Yurei Yanagi), who visits the house to check out the whereabouts of six year-old Toshio (Ryota Koyama). He finds the boy at home alone and the place in disarray and decides to stick around in order to investigate further. The film then moves forward in time (though this is not made clear in the plotting) to focus on another group of tenants, primarily three schoolgirls named Yuki, Kanna and Mizuho (Chiaki Kuriyama, from *Shikoku*), before side-stepping into a police investigation of the girls' dismembered remains and returning to Kobayashi and Toshio for the climax. Part Two of *Ju-on* concerns itself with the fate of an estate agent who has been allotted the unenviable task of trying to sell the property.

Ju-on: The Curse features two exceedingly grisly sequences, neither of which made it into the feature version. In the first, the cadaver of Kanna returns to the house,

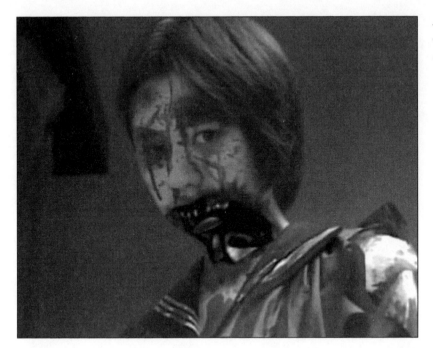

Ju-on: The
Grudge: *Kanna
(Asumi Miwa).*

minus its lower jaw, to confront its erstwhile mother in a scene that is either gut-wrenching or risible, depending on one's tolerance for graphic imagery. The second gives more form to the story than is to be found in the subsequent film. At the climax, Kobayashi finds Kayako Saeki's diaries in the house and reads to his dismay that she has been nurturing a crush on him; soon afterwards, he discovers her dead body in the attic. It is now clear to him what must have occurred: Toshio's father has murdered his mother and left the boy alone. Or so he thinks. Then he receives a phone call; it is Takeo Saeki. "Have you met Kayako yet?" Saeki asks, before telling him, "Your baby's been born." The viewer knows from an episode at the beginning of the film that Kobayashi's wife was heavily pregnant. "I see it's a girl…" Saeki finishes, holding up the foetus in the blood-spattered phone-booth. Kobayashi crumples to the floor. And meets Kayako…

Shimizu revised all of this for *Ju-on: The Grudge*, taking Taka Ichise's advice and replacing the Kobayashi 'wraparound' with that of Rika. The revelation of the murders (and murderer) in the feature film has much less of a visceral punch as a result, but the cast was certainly more attractive.

Ju-on comes supplied with its fair share of shocks, but ambience is more impor-tant to this scare-fest than it was to *Ring*. The 'Saeki' house used in all four films was a real house in the agricultural Saitama district of Greater Tokyo. "In some neighbour-hoods there, you can sometimes find abandoned houses where the owner will rent out the property for film crews to shoot in," Shimizu explained. "The house in *Ju-on* has also been used in a TV drama watched by housewives! I think there's something very scary about that house, but maybe foreigners wouldn't think so. In America and Europe, an attic can be a room where someone lives, but in Japan it's always dark and abandoned. Even the closets in Japan are different, with sliding doors instead of doors that open. Non-Japanese are afraid of what's under a bed, for example. But in Japan, people sleep on the floor!"

Nevertheless, the film was more conventional in its approach to the material, if not in the oblique structure of its narrative, and it allowed its ghosts to spread their terrors further from the confines of the house. But in doing so, it loosened the claus-trophobic ties to the seat of the haunting which had made the V-cinema versions so effective. No reason is given in *Ju-on: The Grudge* for Saeki to have murdered his wife and child so brutally, beyond an allusive hint to the effect that he thought she was hav-ing an affair, and there is no equivalent to the *Se7en*-inspired revelation in the phone-booth. But the numerous encounters with the dead duo are all inventively staged, with one especially evocative shot acknowledging Henry Fuseli's famous painting of 'The Nightmare', as Toshio squats on Rika's bed while Kayako peers down at her from over-head.

Takashi Shimizu perfectly exemplified the Japanese way with supernatural hor-ror in interview: "Timing is very important," he said. "You have to indicate to your actors exactly when a scream should come. Maybe a character hears a strange noise, but they shouldn't scream right away; they might think instead, 'oh — something dropped off the shelf', or, 'it's only the wind'. Doubt and fear will pile up little by lit-tle, and that makes for suspense. You have to calculate this perfectly to control the audience. Also, I think the art of horror is the art of misdirection. You think something is over there, then you realise that something is behind you… and maybe it's not even human…'

Derek Elley's *Variety* review was a little wide of the mark: 'A wannabe scare-fest that hides its lack of originality beneath a deliberately discombobulating structure, Takashi Shimizu's *The Grudge* is a haunted-house one-trick pony. Already a legend among Asiaphiles, and with an English-lingo remake in the works under producer Sam Raimi, pic is an OK entry in Japan's rich psycho-thriller genre but is far from a classic. Producer Taka Ichise was responsible for *The Ring* and *Dark Water*, but *The Grudge* doesn't bear mentioning in their distinguished company.' Ian Berriman's *SFX* review offered a more perceptive reflection: '*Ju-on* is not exactly original — its many scenes of a ghostly female creeping along the floor recall Sadako in *Ring*. But it has far

A Tale of Two
Sisters *(2003).*

more hair-raising moments, and its lack of narrative development is oddly disturbing.
You keep expecting someone — a police officer, a white-coated boffin — to resolve
matters so that everyone can live happily ever after. But it never happens...'

Ju-on was the first horror to come out of Japan in the wake of *Ring* to offer a
viable alternative to the over-familiar theme of the long-haired ghost. Consequently, it
quickly attracted the attention of another Hollywood company in search of product to
which it might lucratively apply a makeover.

In the meantime, Shimizu's film version inspired another sequel in the form of

Ju-on 2 (2003), which sought to move the story out of the confines of the Saeki house and into the big bad media world of TV documentaries about the supernatural (still hugely popular on Japanese television at the time of its production). Host and crew of one such fictional show set up shop in the house to investigate its gory past with the inevitable result that when filming is over, they each have to return to their former lives with a brace of ghosts in tow. The first half-hour of *Ju-on 2* offers up a new set of novel shocks of the now-renowned *Ju-on* variety, and Shimizu makes clever use of spectral occurences which increasingly are manifestations of future events of a violent nature, recalling the reinventions of the ghost story which Nigel Kneale initiated in his BBC teleplays *The Road* and *The Stone Tape*. Thereafter, however, the film descends rapidly into a variant on the old theme of demonic possession as the pregnant star of the show (Noriko Sakai) ultimately gives birth, *It's Alive!*-style, to a miniature Kayako and suffers a particularly vindictive form of post-natal trauma in consequence. Rather than shock and scare, *Ju-on 2* becomes risible as a result and its climactic excesses brought an inappropriate end to an original and intriguing idea.

> Do you know what's really scary? You want to forget something. Totally
> wipe it off your mind. But you never can. It can't go away, you see... and
> it follows you around, like a ghost.
> - **Eun-joo (Jung-ah Yum)**, *A Tale of Two Sisters* (2003)

Despite Nakata's premature predictions of imminent demise, the influence of *Ring* continued to be felt throughout 2003, not least in Korea. Ji-woon Kim's *A Tale of Two Sisters* (*Janghwa, Hongryeon*) inserts a very Sadako-like ghost into an otherwise slick and stylish psychological horror revolving around the antipathy felt by the titled sisters for the supposedly wicked stepmother that their father has chosen to inflict upon them in place of their beloved, but now suicidally deceased, mother. The film reeks of class in every department, not least that of the acting, where almost the whole weight of the (sometimes too) complex tale falls on the diminutive shoulders of twenty-two year-old former model Soo-jeong Lim as the teenage Su-mi, the stronger and more wilful of the sisters. The skin-crawling scene in which the aforementioned ghost makes its creaky presence felt to an insomniac Su-mi would do little to assuage the night fears of anyone who has ever laid awake in bed in the dark, while a second, more *Grudge*-like apparition is also to be found inhabiting a fateful closet.

Obviously, there *is* a ghost in *A Tale of Two Sisters*, but it very much plays second fiddle to a story of paranoid schizophrenia and the idea of the sins of the fathers being visited upon their children. Deeply unsettling and intellectually creepy for much of its length, the film shares its constructional conceit with Henri-Georges Clouzot's

One Missed Call
(2003).

classic *Les Diaboliques* (1955), or even the more recent *The Others*, in that what is depicted is not always what is taking place in reality — but to give more away would be to spoil one of the best and most unexpected last-quarter twists of any genre entry in living memory.

A *Tale of Two Sisters* drew the biggest weekend take in Korean film history when it opened on 13 June 2003, with more than three quarters of a million people turning out to see it. Not surprisingly, DreamWorks has since optioned the remake rights.

Back in Japan, however, things were looking a little less original. *One Missed Call* (*Chakushin ari*, 2003) ostensibly picked up where *Phone* left off, with a *Ring*-like riff of its own on the idea of a haunted cell-phone. In this instance, the recipient of the call is forewarned of his or her impending death by the snatch of conversation that they will utter immediately before the fateful moment. Neat concept, executed initially in a style somewhat similar to that of *Final Destination* (2000). But less than halfway through, things start to go wildly off the rails as a crazy television producer latches onto one of the victims and turns what are meant to be her final few moments into the centre-piece of a paranormal show in which she is subjected to an exorcism by a Buddhist shaman. In yet another nod to *Quatermass and the Pit*, things go horribly awry, the ghost makes its appearance live on air, and the victim perishes on cue. (This being a film by prolific genre funster Takashi Miike, she is encouraged to rip her own head off, which then lies staring into camera as the rest of her body tumbles to the ground behind.)

For all its portentous air and several genuine jolts, *One Missed Call* is nothing more or less than a compendium of the gimmicks introduced into J-horror since 1998,

One Missed Call.

plus a sampling of Western ones for good measure. In Miike's restless hands, the film ploughs ruthlessly through the furrow of recent ghost entries, offering up familiar situations out of everything from *Ring* to *The Grudge*, while changing tempo and style along the way and making as much sense in the final analysis as a *sukiyaki* composed entirely of bits and pieces found lying about. To ensure that his loyal audience were privy to the joke, Miike employed the talents of Kou Shibasaki (from *Kakashi*), Goro Kishitani (who had played Mitsuo Ando in the TV version of *Rasen*), Yatuka Matsushige (from *Rasen*), Renji Ishibashi (from the 'Chess' segment of *Tales of the Unusual*) and others who had featured in Kinji Fukasaku's notorious *Battle Royale* (*Batoru rowaiaru*, 2000), which included Shibasaki herself; if that were not enough, one of the character names in *One Missed Call* is 'Kenji Kawai', after the composer of *Ring*!

Miike's Western-leaning in-your-face approach found favour with *Variety*'s Derek Elley: 'In his first pic since *Audition* that doesn't look as if it was put together during a spare weekend, Nipponese pulp-meister Takashi Miike mines the Asian psycho-thriller vein to fine effect in *One Missed Call*. Blatantly hitching a ride on the Japanese *Ring* and South Korean *Phone*, with copious refs to *Dark Water*, film combines scares and chuckles with good production values. When the panicked Natsumi agrees to go on a trashy TV show that will be broadcast at the exact time of her flagged death, the movie becomes a much tastier blend of shocks, satire and suspense.'

With a haunted hospital lifted straight from *House on Haunted Hill*, a TV show that plays like a terminal version of real Japanese game-show 'Endurance', a perambulating corpse that oozes gore as efficiently as any Hollywood horror, and a climax that owes its extraneous ambivalence to that in *Basic Instinct* (1992), *One Missed Call* has

something for everyone. All it lacks is originality, though few in the packed houses of
Southeast Asia cared about that when it was released during January to March of 2004.

Detective Nakagawa — all the time I was in that house, I felt something
was wrong. What happened there?

- **Karen (Sarah Michelle Gellar)**, *The Grudge* (2004)

Above: The
Grudge (2004):
Takashi Shimizu,
Sarah Michelle
Gellar, Jason
Behr.

Following the lead that had been set by Hollywood's DreamWorks in relation to *Ring*,
The Evil Dead (1981) and *Spider-Man* (2002) director Sam Raimi's Ghost House
Pictures had snapped up the remake rights to Shimizu's *Ju-on*, thinking it to be anoth-
er golden franchise opportunity along the lines of Nakata's film. "I could imagine the
kind of effect that this would have on a Western audience," Raimi enthused after view-
ing the original at the behest of Roy Lee. "We saw it as something that could be great.
On my way out of the screening I told Rob [Tappert, Raimi's partner in the Ghost
House venture] three things: we must work with this director, we must bring this to
Ghost House and we must go into production as soon as possible."

True to their words, Raimi and Tappert hired Shimizu to direct the remake

American poster for The Grudge.

himself. "The thing that was so fantastic was the artistry of the director, who works   *Above:* The
very closely with the producer," Raimi said. "We felt that if we could employ the same   Grudge.
director and producer and support them with a larger budget, English-speaking actors
and all the modern film-making techniques that Hollywood excels at, maybe we could
preserve the original's integrity level and bring it to a wider audience." Given that the
film was also intended to be shot in Japan, but with an American cast, Shimizu was
backed up by his regular producer Ichise and his Japanese crew as well. In fact, the
only real distinction between *Ju-on: The Grudge* and what was now to be known simply as *The Grudge* was an English script by Stephen Susco. By setting its remake in
Tokyo, Ghost House was able to keep the new film's budget down to a more
respectable $10 million, as opposed to *The Ring's* overblown $45 million, and *The
Grudge* went onto the floor on Stage Seven at Toho Studios in February and March of
2004, in a full-scale mock-up of the house in Saitama prefecture where Shimizu had
shot his original.

The Ring at least had the relatively unknown Naomi Watts as its lead, thus
enabling the story to come to the fore, but *The Grudge* offered the Rika role (renamed
Karen) to Sarah Michelle Geller, aka Buffy Summers of television's *Buffy the Vampire
Slayer*. And Buffy kicks supernatural ass, right? Which seemed on the face of it to spike
the makers' guns somewhat almost before the off. Even so, Ichise and Shimizu managed to constrain their star's natural inclination to reach for heavy weaponry when

Above: The
Grudge.

confronted by ghostly adversaries, and with Takako Fuji and Yuya Ozeki returned to their roles as Kayako and Toshio Saeki (and for a *fifth* time, in the case of Fuji), *The Grudge* stayed more faithful to its source than anyone could reasonably have expected.

Whereas *Ju-on* was episodic in construction and effectively open-ended as a result, *The Grudge*, however, follows the route of Verbinski's *The Ring* and attempts to weave the various strands into a single, cohesive whole. In this, it is only partially successful. As the narrative now has to traverse three years in time, Shimizu employs two different flashback techniques, one of which is integrated into the main action but depicts a prior history of the house and a second in which Geller has suddenly to become psychically aware and witnesses, at first-hand, the events that have led up to the veritable epidemic of ghostly occurrences. Most of the set-piece scare sequences are virtually identical to those in the Japanese film, though their impact is lessened in the remake by the overuse of a heavy-handed score by Christopher Young which clumsily telegraphs every fright. As with Rick Baker's corpses in *The Ring*, Western audiences were accorded a moment of graphic shock that did not feature in *Ju-on: The Grudge* (though it is similar to that in *Ju-on: The Curse*). In the stairwell of his office building, Karen's boss is confronted by the figure of Yoko, the social worker who preceded her into the house at the start of the film and subsequently vanished. After shambling past him in shadow, she responds to his entreaties and turns to face him:

The Ghost/Dead Friend *(2004)*.

her jaw has been ripped off, leaving her tongue dangling hideously from what remains of her mouth. This is an effective shock-scene, with Shimizu fading the shot to black after *just* enough of it has been glimpsed for the image to imprint itself onto memory — though that may have had something to do with the battles which Shimizu had to fight with distributors Sony about the level of graphic violence in the film and the necessity for a PG-13 certificate in America.

Bill Pullman's presence, in the role of the schoolteacher played by Yurei Yanagi in the V-cinema version of *Ju-on*, only serves to heighten comparison between Shimizu's *The Grudge* and David Lynch's similarly obtuse *Lost Highway* (1997, in which Pullman had starred), and not favourably so: in restructuring the narrative to meet the 'investigative' requirements of the typical horror-thriller, the audience is enabled to stay several steps ahead of the actors for much of the proceedings. The opposite was true of the original, where it was the very random nature of events which was key to its unnerving success. With one or two exceptions, as when over-familiar CGI effects snake their predictable tendrils across the screen, the *frissons* in *The Grudge* are as ably handled as those in its various predecessors — but Gellar acts throughout as though she is well aware that she is appearing in a spooky movie, which tends to undermine their impact somewhat. For all its adherence to the personnel and precepts of Japanese horror, there are still things that Hollywood seems singularly unable to do, and to make a truly scary movie out of a Japanese original would seem to be one of them.

Variety was similarly unimpressed: 'Pic is a woeful Americanisation of a creaky haunted-house story Shimizu has filmed four times in Japan,' Scott Foundas opined. 'While press notes say pic's titular curse never forgives or forgets, viewers of this Sam

The Ghost/Dead
Friend.

Raimi-produced, sub-*Amityville* scare-fest are likely to hold the real grudge. If ever there was a remake that should have worshipped less faithfully at its predecessor's altar, *The Grudge* is it. Like *Ju-On: The Grudge*, new pic is less of a linear narrative than a series of flashbacks depicting earlier victims. And each of these scenes seems to have been scripted according to the horror-movie rules so deftly skewered by Wes Craven in his *Scream* pictures: a shadow streaks across the room or some floorboards creak; the naïve about-to-be victim goes to investigate and is startled by some sort of red herring; then, finally, the big 'gotcha!' moment occurs and screen fades to black, only to begin again.'

Scary or not, *The Grudge* would go on to take an impressive £39 million dollars during its opening weekend in America in October 2004, with a global gross of $110 million on top of that, thus ensuring itself of the inevitable sequel in due course.

As American studios geared up to recycle more remakes of films which already had come dangerously close to recycling themselves, it was left to the Koreans to bang the last nail into the coffin of the first wave of new Asian horror.

Tae-kyeong Kim's *The Ghost* (*Ryeong*, aka *Dead Friend*, 2004) is yet another tale of a vengeful female ghost which marries the over-familiar scares of *Ring* to the tricksy psychological twist-ending of *A Tale of Two Sisters*. A pre-credits séance conducted by three friends from Sang-Rim high school raises the requisite spectre, though its bearing on the narrative as a whole is made intentionally oblique by a plot which appears to be at variance with what has passed, as a young woman named Ji-won (Ha-neul Kim), who was *not* party to the séance, battles to regain the memory which has been lost to her as a result of some other unspecified trauma.

But Ji-won is more than amnesiac; she seems to have undergone a complete change of personality in the process. Whereas before, she was spiteful, vindictive, arrogant and snobbish, now she is sensitive, kindly, docile and deferential. The cleverest element in Asian psychological horror, helped in no small part by Western unfamiliarity with body language and the social etiquette of the characters, is its sheer inscrutability and how it manages so easily to manipulate the perceptions of the viewer. One is led to assume in *The Ghost* that this change of heart on Ji-won's part is as a result of her accident/plight. The truth, of course, is actually much simpler.

The lesson to be taken from *The Ghost* is to beware of a plot which appears to take off in another direction to its prologue once the credit titles have faded; something has occurred in between which will lead to the unexpected twist at the finale. In this case, it is the revelation that there are *two* ghosts, each of them in possession of a living body. And that the murderous one is the *other* one.

If it were not for the tired use of *Ring* imagery — strands of long, dark hair extracted from plug-holes, shadowy figures appearing stage-left, ominous pools of water — items like *The Ghost* would be elevated to a higher plane of acceptance. As it is, the film has some effective shock scenes and, it must be said, a quite terrifying spook, but they tend not to gel with the story as a whole. A tremendous finale, in which the ghost clambers out of a pool of water on the floor, tries to outdo that of *Ring* and very nearly succeeds, but even that is offset by the fact that it has now all been done, and seen, before. A new iconography is needed to inject some breathing-space into the Asian ghost story before it exhausts itself through repetition. With the genuine empathy towards the genre that is part of the Asian birthright, however, there can be little doubt that one will come.

The Ghost was released in South Korea in June 2004, just ten days after the crew of *The Ring Two* had set up shop again at the horse ranch in Monroe, Washington, which had played such a pivotal role in the DreamWorks original.

If Hideo Nakata had gone to America to try to avoid permanently being tagged as the director of *Ring*, he was in for a shock. As should be obvious by now, the Ring virus has a nasty habit of popping up unexpectedly, and the success of Gore Verbinski's remake had set a whole new strain in motion. Nonetheless, Nakata had not been fazed. "For my first US film, I'm trying to avoid making a horror film," he had said. "For me, horror in the US is very straight and very cruel, so it's difficult to find a suitable project." Find a project he did, though, and at MGM. But the virus had a sting in its flagellum: it was equally fond of *mutating*. Before he could say 'Samara', his American début had been transformed into something entirely different. "I was working on a project called *True Believers*, but somehow it became a Dimension project in

The Ring Two
*(2005): Evelyn
(Sissy Spacek).*

2004. And then Dimension thought it would need more work, or further development. That's why I wanted to find another project... And DreamWorks offered me *The Ring Two*."

The Ring Two

DreamWorks' CEO Walter Parkes had set the tone for the company's sequel to *The Ring* a year earlier, by stating his intention to dispense with what had gone before: "It's a very challenging franchise to create because I don't think in looking at the other *Ring* sequels that there's an obvious story to take. I don't think any of them were nearly as good as the original. We'd start at the beginning creatively by saying, 'Is there a story worth telling?'" The only story worth telling about *The Ring Two* by March 2004 was that Noam Murro, Parkes' original choice of director, had left the production citing the usual 'creative differences' which, in this instance, seemed to revolve around the extent to which Murro wanted to 'flash back' to Verbinski's film.

Featured heavily in the contentious flashbacks would have been Daveigh Chase, the Samara of *The Ring*, who had fully expected to reprise her role. "They're going to

start filming in March," she had said. "But I can't say anything about it. They're wait-ing till the last minute to show me a screenplay. I'm pretty sure I'll get to kill every-body again. That'll be fun!" The last minute came and went, however, and little Daveigh followed Murro out of the exit door.

Opposite: The Ring Two: *the return of Samara.*

Donnie Darko director Richard Kelly had been first in line to replace Murro, but he had declined DreamWorks' invitation. Then somebody came up with the bright idea of offering the film to the now-available Nakata. David Dorfman was signed to revive the role of Aidan alongside Naomi Watts as Rachel, and they were joined for the occasion by veteran Sissy Spacek — ironically, the very actress who had played Carrie in Brian De Palma's adaptation of the King novel. With Nakata on board and the cast set, filming of *The Ring Two* commenced on 13 May 2004, in the Columbia riverport of Astoria, Oregon. The sequel was meant to have been released in November of the same year, but production delays pushed it back to 18 March 2005 in America and 1 April in Britain.

> Have you ever seen something so scary that you just… you had to show it to someone else? Yeah, I mean like, you know, a movie or something? Okay, I've got the scariest freakin' movie you'll ever see…
>
> - **Jake (Ryan Merriman)**, *The Ring Two* (2005)

Even in the able hands of Hideo Nakata, *The Ring Two* (or 2, according to some of the trailers; its makers seemed confused on the issue) proved to be less an addition to an illustrious series — let alone a second instalment in a possible franchise — and more the formula horror movie that fans have long come to expect from Hollywood every time a domestic genre offering turns an inflated profit. Returning screenwriter Ehren Kruger seemingly flicked through his well-thumbed Roladex of tried-and-tested plot-lines to settle on the one where the monster latches onto a particular individual who escaped its clutches first time round, so as to pursue a vendetta which relates tangen-tially to its own prior history. This then leads to a new spate of grisly deaths, as the person in peril again attempts to escape the clutches of a fiend increasingly afflicted with tunnel vision (perhaps appropriate in this instance). *The Ring Two* adheres to these time-honoured precepts in all but the grisly deaths:

Six months after the events of the first film, Rachel Keller (Watts) and her son Aiden (Dorfman) have upped sticks and resettled in the small, out-of-the-way town of Astoria, Oregon. It is not long before the inexplicable demise of a local boy appears to Rachel to bear all the hallmarks of exposure to the very videotape which, accord-ing to *this* film, she thought she had left behind her in Seattle. (In actual fact, she had been instrumental in spreading its curse.) Rather than flee to another small town even

Above: The Ring
Two*: Samara
(Kelly Stables).*

further to the south, Rachel decides to investigate and duly comes to realise that, in the words of the official synopsis, 'Samara is back'… and that 'this time, it's personal'. (Sorry, wrong film.) Specifically, Samara is out to 'possess' Aiden, so that she can experience the mother-love which was denied her in life. In a soporific plot twist as old and self-consciously clichéd as one of Bobby Picket's lyrics for 'Monster Mash', the monster in *The Ring Two* just wants to be loved! At this point, the story abandons all connection with *The Ring* (as well as *Ring*) and cosies down in the well-trodden territory of the feisty protagonist determined at all cost to rescue a loved one from a fate worse than death. This Rachel eventually does by sacrificing herself at the climax in the manner of Anna Morgan in *The Ring*. Or she *did*, until American preview audiences demanded a happier ending and DreamWorks tacked on a revised finale of the 'it-was-all-a-dream' variety, which implies that the curse inexplicably is at an end and that she and her son will now live happily ever after — several unexplained dead bodies permitting, including one currently propped against the steering wheel of a truck which sits with its engine running outside their home…

To say that *The Ring Two* is a travesty is to understate the crassness of Kruger's

approach to the most original notion in Terror cinema since Dr Jekyll turned into Mr Hyde. The film is a prime example of Big Mac movie-making: bloated, predictable and homogenised. An excellent (if faintly preposterous) opening sequence in which another viewer of the video is made fatally aware of the truth of its prophecy (inventively shown from Samara's viewpoint) soon gives way to a facile tale of demonic possession which jettisons every rule of the curse which previous films had scrupulously to live by and in which all the characters are required to act with the consummate stupidity of any wide-eyed teenager who ever set foot in a Hollywood haunted house.

Above: The Ring Two: *Rachel Keller.*

Nakata serves up the required quota of shocks, but mostly they involve arms being grabbed by disembodied hands to the accompaniment of loud chords on the soundtrack and one — that of actor Gary Cole's entrance as an unlikely estate agent at the Morgan ranch — even harks back to the kind of sudden 'door-opening' jolts which traditionally were allotted to Vincent Price in Roger Corman's Poe thrillers of the 1960s. Samara is afforded little history, no real motivation and fewer onscreen appearances than in any episode in the entire series; she is simply a monster on the loose, devoid of personality or feasible rationale. The intricate logic of the video curse is cursorily dispensed with before the second reel is out, as Rachel sets fire to the 'only' copy of the tape while muttering, "Not here, Samara... not here!" A futile act, to be sure, had she any memory of the events of the first film — but Kruger has seen to it that collective amnesia is the order of the day for all concerned. All but the audience for *The Ring Two*, that is. In re-engineering the rules of the deadly game of death, Samara is now enabled to utilise a television set — *any* television set — as the conduit for her re-entry at will into the world of the living, in the same way that Fred Krueger was able to use the dreams of his victims as a corridor between death and life in the *Nightmare on Elm Street* movies. Thus she can pop up in any convenient locale, to grab unwary antagonists and drag them kicking and screaming into her own version of virtual reality. While this concept has echoes of Suzuki's *Loop*, it makes a mockery of the ghost story element which previously had been central to the series. In such a yawningly formulaic scenario, lost opportunities abound — the most blatant being a subplot which has Rachel accused of child abuse and which might just have afforded the film a neat sub-textual reading had the powers-that-be not decided to drop the idea like a wet braid of long dark hair as it was beginning to gain ground.

The obvious tampering of DreamWorks executives after the event was enough to send an already-fractured production spiralling downwards to its doom: continuity is non-existent (Rachel goes about breaking-and-entering in her adopted town of Astoria with apparent impunity); characters who appeared in early cast listings for the film are nowhere to be seen in the extant print, and late cameos were added to paste over the consequent joins in logic (such as that by the aforementioned Cole, and an even more histrionic one by the camp-cast Spacek as Samara's biological mother, Evelyn). With the single, under-utilised exception of Simon Baker as Max (shoehorned into the story to offer ambivalent support to Rachel before being dispatched by Samara in another of the film's lost threads: he takes a time-delayed snap of Aiden/Samara prior to his own death, but the resultant photo is never divulged), the cast gravitate in dumb obedience towards the pay cheques awaiting them at the bottom of the well. In the Damien/Regan role of a young child possessed by an evil spirit, Dorfman is all at sea — literally so, in an *Elm Street*-inspired sequence which turns bath night into a tsunami survival session (Kruger was penning the script to *Dark Water* while working on *The Ring Two*). And with the delays and re-shoots, Dorfman's age and appearance alter more significantly in successive scenes than does his personality under Samara's baleful influence.

According to screenwriter Kruger, Nakata had little or no say in the script with which he belatedly was presented and had merely to translate its puerile ideas to the screen. Only the opening, when the film switches point of view to the *other* side of the television screen as Jake (Ryan Merriman) is drawn inexorably towards destiny and death, manages to evince of the director's unique flair for the surprise angle. Nakata

Above: The Ring
Two: *Naomi
Watts, Hideo
Nakata.*

makes a gallant attempt to return the story to its origins in the briny deeps through the
employment of some evocative seascapes in prelude — "I'm from Japan, which is an
island country surrounded by water. Through natural disasters, water itself can be a
symbol of death, so we have an innate fear of water that influences me. And, of course,
in this movie, water becomes a sign of Samara's evil spirit, because she had been kept
at the bottom of a well for a long, long time," he offered once more — and the screenplay defers to Takahashi in the scene in which Sister Elizabeth (Mary Joy) lets Rachel
into a little of Evelyn's psychological history: "She believed some *thing* had come for her
baby from the waters of the world beyond this one…" But pressure of time precluded
the inclusion of more in the way of the atmospherics that Gore Verbinski had brought
to *The Ring*: Watts was due on the set of Peter Jackson's *King Kong*.

Aside from these token nods to source, *The Ring Two* could as easily have been
served up as an exploitation offering by Dark Castle, with its stale repertoire of shocks,
over-the-top horror set-pieces and predictable suspense scenes. The PG-13 certificate
that its producers required for the American market clearly deprived the end result of
much of its potential — but this is DreamWorks, after all, home of *Shrek*. Even Rick
Baker's make-up effects are well below par, the faces of the two featured victims

inspiring little of the undiluted terror in revelation that was so pronounced in their forebears. (Baker's 'Photoshop' technique was less successfully utilised on Merriman in the prologue than it had been on Amber Tamblyn in the similar sequence in *The Ring* and the shot was eventually truncated, relieving it of its payoff.) The well set, built on Stage 1 of Center Studios in Downtown Los Angeles, is a tangible improvement on its prototype, but the inclusion of extracts from Verbinski's version of the cursed video only makes them look oddly out of place in this largely unrelated context.

It is an easy jibe to suggest that *The Ring Two* is all that one might have expected from a screenwriter with *Scream 3* in his résumé, but there really is no other way to evaluate such a hackneyed and moribund entry in an otherwise noble canon, in which production values overall are every bit the match for the feebleness of its plotting: a mid-film assault on Rachel's Volkswagen by a herd of deer (incorporated to recall the runaway horse of *The Ring*) produces only jeers in an audience for whom their antics are more reminiscent of the fantastic creations of an effects team who previously had worked on *Men in Black* (1997) and *Scooby Doo 2* (2004). The pre-release publicity was similarly old hat, as jaded studio hacks waxed excitedly about spooky happenings on-set in an attempt to hype back to the glory days of the much-troubled *Exorcist* shoot. A Shinto Purification ceremony was reportedly demanded by Nakata to stem the flow of bad vibes. "I've worked on more than thirty movies, and that was a first," Parkes remarked. But *The Exorcist* had Old Nick himself to agitate, whereas *The Ring Two* had only an imaginary bogey-girl. Seems no one thought that through either.

The Ring Two took a better-than-predicted $35.1 million on its opening weekend, more than double that of its predecessor, but word of mouth saw it struggle to reach twice that amount after a month in release, whereas *The Ring* saw a seven-fold increase at the box-office over a similar period in 2002. The dead hand of studio interference is everywhere in evidence in the film. Nakata may have come late to the proceedings as an expedient mechanism for getting the show on the road after Murro's acrimonious departure, but he was clearly unwilling — or unable — to deflect the producers from their intent to turn out a third-generation VHS copy of a digital master. Hiring the director of *Ring* was advanced as a masterstroke by DreamWorks publicists — "When Gore was unavailable, we asked him who he thought should direct this film and he suggested Hideo. We all thought it was a great idea. When Hideo came onto the project, it made perfect sense… like it came full circle," Parkes was quoted as saying — but Nakata was far from the company's original choice. The Japanese director tried to make the best of a bad career move, but despite its featuring one of the scariest teaser-trailers ever to appear on the web, the vitriol heaped upon the film in fan sites and chat rooms right across the Internet was for once justified. Had Parkes and MacDonald desired to kill off the franchise at a stroke, they could have contrived no better means of doing it than by producing this by-the-numbers excuse for a fright film. Manohla Dargis of the *New York Times* conceded that '*The Ring Two* is a dud', while the *Washington Post*'s Stephen Hunter felt that the film had been 'written on a large piece of blank paper by chickens with their feet dipped in ink'. Peter Travers in *Rolling Stone* said of the script that it 'strains credulity at every turn', complaining, in addition, that it was riddled with 'clichéd horror gimmickry', while Nicholas Barber, in *The Independent on Sunday*, concluded that the whole Ring cycle was now 'going round in circles'.

In America, *The Ring Two* was denied the usual première engagement at the last minute. "Who d'you think buys this crap?" Rachel is moved to inquire of her son early in the proceedings, during an interlude at a local flea-market. On the evidence of the box-office, it would appear that the answer to her question was those who rushed to purchase tickets before the reviews came in, more in hope than reasonable expectation.

Would he be interested in doing *another* sequel? Nakata was asked by Javier Lopez before the film's theatrical release in the States. "Yes, I would," he had replied. Hideo Nakata is presently ear-marked to helm a Paramount remake of the Pangs' *The Eye*, for producers Roy Lee, Doug Davidson and Peter Chan — which leads one to the conclusion that the esteemed director of *Ring* has become typecast in the very genre that he sought to leave behind him on vacating Japan, after all.

The DreamWorks version of *Dark Water* opened in America on 8 July 2005 (after premièring in New York on 27 June) and in the UK on 22 July. With the company scheduled also to shoot *A Tale of Two Sisters*, Wes Craven slated to direct a remake of *Pulse*, Sony/Columbia again in pre-production with Ghost House on *The Grudge 2*, and genre outfits Distant Horizon and Rogue Pictures holding the rights to *Don't Look Up* and *Phone* respectively, the Ring virus seems still to be as virulent as ever. And these are the tapes which have landed on America's shores thus far; a whole new slew of indigenous Asian horrors is bound to be following on behind…

As to the saga of *Ring* — as James wrote in closing in his 'Casting the Runes', in relation to a victim of the hex in that story: 'Only one detail shall be added…' O

Day Seven: The Famous Final Scene

"Who is this who is coming?"

> - **M R James**, 'Oh, Whistle, and I'll Come to You, My Lad'
> *Ghost Stories of an Antiquary* (1904)

Suddenly, as I watched, one of the shadows that danced round and about the pool and reeled to the blattering wind and the thunder peals, detached itself and rose slowly out of the pond and, dripping, passed through the door of the farmhouse.

> - **N Dennett**, 'Unburied Bane' *Horrors* (1933)

The reader should have noticed by now that all mention of what takes place at the climax of the various film versions of *Ring* has thus far been rigorously eschewed from the narrative of this book. Having now reached Day Seven, however, the genie must at last come out of the bottle. Be it 12.48, 7.08, 8.55, 10pm or any other of the times allotted by film script and fate, the hour is here at hand. The minutes tick by.

Let us now go back aways, and fill in the bits that consciously were missed. Surely you did not think, my friends, that like Reiko or Rachel, you had *escaped* the curse…?

INT. RYUJI'S APARTMENT — MORNING

Ryuji is busy scribbling away at his notes again. His hand suddenly ceases. Ryuji spins around to face the TELEVISION SET, eyes dancing worriedly as he hears a faint…

No.

Breath rattling fearfully in his throat, Ryuji spins around to face the TELEVISION SET. He gets out of his seat for a better look, falling to his knees on the tatami.

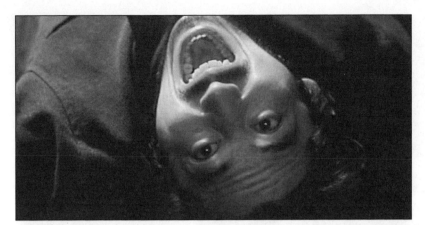

Ring *(1998)*, Ring 2 *(1999)*, The Ring *(2002) – the seventh day...*

Above: Ring.

The image that fills the screen is the last scene from the videotape; the shot of the well.

The sound from before comes louder now, more insistent, a metallic screeching that both repulses and beckons him closer. Ryuji crawls on all fours towards the screen, stares at its unchanging image with terrible foreboding.

There is a flash of MOTION as something shoots out of the well. A hand. First one, and then another, as Sadako, still in her grimy white dress, face hidden beneath long, oily strands of hair, begins slowly pulling herself out. The television screen jumps unsteadily, fills with static as if barely able to contain her image.

CUT back and forth between Ryuji, who is beginning to visibly panic, and the television, which shows Sadako lurching ever closer.

RYUJI
(almost frantic)

Why?!

The TELEPHONE rings, and Ryuji spins round towards it, breath catching in his throat. He looks at the phone, over his shoulder at the television, back to the phone.

RYUJI

That's it! Asakawa…

Ryuji scrambles wildly towards the phone. He takes the receiver but is unable to do more than clutch it fearfully as his gaze is drawn inexorably back to the television. Sadako's shrouded face has filled the entire screen… and then, television popping and crackling, she jerks forward and emerges from the television onto the floor of Ryuji's apartment. Ryuji backs away, screaming in terror.

Above: Ring.

RYUJI

Aaargh!

Sadako lies prone, collapsed, hair splayed out like a drowned corpse. Only her FINGERS are active, crawling, feeling. The TIPS of her fingers are little more than bloodied stumps, not a single fingernail on them. She uses the strength in those fingers to pull herself forward, coming jerkily to her feet. The joints of her body twist unnaturally, more insect-like than human.

Ryuji flings the phone aside and begins scrambling about the apartment as if looking for cover. The strength has already begun to fade from his body, however, and his movements are clumsy, exaggerated. He falls to the floor, panting heavily.

Sadako turns to regard him, and for just an instant we can see beneath her impenetrable shroud of hair; a single EYE burns with manic, unbridled hatred.

Its gaze meets Ryuji's and his face twists into a grimace as he SCREAMS loudly.

- **Javier Lopez**, adaptation of Hiroshi Takahashi's screenplay of *Ring*
(1998)

So just what was it that invested *Ring* with the power to terrify audiences more than any film since *The Exorcist* back in 1973? In truth, there is not much of consequence in its ninety-six minutes of screen time to justify its reputation as a shocker; the 'cursed' video at the centre of the tale makes for unnerving viewing, and prior knowledge on the part of the audience that something 'monstrous and horrible' is destined to befall any who are exposed to it (which cleverly includes those watching in the audience) plays a cumulative part in creating a climate of fear. But no clue is forthcoming as to what that climactic terror might be, and no examples of its effect on previous observers of the tape are allowed to intrude on the narrative beyond the glimpse of a dead teenager that is offered up at the very beginning of the film — all of which would seem at first to substantiate the charge that screenwriter Takahashi had levelled against Hideo Nakata, that he was 'not a good horror film director'.

In contravention of the old adage that less is more — that what remains unseen must by implication be more frightening than anything that the film-maker can visualise, *Ring* made good on its promise. It delivered the goods. And its last act installed it forever in the horror hall of fame. *Ring's* exalted place in the cinema of Terror rests wholly on its famous final scene — its *Jamesian* moment of climax:

> ...For some reason it was hateful to him from the first, but he had gazed at it for some moments before any feeling of anxiety came over him; and then it did come, stronger and stronger — a horror lest something might emerge from it, and a really agonising conviction that a terror was on its way, from the sight of which he would not be able to escape. Oh yes, far, far down there was a movement, and the movement was upwards — towards the surface. Nearer and nearer it came, and it was of a blackish-grey colour with more than one dark hole. It took shape as a face — a human face — a *burnt* human face: and with the odious writhings of a wasp creeping out of a rotten apple there clambered forth an appearance of a form, waving black arms prepared to clasp the head that was bending over them.
>
> - **M R James**, 'Mr Humphreys and his Inheritance'
> *More Ghost Stories of an Antiquary* (1911)

...Then he dozed, and then he woke, and bethought himself that his brown spaniel, which ordinarily slept in his room, had not come upstairs

Ring: *the coming of Sadako.*

with him. Then he thought he was mistaken: for happening to move his hand which hung down over the arm of the chair within a few inches of the floor, he felt on the back of it just the slightest touch of a surface of hair, and stretching it out in that direction, he stroked and patted a rounded something. But the feel of it, and still more the fact that instead of a responsive movement, absolute stillness greeted his touch, made him look over the arm. What he had been touching rose to meet him. It was in the attitude of one that had crept along the floor on its belly, and it was, so far as could be recollected, a human figure. But of the face which was now rising to within a few inches of his own, no feature was discernible,

Above: Rie Inou.

only hair.

-**M R James**, 'The Diary of Mr Poynter' *A Thin Ghost and Others* (1919)

The finale of *Ring* is a show-stopper in the history of the horror film; a sequence to match the unmasking of the phantom in *The Phantom of the Opera* (1925), King Kong crashing through the gates of the great wall on Skull Island in *King Kong*, the strangling of the psychiatrist in *Dead of Night*, Asa the witch being raised from the dead in *La maschera del demonio* (1960), the shower-bath murder of Marion Crane in *Psycho*, the blood raining down on the lovers in *Angel Heart*, or the final render of the 'face' of the Jersey Devil in *The Last Broadcast* (1998) — all of them moments when the veil of reality is suddenly, shockingly, cast aside and a descent into nightmare begins...

It was a simple trick, but a clever one: once again, a television set crackles into life; the video appears on the screen; it is the scene of the well... But this time — *this* time — it is not the same scene. This time, a figure climbs out of the well; walks jerkily towards the camera; fills the frame, its face shrouded by long tresses of dark hair... Then it *crawls through the screen towards the viewer...*

As the image on the video flops physically onto the floor of Ryuji's apartment, like some hellish foetus dragging itself into the living world on torn and bloody fingernails, the physically impossible is brought searingly into being.

The boundary has been crossed; the limit reached. The line between the known and the unknown erased. This is the arc of Terror. And the stroke of genius which hardcore horror fan and *Ring* scriptwriter Hiroshi Takahashi conjured out of the air in a moment of pure homage, echoing of *Poltergeist* and David Cronenberg's gross-out *Videodrome* (1983) with its organic videotapes, was the final spark of inspiration that was needed to shift the film onto a new level of fright.

All well and good, but the figure of Sadako herself required to rise to the challenge of such an entrance — especially when the fulfilment of the video prophecy represented her only appearance on screen in 'ghost' form (at least in the original film). She did not disappoint. Before familiarity and repetition in any number of similar films since — up to and including *The Grudge*, not to mention the slapstick of *Scary Movie 3* (2003) — lessened the effect and emblemised the image in the style of Dracula or Frankenstein's monster, the apparition of Sadako at the climax of *Ring* was a terrifying creation: a classic Japanese ghost, clad in white and with dark, waist-length hair. But the hair hangs down over the face, entirely obscuring the features. On first viewing, this image demanded a moment or two of perceptive adjustment; was her head facing *backwards*, like that of Regan in the most notorious sequence from *The Exorcist*? When eventually it registered, it also became clear that Nakata had pulled off a masterful double-bluff, satisfying audience expectation by producing a monster out of his hat but remaining true to the adage that things unseen are more frightening than things seen by keeping its face hidden. In this, he corrected his misjudgement at the climax of *Don't Look Up*, where Dan Li's 'ghost actress' is a good deal less scary in the flesh than were the blurred images of her earlier in the piece. "Takahashi, who co-wrote the screenplay, said that *Ghost Actress* was not frightening at all," Nakata explained. "The ghost shows her whole face, but the image was maybe not very powerful. In *Ring*, we have this evil character who shows only one eye and her hair, and I think that's the most powerful image."

As personified by thirty year-old Kabuki actress Rie Inou, Sadako is the very epitome of sentient malevolence as she heaves herself upright to stand, lop-sided and lethal, in front of the petrified Ryuji. Nakata affords the viewer a brief glimpse of a dilated eye, burning with an intense and otherworldly hatred, and then it is over. This one brief shot of (part of) Sadako's face has since become trite through over-exposure in every article related to the film, but its initial employment in *Ring* was powerful enough to convince most viewers of Ryuji's fate as he stared into the face of the Gorgon.

If *Don't Look Up/Ghost Actress* had fallen foul of one of the unwritten rules of the Terror film, *Ring* put things to rights. "I went in a completely different direction," the director went on. "Okay — let's cover her face up completely. Again, we had to show something, so we decided just to show the one eye. But probably the new thing is about just covering up the face completely…"

Nor were any elaborate effects deployed to enhance the sense of apprehension and dread felt by Reiko's ex-husband during Sadako's emergence from the well, other than a camera trick which had been in play since the time of silent screen magician Georges Méliès: Inou merely walked backwards towards the well in the exaggerated motion that is part of *neo*-Kabuki, and the film was played *in reverse*. (The American *Ring* found itself unable to top such simple sleight-of-hand, especially when its version of Sadako was a juvenile unversed in oriental dance techniques, and opted instead to concentrate effort on what transpires *after* Samara has entered Noah's room.)

Takahashi's original draft for *Ring* had called for a prologue to this climactic scene, which was to have taken place while Ryuji was still seated at his desk.

INT. RYUJI'S APARTMENT — MORNING
Ryuji is busy scribbling away at his notes again. His hand suddenly ceases,

cheeks draining of colour as the faintest of sounds reaches his ears and fills him with dread.

No.

Just then his hand jerks into life, moving with a will of its own. Ryuji watches, shocked, as a series of jagged, spiky letters forms on the page.

H... E... L... L...

When the hand finally ceases writing Ryuji sits a moment in stunned silence. He then spins around to face the TELEVISION SET, where the last scene from the videotape — the shot of the well — has appeared onscreen.

- **Javier Lopez/Hiroshi Takahashi**, scene deleted from the screenplay of
Ring (1998)

When Reiko later arrives at Ryuji's apartment, she was to have found the scribbled note, which in the earlier scene had been completed out of shot. On it, she reads: 'Hell is *real*'. Both of these episodes were deleted from the script prior to filming, which had the effect of making the appearance of Sadako all the more unexpected.

So much for *Ring*. But what about the others — *Ring: The Final Chapter*, *The Ring Virus*, *Ring 2*, *Ring 0: Birthday* and *The Ring*? What horrors unfolded in those?

Ring: Saishusho has no 'famous final scene' as such, as the story takes a different route from the point when Asakawa climbs down into the well. Neither is the corpse

Below: Ring: Saishusho *(1999).*

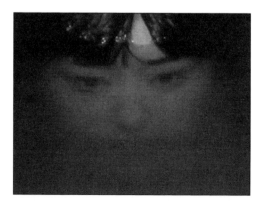

of Sadako discovered there, nor anywhere else for that matter. The finale with the TV set is nowhere to be seen in this version, as the climactic twist of *Ring* has to be subverted to the need to continue the story into *Rasen* territory, and the death that usually follows the discovery of the well and exhumation of Sadako's body is merely accomplished by the second-hand news that another schoolgirl has since died. The serial does, however, offer up the requisite shock in the well, when Asakawa sees Sadako's face floating just below the surface of the water and moments later, her hands lunge at his throat...

(Fuji Television's version of *Rasen* went some way towards correcting the omission by including a sequence in which Ando stares at a television while Sadako climbs out of the well; as he kneels close to the set, her hands suddenly thrust through the screen and she attempts to strangle him. Shot in profile, with two arms projecting from a box, the brief sequence required no special effects.)

The Ring Virus also went its own way for much of its length, but it chose to defer to Nakata for its finale. In this version, there is quite a change of emphasis, however, and the significantly more in-your-face approach of director Dung-bin Park is worth noting: Choi is at home, as per Ryuji in *Ring*, but before the television set can flare into unholy life, he begins to realise that he has made a mistake and that the curse is not at an end. He creeps towards the set and removes the tape, his gaze lingering on the word 'copy'. Only when he returns to the side of the room to phone Sun-joo does the television turn itself on. He stares at it fixedly, fear whitening his eyes... Park

Above: The Ring Virus *(1999): Eun-kyung Shin.*

now goes one better than Nakata. He dispenses with the slightly offset view that was decided upon for *Ring* and favours instead a full-on shot of the screen as Eun-suh emerges. Cutting back and forth between a slow zoom towards Choi and the materialised Eun-suh, he holds the angle as she crawls along the floor towards camera — a wide-angle lens emphasising her clawed hands as she reaches out to her shaken victim. The requisite shock-cut to a green-faced Eun-suh at the moment of Choi's death is effective, if a little odd, but the scene of her birthing through the screen is a definite improvement on a classic original.

Ring 2 was invested with a climax as weak as that of *Ring: The Final Chapter*.

Nakata had made much in interview of the metaphorical aspects of the well, with its mythic association as a gateway to the underworld as well as its Freudian connection to the subconscious mind. In *Ring 2*, he attempted to heighten the psychological angle by shooting the well as though it were deeper, danker and more symbolic in nature. As an alternative to the straight scare tactics which he had employed in its

Ring 2.

predecessor, it was a failure on all counts:

Having been subjected to Dr Kawajiri's mad experiment by the pool, a psychic Mai Takano wakes up in a dream with Yoichi by her side, and both are clinging onto the side of the well. 'Frolic in brine — goblins be thine' chants on the soundtrack. Takano looks down, then she and the boy leap feet-first into the swirling waters. A rope appears from above, followed by the shade of Ryuji — but from the depths, in his case; he says to her: "Give your fear to me…"

All of this already is too spiritualistic and surreal, and it is difficult to believe that it is the work of the same director who was responsible for *Ring*. Takano begins to climb out of the well again as black hair floats to the surface of the water. As she and Yoichi cling desperately to the interior face of the well, the figure of Sadako emerges, reaches out for the wall and starts to crawl up, spider-like, towards them. But this goose-bump moment is quickly dissipated when Takano turns to look at the ghostly figure who has now reached her side: in place of a death's head is the clay face that was reconstructed from Sadako's skull by the forensic scientists earlier in the film. "Why are you the only one saved?" Takano is asked, inconsequentially, then the 'puppet' Sadako releases its grip on her arm and plummets back into the well, and what should have been a frenzied nightmare of terror as Takano and Yoichi try vainly to escape the clutches of a demon that 'doth close behind [them] tread' is effectively thrown away for the sake of an arty visual allusion.

Things improved somewhat in Norio Tsuruta's *Ring 0: Birthday*, which attempted to replicate the shock level of the original's climax to no small degree of success:

With the re-energised figure of Sadako now stalking the forest and dispatching

Ring 0: Birthday
(2000).

her erstwhile pursuers, one by one, as she goes, Miyaji and Etsuko take refuge in the empty house. Miyaji looks out of a window and sees Sadako standing amid the trees. She runs to barricade the door but Sadako is already in the hallway. Miyaji collapses to the floor and clambers back into the room where Etsuko cowers, petrified, against a wall. They stare at the doorway — and Sadako springs suddenly into view. As the demon makes its inexorable approach to where the women lie huddled together in sheer terror, its body twitches and stretches, creaks and contorts in spasm, like some unholy insect uncoiling itself for the feast...

Miyaji pulls out her pistol, but instead of trying to kill (or face) the unearthly thing that now towers above them, she shoots Etsuko before turning the gun on herself...

The sequence is a bone-chilling elaboration of the Kabuki trick that Rie Inou pulled in *Ring* when she clambered out of the well to walk, crab-like, to camera. No CGI was involved in this instance either; it is a pure piece of physical contortion. But the image is grotesque in the extreme — the stuff of nightmare. The idea that someone would blow their brains out as a viable way of erasing a sight that their mind simply cannot contain only serves to compound the horror. The cinematic ghost story never had it so good.

DreamWorks' *The Ring* was stuck with simply having to reprise what, by then, was a well-known and much-imitated routine. Samara's emergence from the TV screen was re-enacted virtually shot-for-shot to Nakata's template for Sadako, but when she stands erect, Verbinski *does* opt for a little help from CGI in order to depict the girl as though she were an electronic image and therefore subject to technical glitches. This proves to be very effective in the American film, which is altogether rooted in too much reality in the first place and in which a more solid Samara would have appeared less of a threat, and an additional jolt is provided when she suddenly 'leaps' forward, in imitation of a jump-cut in the living tape. (This holographic representation of Samara in *The Ring* is actually an extension of the scene in *Kanzenban* where Sadako walks 'through' Ryuji's girlfriend before turning and strangling him.)

In other respects, though, the sequence is less than convincing. The water that drips around a live television set as Samara makes her entrance through the tube disturbs the equilibrium even of those who are not themselves electrical engineers, and the puddles that remain physically present after Sadako's appearances (such as during the death of the resort manager) hark back to the incongruous materialisation of a real fly *outside* of a monitor screen earlier in the piece. It is almost as though the filmmakers were trying to cling onto some scientific rationale for the events which they were required to depict and were unable, in the final analysis, to give themselves over to a supernatural explanation. The strength of the Japanese original derives from its cultural willingness to surrender itself to the inexplicable; that is the root of its power to terrify. Faced with the uncanny in *The Ring*, it is difficult to escape the impression that what its director really wanted to be able to do was to call in the marines.

The Ring Two lifts its climax from Nakata's own *Ring 2*, as Rachel clambers up the side of the well with an organic Samara in hot pursuit. The sequence is a technical advance on that of its forerunner and might have compared favourably with that of the 'double-jointed' Sadako at the close of *Ring 0: Birthday* had the CGI-aided design of Samara's creepy-crawly 'spider-walk' not already been done to death in numerous sci-fi shockers from *Alien3* (1992) on. Nakata denied the use of CGI in interview ("There was a discussion about how to achieve Samara's movements — maybe even CGI — but I felt it wouldn't work in the scene"), just as Jacques Tourneur used to decry the incorporation of a rubber monster into his own *Night of the Demon*, but the use of computer imaging to enhance the contortions of stuntwoman Bonnie Morgan as she scrambles along a well constructed on the Universal Studios lot in Hollywood are there for all to see. Having nevertheless managed to out-climb her arachnid-like nemesis, Rachel then dislodges the one loose brick in the entire well to send a torrent of water flooding implausibly down upon the head of the relentless Samara, which sends her plummeting back from whence she came. No problems there, then.

What was unique about Hideo Nakata's *Ring* was that it made a serious attempt to suggest a fulfilment of its curse which was so terrifying to behold that those who were witness to it could reasonably be believed by an audience to have died of fright.

The idea of 'dying of fright' has been a staple of the literary ghost story for almost two hundred years, and readers have thought little of such an outlandish concept on the page, where imagination kicks in to conjure the degree of horror in the relevant vision that might just produce the desired effect. Many of the protagonists in

The Ring: the coming of Samara.

the stories of M R James died of fright (the physical injuries that they would suffer as a result of tangling with one of his spectral entities were usually brought about *after* death), as did those of his mentor Sheridan Le Fanu, while H P Lovecraft preferred to go the more modernist route of having those who came face-to-face with one of his eldritch monsters turn into gibbering wrecks, their sanity sacrificed to a single moment of cosmic revelation.

Films, on the other hand, have always fought shy of such a notion, and were it to be considered at all, invariably it would be reserved for a minor character in the narrative, whose nervous disposition was less well-attuned than that of a hero when it came to the matter of facing down a particularly unsavoury example of the supernatural unknown. When push comes to shove, those who have had to stare into the face of the Gorgon in horror films habitually have shied away from the image, sometimes committing suicide by accident or design, rather than 'die of fright': in John Irvin's *Ghost Story*, those who found themselves in the putrescent presence of Alma Mobley quickly toppled off high places, while burly Oliver Reed also preferred to throw himself out of a window at full pelt in Dan Curtis' *Burnt Offerings* (1976), rather than be caught quivering in a corner like a girlie. There are myriad other examples. Conversely, in the determinedly realistic *The Exorcist*, those who were confronted by one of the most terrifying visages ever put onto film barely turned a hair at the sight, any more than they were diverted from their ability to recite prayers in Latin by its voluminous projectile vomiting.

The reason for this requires no explanation and takes the form of a 'Catch 22': the viewer, unlike the reader, has to be privy to the *same* sight in most cases, and unless he or she is also found dead of fright after a screening of the film in question, the alleged Terror that a protagonist is required to face can hardly be as bad as has been made out. Therefore, it has always been easier in films to supply otherworldly denizens with fangs and claws with which to assault a victim, rather than rely on facial features alone.

Ring changed that precept. Admittedly, it did so by allowing itself the safety margin of only revealing a tiny (but always unsettling) part of its demon's face and leaving the rest to the imagination — cleverly placing itself between the two stools of story and film in the process — but it managed nevertheless to provide a climactic Terror which, while it may not have induced the same effect on the viewer as on those confronted onscreen, was still convincing enough for one to believe that the percipient of it might well have died of fright in context, were they to have been faced with it in reality.

Asian horrors as a whole have done a good job of maintaining this pitch of terror in subsequent films. *Ring* is no longer alone in featuring imagery which is a fair match to the worst nightmares of the susceptible viewer. *Ring 0: Birthday*, in fact, produced the

Ring: the evil eye...

most frightening single shot of Sadako in the entire canon, while *Ju-on*, *The Eye*, *One Missed Call* and *A Tale of Two Sisters* have all done their bit towards providing entries for a growing catalogue of new terrors. Only *The Ring* stumbled and fell when it chose to sideline its stunt-girl, once she had cleared the television, and go instead for a close-up of Daveigh Chase looking like nothing so much as a hideous dwarf.

Ring's 'final scene' is justifiably famous now, and not merely because it represents a high-water mark in the cinema of Terror, but because it overcame the artificial boundary which had been placed on the fright-film since its inception — that what is seen is never as frightening as what can be imagined.

It is hard to imagine a more frightening image than Hiroshi Takahashi dreamed up for the climax to *Ring*. But there can be no doubting now that he, or someone like him, will do exactly that.

Not since *The Exorcist* has a single horror film had so much impact on the genre as a whole, and even the DreamWorks franchise — intent as it seemingly is on descending into formula cliché — has failed to diminish the power of the movie that started it all, or to dampen the enthusiasm and invention of others in Japan or the Far East who wish to follow in its sodden footsteps. Those who saw *Ring* before the word was out, the secret exposed, the fright revealed, will have that image of Sadako materialising from the TV screen, long, lank hair hiding her features, fingers crabbed and bloody, etched indelibly into their cinematic consciousness for all time. It was a sight that elicited a real thrill of fear. A pleasing terror.

M R James would have approved. ⭘

Epilogue: Day Eight

When the brain is in a stressful tense state, it needs to have down time. And the release after a scary movie can bring the brain down.

- Joseph LeDoux, PhD, Center for Neural Science, New York University

What we are left with at the climax of *Ring* is not merely the residue of a single human soul which has managed to 'survive' death by imprinting itself onto the ether and thus onto radio-waves, like the traditional ghost, but a perpetuating malignance whose very existence depends upon a ritual and repetitious destruction of living beings. This is the Dracula myth reborn for the electronic age.

The great literary monster of the nineteenth century was Bram Stoker's Count Dracula, a creation which tapped into a number of diverse cultural fears and coalesced them into a single understandable metaphor. In Stoker's day of 1897 (the date of publication of the novel), they were typically sex, death and prevailing concerns about the hereafter, but there was also the pestilential threat which was thought to be posed by immigration and its potential to destroy the British Empire from within. Like Robert Louis Stevenson's 'Mr Hyde' of thirteen years before, Dracula was more than a bogeyman concocted for commercial gain from out of a few shards of history and legend to frighten avid readers of Victorian 'shilling shockers' — he was instead the product of neurosis, both real and imagined, and what he represented struck a chord that resonated on a deeper level than that of the similar stories of vampire-monsters which had preceded him.

Koji Suzuki is a serious author, not given to churning out tales of horror on demand or rehashing hackneyed themes simply in order to feed the insatiable appetites of genre fans and, in *Ring*, he had taken the conventional ghost story of the restless spirit in the unquiet grave and combined it with the multiplicity of fears which are being inspired by modern technology: the proliferation of unsavoury images and their malign impact on the young; the fact that nothing exists in material form any more, that all imagery is ethereal and held on erasable databases, such as hard drives or other removable media; the fact that all of us are eavesdropped upon — that someone, somewhere is watching us 24/7, via spy satellites, security or speed cameras, Internet, cell-phone and even e-mail monitoring, chip-and-pin... *Someone is watching us.*

Sadako is not a metaphor for the supernatural unknown, but for the technological unknown; she taps into genuine concerns about the increasing use of high technology, inasmuch as it appears, more and more, to be taking things out of our own control and placing them in the hands of others. The more that it infiltrates our everyday lives, the more it puts previously familiar objects beyond the realm of our understanding. This is akin to the science fictional fears of the 1950s, where energy, for example, began to be produced by the largely inexplicable process of atomic fission, when previously it was the product of a natural resource ignited at high temperature.

Suzuki's revolutionary idea, dredged up from his thoughts and feelings about being restricted to home and pestered by the prevalence of digital media in his own daily life, is that no longer is the ghost confined to the metaphorical 'haunted house' — the ghost, quite literally, is now in the machine, along with similar phantom images of spouse and children, relatives and friends and a billion other Web wanderers, all watching or being watched. Sadako's 'ghost' is anywhere and everywhere, at one and the same time. All it needs to manifest itself is an electronic means of transmission. Television and video are the ageing conduits in the novel, but any form of data transfer will suffice; anything transmissible into which her will can burrow, like a virus in the bloodstream. Thus, she is able to propagate a vampiric contagion, the victims of which must inevitably die or become carriers and infect others with the self-same disease. This deep and instinctive fear is what *Dracula* was actually predicated upon, not the superficial glaze of Gothic monster and imperilled heroine, but fear of the *other* — of infection and infraction, one of the great Gothic staples.

It is no accident that Sadako's appearance in fiction should coincide with the rise of Islamic fundamentalism: just when you thought it was safe to switch on your television set again, up pops Osama in another grainy video full of coded references and obscure imagery, but always with the same doom-laden warning. (Unlike her Japanese cousin, Samara in the remake is kept confined in a makeshift cell, and is brutalised and finally murdered by her captors.) The Terror that Bin Laden inspires feeds into the lifeblood of Western civilisation. It topples buildings and kills thousands. It stands next to you in the bus queue and blows you to oblivion. It wants to suck out your thoughts and beliefs and replace them with its own. It is everywhere and nowhere, and it cannot be killed, because it is an *idea* — an ideology — not a person or a movement: "Ideas are life-forms, with energy of their own," Ryuji explains in *Ring*, in concise expression of the novel's central theme. "You mean the thoughts in our heads can turn into living beings?" asks Asakawa. "That's about the size of it," his friend confirms. The ideological undertone in the story is overtly politicised in *The Ring*, where the Arabic-sounding Samara is not even racially related to her infertile parents, who 'adopted' (bought?) her during a trip to unspecified foreign parts. Thus, she brings with her a genetic baggage of hatred and rage against all things American. In DreamWorks' version of events, Samara's ire has no discernible source: "But I can't help it. And it won't stop," she tells her psychiatric inquisitor, thus perpetuating the myth of an unfathomable evil, emanating from beyond America's shores, that 'never sleeps'.

(Four years after the publication of Suzuki's novel in Japan, members of a religious sect named Aum Shinrikyo, on the orders of self-styled guru Shoko Asahara, released a quantity of the nerve agent sarin into the Tokyo subway system after having performed a trial run of the gas in a residential district the year before. These two attacks killed a total of nineteen people and injured over 6,000 more.)

This *tenor* of genuine unease — this tapping of a real, if essentially unspoken, dread among the populace at large is what gives *Ring* its currency. Koji Suzuki has reinvented the ghost, and its spectral threat now hovers over us all. His novel in consequence, like Stoker's before it, represents a cornerstone in the larger Literature of Terror.

With Hollywood films becoming ever more the celluloid equivalent of junk food, the rise and rise of Asian cinema in recent years has been a breath of fresh air; another reading of *Ring* might see it as a commentary on the fight against the 'virus' of empty, effects-driven spectacles, to which the American industry is so mindlessly devoted. Far Eastern horrors conversely are derived from a long tradition of *story*telling, and remain narrative-based, whereas writers have never commanded much respect in Hollywood dream-factories. The ghost story, in particular, is a medium which has always belonged exclusively to its practitioners; it is a very specific craft, the secrets of which have been vouchsafed to only the favoured few.

The repetitive and predictable nature of video game spin-offs from feature films, as well as the inevitable behind-the-scenes extras which are now included on every DVD, have done much to expose the tired, mechanistic inadequacies of the average American studio production which might otherwise have remained hidden from view by a veneer of characterisation or a salvo of savvy dialogue. Hollywood product has become bland and conservative, fat and bloated, in its imperious grip on the world's multiplexes. But apparent behind the New Age clothes of digital magic is now the naked cynicism of a money machine that is dedicated to the endless recycling of tried and tested formulae. Audiences wanting more than eye-candy to keep themselves amused for 100 minutes in their local cinema have started to look to the East for what Hamish McAlpine, CEO of Asian importer Tartan Video, calls 'brain-food'.

Horror has led the way, but megabucks hits like Yimou Zhang's *Hero* (*Ying Xiong*, 2002), featuring Jet Li, and *The House of Flying Daggers* (*Shi mian mai fou*, 2004) have spared no blushes in their elbowing aside of American releases in the European marketplace. Hollywood may try to emulate the success of *Ring*, *The Grudge* or *Dark Water* simply by cloning them or adding an acceptable American presence to the mix, as the entrepreneurial Joe Levine did with Raymond Burr in the original *Godzilla*, but the results invariably are club-footed and stumbling. The proletariat often votes with its feet, and the most original and inventive exercises in the cinema of Terror are all to be found on a path to Southeast Asia.

Above: Ring *(1998).*

Well before *Ring*, the Japanese showed themselves to be past masters of this arcane art; after it, they have consolidated that status into one of world leadership. The ghost story has never been so popular, nor so vibrant with ideas, since its glorious heyday in the Edwardian era in England. Thanks to Koji Suzuki, Hideo Nakata and others, we are witnessing a veritable renaissance in the tale of Terror. *Things* can only get better.

On the morning of 10 August 2002, a mock funeral service was held for Sadako at the museum of popular culture which is a feature of the Laforet shopping centre in the fashionable Harajuku district of Tokyo. Among those who attended the ceremony were Koji Suzuki and Tsugihiko Kadokawa, chairman of Kadokawa Shoten.

Needless to say, the whole thing was a publicity stunt initiated to bid farewell to the 'old' Sadako and usher in the new via an exhibit entitled 'Ring to *The Ring*', which had principally been designed to promote the DreamWorks remake that was due to open in Japan that November. Suzuki was called upon to make a speech to the gathering which conceded that the tragic figure whom he had created originally to sire a curse had been transformed in the intervening years into a monstrous archetype whose impact had now been felt across the globe: "Sadako's physical body has died, but her spirit has crossed the oceans where it was reborn as Samara," he dutifully declared, before moving on to acknowledge (with his tongue planted firmly in his cheek) the unexpected outcome of his endeavours. "The moment I created the character of Sadako, I did a great wrong to all the women of Japan who share her name. For this, I have stood before a shrine and apologised wholeheartedly." The shrine in question was a display prop, which featured a portrait of Sadako Yamamura in typical pose.

Sadako's spirit had indeed crossed the oceans, but true to the unpredictable nature of her curse, it had not been replicated in its original form. Ehren Kruger christened *his* villain Samara, thus making a 'copy' and preserving the integrity of the master.

The Ring is a mutation, and its limited virulence will run a course like that of Jason or Freddy or *Halloween's* Michael Myers, or Alien or Predator and more. By 'burying' Sadako in her prime, her creators have actually assured her of immortality as an icon of the new Gothic cinema.

The curse will go on. Sadako will rise again.

The Ring is dead. Long live *Ring*. O

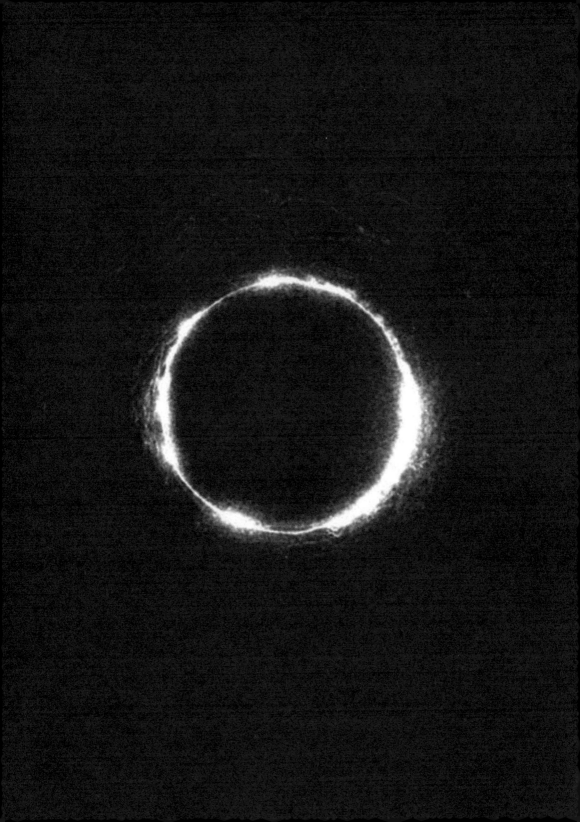

Appendix: Cast and Credits

1995

Ring: Kanzenban (Ring: The Complete Edition)

Cast

Kazuyuki Asakawa ....Katsunori Takahashi	Copy Editor ....Takayuki Godai
Ryuji Takayama ....Yoshio Harada	Yoshino.....................Shigeyuki Nakamura
Sadako Yamamura ....Ayane Miura	Heihachiro Ikuma................Koji Shimizu
Shizuka Asakawa................Mai Tachihara	Taxi Driver........................Akira Sakamoto
Mai Takano ....Maha Hamada	Kei Yamamura ....Tadayoshi Ueda
Jotaro Nagao ....Tomorowo Taguchi	Shuichi Iwata ....Nattsu Tanabashi
Tomoko Onishi.................Akiko Hinagata	Takehiko Nomi.......................Kazu Itsuki

With Kyoko Donowaki, Kikuko Hashimoto, Koichi Koshimura, Aya Mizuno, Miho Morikawa, Seiroku Nakazawa, Ko Seno, Kansuke Shimizu, Yuka Takejima, Yuka Torashima, Manami Umeda, Yoshinari Yoshie.

Credits

Director: Chisui Takigawa/Producer: Ryunosuke Endou/Screenplay: Joji Iida, Taizou Soshiya/Based on the novel by Koji Suzuki/Music: Yoshihiro Ike/Cinematography: Kazumi Iwata/Lighting: Susumu Mikajiri/Sound: Naoki Sugiyama/Video Engineer: Keiji Takimoto/Sound Effects: Shinichi Sako/Editor: Ichiro Chaen/Set Design: Kazuo Yanagawa. **Fuji Television. 95 minutes.**

1998
Ring

Cast

Reiko Asakawa	Nanako Matsushima	Sadako Yamamura	Rie Inou
Mai Takano	Miki Nakatani	Hayatsu	Hiroyuki Watanabe
Ryuji Takayama	Hiroyuki Sanada	Kazue Yamamura	Miwako Kaji
Tomoko Oishi	Yuko Takeuchi	Junior High Schoolgirls	Yoko Kima
Masami Kurahashi	Hitomi Sato		Asami Nagata
Takashi Yamamura	Yoichi Numata	Senior High Schoolgirls	Keiko Yoshida
Yoshino	Yutaka Matsushige		Yoshiko Matsumaru
Koichi Asakawa	Katsumi Muramatsu		Yoho Naose
Yoichi Asakawa	Rikiya Otaka	Yoko Tsuji	Maki Ikeda
Shizuko Yamamura	Masako	Takehiko Nomi	Takashi Takayama
Dr Heihachiro Ikuma	Daisuke Ban	Yamamura as a Teenager	Toshiliko Takeda
Omiya the Cameraman	Kiyoshi Risho	Sadako as a Young Girl	Chihiro Shirai
Okazaki	Yurei Yanagi	Town Hall Moderator	Mantaro Koichi
Reiko's Aunt	Yoko Oshima	Press Representatives	Shinkichi Noda
Ryomi Oishi	Kiriko Shimizu		Kazufumi Nakai

Credits

Director: Hideo Nakata/Producers: Takashige Ichise, Shinya Kawai, Takenori Sento/ Screenplay: Hiroshi Takahashi/Based on the novel by Koji Suzuki/Associate Producer: Makoto Ishihara/Music: Kenji Kawai/Cinematography: Junichiro Hayashi/Production Designer: Iwao Saito/Sound: Yoshiya Obara/Production Manager: Tetsuya Nakamura/ Assistant Director: Kuni Risho/Make-up: Yoshiichi Matsui, Takuya Wada/Special Effects: Hajime Matsumoto/Visual Effects: Hajime Matsumoto/Executive Producer: Masato Hara. **Kadokawa Shoten/Asmick Ace/Omega Project. 96 minutes.**

Rasen (Spiral)

Cast

Mitsuo Ando	Koichi Sato	Sadako Yamamura	Hinako Saeki
Mai Takano	Miki Nakatani	Ryuji Takayama	Hiroyuki Sanada
Yoshino	Yutaka Matsushige		
Reiko Asakawa (archive footage)			
	Nanako Matsushima		

With Tomohiro Okada.

Credits

Director: Joji Iida/Producers: Takashige Ichise, Shinya Kawai/Screenplay: Joji Iida/Based on the novel by Koji Suzuki/Cinematography: Makoto Watanabe/Production Designer: Iwao Saito/Editor: Hirohide Abe/Visual Effects: Hajime Matsumoto.
Kadokawa Shoten/Asmick Ace/Omega Project. 97 minutes.

1999
Ring: The Final Chapter (Ring: Saishusho)

Cast

Kazuyuki Asakawa	Toshiro Yanagiba	Nao Matsuzaki	Herself
Ryuuji Takayama	Tomoya Nagase	Tomoko Ooishi	Aya Okamoto
Rieko Miyashita	Hitomi Kuroki	Tomoko's Father	Toshihiko Yamamoto
Akiko Yoshino	Kotomi Kyono	Professor Kaneda	Fumiyo Kohinata
Mai Takano	Akiko Yada	Officer Kashiwada	Tetsu Watanabe
Professor Jotaro Nagao	Kei Yamamoto	Yagi	Sadahiko Takamoku
Kawamura	Takayuki Kato	Dr Heihachiro Ikuma	Shozo Uesugi
Yoichi Asakawa	Yuuta Fukayama	Dr Ikuma's Wife	Sumie Sasaki

With Tamae Oonishi, Satomi Nagano, Mansaku Ikeuchi, Tomoka Higata, Watanabe Kenkichi, Takahiro Hirano, Shigeo Matsuzawa, Yuuko Yamamoto, Aiko Konoshima, Munehisa Fujita, Fumie Noguchi, Shozo Inagaki, Hideyuki Akabane, Miyuki Shindo, Tadaharu Kutomi, Tae Kimura, Sawa Suzuki, Katsuya Kobayashi, Yuriko Hirooka, Chieko Ichikawa, Rie Ozawa, Shinsho Nakamaru, Kenzo Kawarazaki, Chiharu Niiyama, Masatane Tsukayama, Yuki Inomata, Rie Takarai.

Credits

Directors: Yoshihito Fukumoto, Hidetomo Matsuda, Hiroshi Nishitani/Producers: Sosuke Osabe, Kenji Shimizu/Screenplay: Koji Makita, Naoya Takayama/Based on the novel by Koji Suzuki/Music: Toshiyuki Watanabe.
Fuji Television. 12 x 54 minutes.

Ring (*aka* The Ring Virus)

Cast

Sun-ju Kim	Eun-kyung Shin	Eun-suh Park	Du-na Bae
Yeol Choi	Jin-yeong Jeong		

With Seung-hyeon Lee, Chang-wan Kim, Ggoch-ji Kim, Yeon-su Yu.

Credits

Director: Dong-bin Kim/Producer: Mauricio Dortona/Screenplay: Dong-bin Kim/Based on the novel by Koji Suzuki/Music: Il Won/Cinematographers: Mauricio Dortona, Chul-hyun Hwang/Editor: Mauricio Dortona.

AFDF. 108 minutes.

Ring 2

Cast

Mai Takano	Miki Nakatani	Ryuji Takayama	Hiroyuki Sanada
Masami Kurahashi	Hitomi Sato	Shizuko Yamamura	Masako
Kanae Sawaguchi	Kyoko Fukada	Koichi Asakawa	Katsumi Muramatsu
Dr Kawajiri	Fumiyo Kohinata	Dr Heihachiro Ikuma	Daisuke Ban
Detective Omuta	Kenjiro Ishimaru	Sakuma	Reita Serizawa
Okazaki	Yurei Yanagi	Inspector	Taro Suwa
Yoichi	Rikiya Otaka	Nurse	Yoshiko Yura
Takashi Yamamura	Yoichi Numata	Sadako Yamamura	Rie Inou
Reiko Asakawa	Nanako Matsushima		

With Shiro Namiki, Yoko Chosokabe, Takashi Nishina, Shinmei Tsuji.

Credits

Director: Hideo Nakata/Producer: Taka Ichise/Screenplay: Hideo Nakata, Hiroshi Takahashi/Music: Kenji Kawai/Cinematography: Hideo Yamamoto/Editor: Nobuyuki Takahashi/Make-up: Yuuichi Matsui.

Kadokawa Shoten/Asmick Ace/Omega Project. 95 minutes.

Rasen (TV series)

Cast

Mitsuo Ando	Goro Kishitani	Miwako Ando	Risa Junna
Mai Takano	Akiko Yada	Toru Kawai	Takeshi Masu
Natsumi Aihara	Takami Yoshimoto	Misaki Nishijima	Risa Sudo
Okada	Takashi Naito	Imanishi's wife	Aya Enyoji
Kumiko Nishijima	Yuka Nomura	Imanishi	Go Kageyama
Kyosuke Ota	Seiichi Tanabe	Tsutomu Kasahara	Hiroshi Okouchi

With Mayuko Azusa, Yasuhide Tonesaku.

Credits

Directors: Takao Kinoshita, Hiroshi Nishitani/Producers: Kenji Shimizu, Sousuke Osabe/Screenplay: Kazuhiko Tanaka, Koji Takata/Original Music: Dennis Martin/Technical Producer: Toshiyuki Sasaki/Technical Director: Yoshihiro Kitayama/Cinematography: Kisaku Isogai/Lighting: Hiroshi Hanamura/Sound: Masahiko Nishikiori/Editor: Masaaki Yamamoto/Sound Effects: Yoshihiko Fujimura, Kazuyuki Ishii/Set Production: Kazuhiko Sakamura/Design: Kazuo Yanagawa.

Fuji Television. 13 x 45 minutes.

2000
Ring 0: Birthday (Ring 0: Bāsudei)

Cast

Sadako Yamamura	Yukie Nakama	Shizuko Yamamura	Masako
Toyama	Seiichi Tanabe	Kiyomi	Masami Hashimoto
Shoko Miyaji	Yoshiko Tanaka	Sudo	Kazue Tsunogae
Etsuko Tachihara	Kumiko Aso	Girl	Chinami Furuya
Wataru Kuno	Ryuji Mizukami	Miyaji's Co-Worker	Go Shimada
Yusaku Shigemori	Takeshi Wakamatsu	Yumiko Kanai	Tsukasa Kimura
Aiko Hazuki	Kaoru Okunuki	Nurse	Yukimi Koyanagi
Heihachiro Ikuma	Daisuke Ban	Okubo	Yoshiyuki Morishita
Kaoru Arima	Junko Takahata	Male Teacher	Yoji Tanaka
With Masato Oba.			

Credits

Director: Norio Tsuruta/Producers: Shinji Ogawa, Masao Nagai, Takashige Ichise/Screenplay: Hiroshi Takahashi/Based on the short story 'Birthday' by Koji Suzuki/Cinematographer: Takahide Shibanushi/Lighting: Yoshimi Watabe/Music: Shinichiro Okata/Set Design: Shiro Yamaguchi/Editor: Hiroshi Shinaga/Clothing: Atsuko Sugiyama.

Kadokawa Shoten/Asmick Ace/Omega Project. 99 minutes.

2002

The Ring

Cast

Rachel Keller	Naomi Watts	Donna	Stephanie Erb
Noah Clay	Martin Henderson	Babysitter	Sara Rue
Aidan Keller	David Dorfman	Grad Student	Lindsey Stoddart
Richard Morgan	Brian Cox	Orderly	Joe Sabatino
Dr Grasnik	Jane Alexander	Cashier	Joanna Lin Black
Ruth Embry	Lindsay Frost	Girl on Ferry	Maura McNamara
Katie Embry	Amber Tamblyn	Girl's Father	David Povall
Rebecca Kotler	Rachael Bella	Ship's Mate	Keith Campbell
Samara Morgan	Daveigh Chase	Ferry Worker	Chuck Hicks
Anna Morgan	Shannon Cochran	Dave	Michael Spound
Teacher	Sandra Thigpen	Painter	Gary Cervantes
Innkeeper	Richard Lineback	Nurse	Aixa Clemente
Girl Teens	Sasha Barrese	Cal	Art Frankel
	Tess Hall	Darby	Billy Lloyd
Kellen	Adam Brody	Mourners	Coleen Maloney
Harvey	Alan Blumenfeld		Catherine Paolone
Beth	Pauley Perrette	Librarian	Guy Richardson
Doctor	Joe Chrest	Video Store Clerk (deleted scene)	
Library Clerk	Ronald William Lawrence		Maury Ginsberg

Credits

Director: Gore Verbinski/Producers: Laurie MacDonald, Walter F Parkes/Screenplay: Ehren Kruger, Scott Frank/Based on a novel by Koji Suzuki/Associate Producer: Benita Allen-Honess/Music: Neil Brand/Additional Music: James Michael Dooley, Henning Lohner, Martin Tillmann, Hans Zimmer/Cinematography: Bojan Bazelli/ Production Designer: Tom Duffield/Art Director: Patrick M Sullivan Jr/Editor: Craig Wood/Sound Mixer: Lee Orloff/Production Manager: Bill Johnson/Assistant Director: Benita Allen-Honess/Make-up: Jean A Black, RaMona Fleetwood, Amy Schmiederer/Special Make-up Effects: Rick Baker, Bart Mixon, Kazuhiro Tsuji, Chad Waters, Eddie Yang/Hair Stylists: Medusah, Roxanne Wightman/Costume Designer: Julie Weiss/Special Effects: Terry Chapman/Special Effects Supervisor: Burt Dalton/Stunts: Daniel W Barringer, Debbie Evans, Lisa Hoyle, Robert Jauregui, Darwin Mitchell, Julia Seaver, Matthew Taylor/Stunt Coordinator: Keith Campbell/Executive Producers: Roy Lee, Mike Macari, Michele Weisler.
DreamWorks SKG. 115 minutes.

2005

The Ring Two

Cast

Rachel Keller..........................Naomi Watts

Max Rourke...........................Simon Baker

Aidan Keller.......................David Dorfman

Emily.............................Emily Van Camp

Dr Emma Temple...........Elizabeth Perkins

Evelyn...................................Sissy Spacek

Male Reporter.........................Jesse Burch

Anna Morgan................Shannon Cochran

Martin Savide.............................Gary Cole

Cop #2............................Stephen Holland

Sister Elizabeth............................Mary Joy

Betsy....................................Kelly Overton

Jake...................................Ryan Merriman

Babysitter.........................Adrienne Smith

Samara................................. Kelly Stables

Samara (archive footage)... Daveigh Chase

Doctor..................................James Lesure

Young Evelyn.....Mary Elizabeth Winstead

Detective...........................Kirk B R Woller

Father of Emily.............Cooper Thornton

Mother of Emily.............Marilyn McIntyre

Printing Staff.....................Michael Chieffo

Young Detective.................Steven Petrarca

Desk Sergeant................Michael Dempsey

Coroner Attendant.......Jeffrey Hutchinson

Adoption Counselor........Chane't Johnson

Nurse....................Michelle Anne Johnson

Head Nurse................................Teri Bibb

Second Nurse............................Jill Farley

Young Nurse....................Aleksa Palladino

Desk Man............................Victor McCay

Rental Car Owner..........Brendan Quinlan

Father of Jake.............Brendan Tomlinson

Mother of Jake......................Phyllis Lyons

Cop #1.................................Ted Detwiler

Game Attendant..........Omer Stephens III

Marble Man....................Jonathan Coburn

Baby Samara...............Caitlin Mavromates

With Meagen Fay, Alyssa Miller, Madison Miller, Rachel Miller.

Credits

Director: Hideo Nakata/Producers: Laurie MacDonald, Walter F Parkes/Screenplay: Ehren Kruger/From the novel *Ringu* by Koji Suzuki/Music: Hans Zimmer, Henning Lohner, Martin Tillman/Cinematographer: Gabriel Beristain/Production Designer: James D Bissell/Art Director: Christa Munro/Editor: Michael N Knue/Sound Recordists: Tim Gomillion, Dennis Rogers/Sound Mixer: David MacMillan/Production Manager: Michele Imperato/Assistant Director: Doug Metzger/Make Up: Debbie Zoller, Joel Harlow/Special Makeup Effects: Rick Baker, John Calpin, Bart Mixon, Barney Burman, Jamie Kelman/Hair Stylist: Gail Rowell-Ryan/Costume Designer: Wendy Chuck/Special Effects: Peter Chesney, Tom Chesney, Sandra Stewart/Stunt Coordinator: Keith Campbell/Executive Producers: Roy Lee, Mike Macari, Neil A Machlis, Michele Weisler.

DreamWorks SKG. 110 minutes.

Bibliography:

The *Ring* films and the sub-genre of so-called 'J-horror' to which they belong are a relatively new phenomenon, and what has been written about them has largely been confined to fan-magazines or musings on the Internet. In the former category, *Video Watchdog*, *SFX*, *Asian Cult Cinema* and *Little Shoppe of Horrors* deserve a mention as having been of benefit to me in the creation of this first book to deal specifically with the Ring cycle. Also referenced were the works of M R James, Lafcadio Hearn, H P Lovecraft and others, all of which are widely available. There are several books of note on Japanese cinema in general, but this list mainly is comprised of ancillary publications which also were instrumental in aiding me with the task. My thanks go to their authors and creators.

Clairvoyance and Thoughtography, T Fukurai (Rider & Co, London, 1931)
Dorama Encyclopedia, The: A Guide to Japanese TV Drama Since 1953,
Jonathan Clements & Motoko Tamamuro (Stone Bridge Press, Berkeley, 2003)
Horror: The Aurum Film Encyclopedia: vol 3, Editor: Phil Hardy (Aurum Press, London, 1985)
Japanese Cinema Encyclopedia: Horror, Fantasy, Science Fiction, Thomas Weisser & Yuko Mihara Weisser (Vital Books, Miami, 1998)
Literature of Terror, The: vols 1 & 2, David Punter (Addison Wesley Longman Limited, 1996)
Ring, Koji Suzuki (Harper Collins, London, 2003)
Ring, The: vol 1 (*Manga*), Art: Misao Inagaki (Dark Horse Manga, Milwaukie, 2003)
'Sadako: Ring 0, The', ***Increasing the Fear Magazine*** (Kadokawa Publishing, Tokyo, 2000)
Spiral, Koji Suzuki (Vertical, New York, 2004)
Spiral (*Manga*), Art: Meimu (Dark Horse Manga, Milwaukie, 2004)
www.imdbpro.com
www.theringworld.com
www.variety.com